Human Motives

Human Motives

Hedonism, Altruism, and the Science of Affect

Peter Carruthers

Great Clarendon Street, Oxford, OX2 6DP,
United Kingdom

Oxford University Press is a department of the University of Oxford.
It furthers the University's objective of excellence in research, scholarship,
and education by publishing worldwide. Oxford is a registered trade mark of
Oxford University Press in the UK and in certain other countries

© Peter Carruthers 2024

The moral rights of the author have been asserted

All rights reserved. No part of this publication may be reproduced, stored in
a retrieval system, or transmitted, in any form or by any means, without the
prior permission in writing of Oxford University Press, or as expressly permitted
by law, by licence or under terms agreed with the appropriate reprographics
rights organization. Enquiries concerning reproduction outside the scope of the
above should be sent to the Rights Department, Oxford University Press, at the
address above

You must not circulate this work in any other form
and you must impose this same condition on any acquirer

Published in the United States of America by Oxford University Press
198 Madison Avenue, New York, NY 10016, United States of America

British Library Cataloguing in Publication Data
Data available

Library of Congress Control Number: 2023942445

ISBN 978–0–19–890613–1

DOI: 10.1093/oso/9780198906131.001.0001

Printed and bound in the UK by
Clays Ltd, Elcograf S.p.A.

Links to third party websites are provided by Oxford in good faith and
for information only. Oxford disclaims any responsibility for the materials
contained in any third party website referenced in this work.

For Fred and Blythe
Friends, family, and joy in nature

Contents

Preface	ix
1. Introduction	**1**
1.1 The Theoretical Terrain	1
1.2 Why It Matters	4
1.3 The Way Ahead	7
2. The Science of Affect	**10**
2.1 The Scope of Affect	11
2.2 The Input: Appraisals of Value	12
2.3 Output (1): Behavior	15
2.4 Output (2): Arousal	19
2.5 Output (3): Valence	20
2.6 Output (4): Affective Learning	26
2.7 Top-Down Influences on Affect	34
2.8 Conclusion	39
3. The New Hedonism	**40**
3.1 Prospective Decision-Making	40
3.2 How Valence Works	43
3.3 Future-Directed Pleasure	47
3.4 Concerns about Consciousness	49
3.5 Other Forms of Decision-Making	54
3.6 Difficult Decisions	60
3.7 Conclusion	62
4. Traditional Critiques Critiqued	**64**
4.1 Evolutionary Arguments	64
4.2 Self-Sacrifice: Spontaneous and Reflective	68
4.3 Desire and Satisfaction	72
4.4 The Experience Machine	74
4.5 Experimental Evidence	76
4.6 Two Forms of Hedonism	81
4.7 Conclusion	83
5. Feelings Versus Representations of Value	**85**
5.1 Valence as Feeling: An Initial Concern	85
5.2 Valence as Representation of Value	86
5.3 Valence and Consciousness	92
5.4 Theories of Representation	95
5.5 Erroneous Emotions	100

viii Contents

5.6 Erroneous Pleasures and Displeasures	106
5.7 Merely Sub-Personal or Extended Egoism: A Dilemma	109
5.8 Conclusion	113

6. Indicatives Versus Imperatives — **115**

6.1 Two Forms of Imperativism	115
6.2 Imperative Versus Indicative Content	121
6.3 Consummatory Pleasure Is about the Present	127
6.4 Valence and Imperatives in the Brain	132
6.5 Alleged Counter-Examples to Evaluativism	134
6.6 Conclusion	138

7. Pain: A Test Case — **140**

7.1 The Science of Pain: A Primer	140
7.2 The Sensation of Pain	145
7.3 The Painfulness of Pain	152
7.4 Erroneous Pains	155
7.5 Pain's Transparency	157
7.6 Pains as Reasons	159
7.7 Conclusion	163

8. Moral Motivation — **164**

8.1 Kinds of Moral Motivation	164
8.2 Prosociality and Altruism	166
8.3 Equality and Fairness	171
8.4 Social-Group Cognition	177
8.5 Norm Psychology	182
8.6 Conclusion: Scaling Up	188
8.7 Addendum: Weak Humeanism	189
8.8 Summary: The Case against Hedonism	191

References	195
Index	219

Preface

This book has been a while in the making, even if not nearly so long in the writing. I first began to get interested in the science of affective states like desire and emotion around 2009, when I was writing a book on self-knowledge and needed to say something about our knowledge of our own such states (Carruthers 2011). Luckily, since that project was funded by the National Science Foundation, I was able to have Brendan Ritchie working with me as a research assistant for the year. He knew a lot more about the field than I did. (Brendan had worked as an undergraduate research assistant for Tim Schroeder while the latter was writing his book, *The Three Faces of Desire*.) As a result, he was able to put me right on a lot of points, correcting my many misunderstandings of the field.

Thereafter I left the topic aside for the next few years while I worked on other issues, having to do with consciousness, working memory, and conscious thought (Carruthers 2015, 2019). But I then began to do serious work in the area again, focused initially on epistemic emotions like uncertainty (Carruthers 2017) and curiosity (Carruthers 2018d, 2020, 2024). But my reading of the field had led me to think that the nature of positive and negative valence (arguably, pleasure and displeasure by other names), which are described by many as the "common currency" of decision-making, is critical in evaluating the debate between motivational hedonism and its critics. (Motivational hedonism is often called "psychological hedonism" in the philosophical literature; it is the doctrine that all human actions are undertaken to secure good and avoid bad experiences for oneself.) For on some views, it appears that decisions taken to maximize the balance of positive over negative valence are about securing good (and avoiding bad) feelings for oneself; whereas on other views valence is an imperative-like urge to secure or avoid specific types of experience. Both kinds of account seem to lead straight to motivational hedonism. In contrast, I came to feel that valence is best understood representationally, serving to *represent* actions or outcomes as good or bad. This sort of account would warrant motivational pluralism, allowing that people can have many goals besides their own pleasant experiences and avoidance of their own unpleasant ones. The result was a pair of papers (Carruthers 2018c, 2023) which can be regarded as preliminary studies for the present book. Note that these papers were published after a delay of two and three years, respectively, following final acceptance by the journals in question. (That is, they were completed and accepted in 2016 and 2020, respectively.) So they are not as recent as they may seem. As a result, my views have matured and altered quite a bit since then.

Work on this book was facilitated by a Scholar's Award from NSF's *Science and Technology Studies* program (award # 2143473) covering the academic year 2022–23, as well as by a sabbatical semester from the University of Maryland in Spring 2022. I am grateful to both institutions for their support. Valuable initial feedback on some of the ideas presented in this book was provided by a group of graduate students at Maryland who attended a seminar I taught on the topic in Fall of 2021. (Special thanks go to Ken Glazer, who wrote a thoughtful critique of some my initial formulations.) In addition, I am grateful to the following individuals for their comments, criticism, and advice on some earlier drafts of this material: Luca Barlassina, Lia Curtis Fine, Joe Gurrola, Chris Masciari, Lixing Miao, Dan Moller, Shen Pan, Aida Roige, Elizabeth Schechter, Nicholas Shea, Julius Schönherr, Rachel Singpurwalla, Moonyoung Song, Louis Trost, and Xiaohui Yu. I am especially grateful to two anonymous reviewers for Oxford University Press for their thoughtful comments on the manuscript. In addition, some of the material in Chapter 6 is drawn from my 2023 paper cited above. I am grateful to the editors and publisher for their permission to make use of it.

1
Introduction

This short opening chapter introduces our topic, drawing distinctions and elucidating the main claims that are at stake. It also describes why these issues matter, as well as outlining what I take to be the appropriate methodology for resolving them.

1.1 The Theoretical Terrain

Why do human beings do what they do? What are the ultimate well-springs of human action? For many of us the answers to these questions seem obvious. People do what they do for all sorts of reasons, and different individuals have all kinds of intrinsic goals in life. This is *pluralism* about human motives. Some people want to be rich (for its own sake, not only as a means to other goods). Some want fame. Some want the respect of their colleagues. Many want their children and spouses to be healthy and happy. Some want to save the whale, or to preserve Monarch butterflies; others to protect ancient monuments or wilderness lands. Most pluralists will also allow that people (or at any rate, some people) are intrinsically motivated to do what they believe to be morally right—or morally required—and to avoid doing what they take to be morally wrong or forbidden. Moreover, pluralists will likely agree that many people are also, to some degree, altruistic—wanting to benefit or reduce the suffering of at least some other people, and wanting this for its own sake.

Contrasting with motivational pluralism is motivational *egoism*. (Philosophers generally refer to this view as "*psychological* egoism," although this is somewhat less descriptively accurate.) This is the doctrine that all human actions are undertaken, ultimately, to insure the actor's own benefit, where benefits can take various forms, including health, wealth, fame, and respect. A more specific form of motivational egoism, however (and the version this book will mostly be concerned with), is motivational *hedonism*. This is the view that all human actions are aimed at securing good experiences and/or avoiding bad experiences for oneself. Hedonism cashes out the "benefit to self" of egoism in experiential terms. Put differently: all actions

Human Motives: Hedonism, Altruism, and the Science of Affect. Peter Carruthers, Oxford University Press.
© Peter Carruthers 2024. DOI: 10.1093/oso/9780198906131.003.0001

are selected to achieve one's own pleasure and/or to avoid one's own displeasure—where pleasure and displeasure are understood broadly, to include not just good and bad feelings caused by bodily states (drinking when thirsty, eating when hungry, sensuous touch, orgasm, pain, nausea, physical exhaustion, and so on) but affective states more generally (including joy, cheerfulness, love, humor, pride, enjoyment, boredom, fear, anger, grief, guilt, and sadness).

Both egoism and hedonism have an extended history, reaching back at least to the Ancient Greeks, and some form of egoism has arguably been the dominant view in the social sciences throughout much of the twentieth century and beyond (Doris et al. 2020). Moreover, egoism continues to be an influential strand in popular culture, in part through the "objectivist" writings of Ayn Rand. So does hedonism (albeit rarely under that name), with self-help books routinely advising people to "give back" to the community because doing so will make them feel good, for example. But hedonism, in particular, has undergone a resurgence recently among social psychologists, with the rise of theories of decision-making that emphasize prospection of the future together with affective responding to those simulated actions and outcomes (Gilbert & Wilson 2007, 2009; Miloyan & Suddendorf 2015). Indeed, although I will argue that hedonism is false, it will nevertheless emerge as the most defensible form of egoism.

It is important to realize that egoism and hedonism are *modal* theses. They claim that human actions *cannot* be motivated by anything other than self-interest (in the case of egoism), or by one's own anticipated hedonic states (in hedonism's case). In fact, they claim to state laws of human psychology. Hence the force of the *cannot* in question is only as modally strong as those of any other special-science laws. These generally admit of exceptions due to breakdowns or variability at lower levels of causal organization (Pietroski & Rey 1995). Relationships among mental states, in particular, are always to some degree stochastic, reflecting random fluctuations in base-rates of neuronal firing in the underlying brain networks (Prather 2014; Bays 2015).

Descriptions of someone as "selfish" or "egotistical," in contrast, are merely factual statements. A selfish person is someone who is *often* or *generally* motivated by self-interest; and a selfish action is one that *is* motivated by self-interest. Likewise, a hedonist in the ordinary colloquial sense is merely someone who generally, or on the whole, pursues pleasures and enjoyments rather than other goods. Motivational hedonism, in contrast, claims that no one, ever (normally), pursues anything other than pleasure and avoidance of displeasure; and that this is true because of the underlying structure and normal functioning of human motivational systems.

Since motivational hedonism will loom so large in the discussion that follows, it may be worth pausing here to emphasize its distinctness from hedonism colloquially understood. As already noted, motivational hedonism is a claim about the universal well-springs of human action. It claims that every action, no matter how seemingly selfless or altruistic, is about securing pleasure for oneself, or avoiding displeasure, or both. What one might call "colloquial hedonism," in contrast, is an optional lifestyle choice, involving avoidance of work, absence of long-term goals, and attempts to maximize short-term enjoyment. A hedonist, in this sense, is someone whose life is devoted to the pursuit of bodily and social forms of pleasure. A hedonist's life is one that is devoted to "wine, women, and song," as the old (sexist) adage had it; or in more contemporary terms (the terms used in the 1970s and 80s, anyway), a life of "sex, drugs, and rock-and-roll"—classically represented by Bacchus, the Roman god of food, drink, and fertility. A *motivational* hedonist, in contrast, is someone who endorses a specific theory of human psychology, according to which even Mother Teresa does what she does to secure good feelings for herself (pride, perhaps, or the pleasure that comes from making a difference), or in order to avoid bad ones (such as guilt or shame).

A couple of additional points are worth emphasizing. One is that motivational hedonism is quite distinct from hedonic *utilitarianism*. This is the view that only good and bad hedonic states matter morally, and that an overall positive balance of them should be maximized. Indeed, it might be problematic for hedonic utilitarians to endorse motivational hedonism, if one assumes that "ought" implies "can," for motivational hedonists think that people *can't* do other than pursue *their own* hedonic good. Of course, one could also claim that hedonic-utility is actually maximized if everyone just pursues their own hedonic maximization. That would be a fortuitous outcome: in acting as they must (motivated by the only thing that *can* motivate them, allegedly) people would also be acting rightly (provided that they do so effectively, of course). Although utilitarians have not generally endorsed such a claim, weaker versions of it are central to classical economics. If the market operates freely, and everyone acts for their own economic interests, then the economy as a whole will flourish. (This is Smith's [1759] "invisible hand.") However, even classical economists generally stop short of endorsing either variety of motivational egoism, allowing that people have intrinsic—non-self-interested—concerns for family and friends, for example.

Another point to mention is that even if one were to succeed in showing that motivational egoism and hedonism are false, that would still leave intact normative analogs of those views. One could still claim that one *ought* to

4 Human Motives

care only about oneself, or *ought* to act only to secure good and avoid bad hedonic states for oneself. I can, myself, see little that is attractive in such views. But in any case, no attempt will be made to argue against them here. What a successful critique of motivational forms of egoism and hedonism *would* do, however, is underpin the possibility of non-consequentialist forms of moral evaluation of actions and agents, as we will see next. If one thinks, as most of us do, that duties should generally be performed irrespective of one's own interests or enjoyment, and that intrinsic concern for other people is required in order to be a good person, then one needs it to be the case that motivational egoism and hedonism are false. Happily, they are. Or so I think the science of affect demonstrates when properly interpreted.

1.2 Why It Matters

The theoretical stakes surrounding these issues are quite high. For if either motivational egoism or motivational hedonism is true then arguably there are no morally good actions, and nor are there any virtues of character or morally good people. For most of us think that intent is critical for each. Morally worthy actions should aim at worthy ends for their own sakes, not merely out of self-interest or to make oneself feel good. And good people are people who not only value the right things, but reliably act in order to secure those values, and not (or not just) to secure their own benefit or pleasure. All we will be left with are consequentialist notions of good action and good character (that is, actions and people that give rise to good consequences, whatever their underlying motives might be).

Consider someone who very publicly makes a large donation to charity, but who does so only because it will increase her chances of winning an upcoming election. (Perhaps she is caught on tape, in an unguarded moment, saying exactly this.) While we would evaluate the consequences of the action as good—assuming the charity is a worthy one, it is better that the money be given than not—we would be unlikely to think any better of the agent for it. On the contrary, knowing that the gift was entirely self-interested, we are likely to think *worse* of her because of it. Likewise, consider someone who repays a large loan to an acquaintance, not because justice requires it, but merely to avoid the inconvenience of having to contest it—if he could have gotten away without having to repay, then he would have done so. (Again, perhaps he is caught on tape saying just this.) We would surely think worse of him as a result.

Admittedly, the heavy reliance that people in developed cultures (especially in the West) place on agents' intentions when morally evaluating them appears not to be a cultural universal. Although most small-scale societies, too, place some reliance on the intention behind an action in at least some contexts, this seems not to be true of all; and the differences in moral evaluation between intentional and accidental harms tend to much smaller than they are in large-scale societies (Barrett et al. 2016).

It does appear, however, that modulating one's social evaluations of others by their intentions might be the default setting in human development. This is because infants as young as eight months prefer an agent who tries, but fails, to help another over one who tries, but fails, to hinder the goal of another (Hamlin 2013; Kanakogi et al. 2017). Note that the outcome in these cases is the same. Likewise, eight-month-old infants prefer an agent who tries to help another but fails (because acting on a false belief) over an agent who accidentally provides such help (Woo & Spelke 2023); and infants as young as ten months prefer an agent who intentionally, versus accidentally, helps another; and conversely, they also prefer an agent who accidentally, versus intentionally, harms another (Woo et al. 2017).[1] It may be that these are initial innate tendencies that can be weakened by later cultural input. Whether or not that is true, it remains the case that the vast majority of the people in the world now think that moral evaluation depends critically on the agent's intention when acting.

Accepting either egoism or hedonism would come with steep theoretical costs for most of us, then. But in practice those costs could be limited (for motivational hedonists, at least). This is because arguably the underlying function of evaluating others in terms of intent is to predict future patterns of behavior, enabling us to select reliable friends and cooperators while avoiding those who are likely to hurt or betray us. And this function could just as well be served by paying attention to people's proximal, or instrumental, intentions when acting. Even if everyone aims ultimately to secure their own pleasure and avoid their own displeasure, it makes a good deal of difference in practice whether what gives someone pleasure is helping others versus becoming rich, or whether what makes someone feel bad is breaking a promise rather than mere loss of reputation. Motivational hedonists, especially, can thus retain many of the practical benefits of evaluating actions

---

[1] Admittedly, these findings are only known to hold true among infants in the West. Such studies have not yet been attempted in small-scale societies. However, infant false-belief studies *have* been validated cross-culturally (Barrett et al. 2013).

6 Human Motives

and agents in terms of intentions by focusing on proximal rather than ultimate intentions.[2]

That motivational egoism and hedonism come burdened with theoretical costs is not in itself a strike against those views. For each makes an empirical claim about the psychological roots of human motivation—one that may now seem scientifically grounded, as we will see. So our ordinary intuitions should carry no weight in this debate. Indeed, whenever folk-beliefs come into conflict with established science, it is the former that should give way. Scientific findings do need to be interpreted, however, and scientists themselves sometimes over-interpret or misinterpret their own data.

Moreover, the project of this book is to understand what really, truly, motivates people, not to describe and regularize our ordinary concepts and beliefs (which is what most philosophical treatments are concerned to do). So, let the chips fall where they may. If the best scientific account turns out to support hedonism, then we will have to live with the consequences and adjust our beliefs accordingly. Happily, however, I think the best interpretation of the science supports motivational pluralism. Or so I will argue over the course of this book.

Egoism and hedonism don't just provide challenges to our ordinary moral beliefs; they are also socially damaging. This is because theories of human psychology (especially motivation-relevant psychology) are apt to be self-fulfilling. For example, believing that intelligence is malleable rather than a fixed quantity can cause people to do better in school; and interventions that induce beliefs in malleability can improve performance (Blackwell et al. 2007). Moreover, people who believe willpower to be a depleting resource—rather than nonlimited—can perform worse in a series of attentionally demanding effortful tasks; and interventions to induce nonlimited beliefs can likewise improve performance (Job et al. 2015). So we can be confident that people who believe that all actions are ultimately selfish will be apt to behave in a more selfish manner; and conversely, that work persuading people of the falsity of motivational egoism and hedonism will increase the likelihood of prosocial action. Although to the best of my knowledge this specific prediction has not been directly tested, a closely related one has. Economists believe that people are mostly motivated by self-interest, and Frank et al. (1993) found that taking a class in economics causes people to

---

[2] Indeed, as we will see in Chapter 2, it is possible for people to have other-regarding values and cares while at the same time all of their decisions are about maximizing their own hedonic utility, as motivational hedonists claim. So it would be possible to understand good *agents* to be those who possess the right *values*, even though all actions are nevertheless hedonically motivated and self-interested. This would pull apart the evaluation of agents from the evaluation of actions, of course, which would itself be a theoretical cost for most of us.

become *more* self-interested. Convincing people of the falsity of motivational egoism and hedonism, then, should lead them to become *less* self-interested.

1.3 The Way Ahead

Egoism and hedonism are perennially tempting, and have proven remarkably difficult to refute. Those who have attempted to critique them have mostly focused on motivational hedonism, regarding this as the most plausible (and most widely endorsed) form of egoism (Butler 1726; Broad 1952; Nagel 1970; Feinberg 1984; Batson 1991, 2019; Sober & Wilson 1998). Moreover, the most recent iterations of motivational egoism to emerge out of scientific psychology have likewise taken a hedonic form. Indeed, we will see in Chapter 2 that non-hedonic forms of egoism are scientifically deeply problematic. So I, too, will focus on the case for and against motivational hedonism in this book.

Chapter 2 will lay out the basics of the recent science of affect, and Chapter 3 will show how it can be (and has been) taken to support motivational hedonism. These two chapters will also, at the same time, demonstrate the scientific basis for at least a weak form of Humeanism about motivation, according to which all of our motives are grounded in affect ("the passions"), thereby resembling views that Blackburn (1999) has defended on other grounds. Chapter 4 will then show that the resulting form of hedonism is immune to the critiques that have been mounted by philosophers in the past, as well as being immune to the experimental findings in psychology that have been intended to refute hedonism.

Chapter 5 then begins consideration of the nature of the positive and negative valences (pleasure and displeasure) that are common to all affective states, examining two types of theory. It will contrast an intrinsic-feeling account (which would support motivational hedonism) with an account that construes valence as a nonconceptual representation of value (which entails pluralism). According to this latter view, when we select an option because of anticipatory joy or guilt, we are choosing it because that option seems good to us (in a quasi-perceptual manner), or seems bad, not because it will make us *feel good* or *feel bad*. Chapter 6 then contrasts this representational view with an imperativist account (which sees valence as an imperative-like urge to do something or to forebear from doing something). In some versions this, too, entails motivational hedonism. The value-representing view of valence will emerge as the overall winner from these comparisons.

8 Human Motives

Chapter 7 will then examine a test case for the value-representing account of valence, specifically the case of physical pain, about which much has been written by philosophers lately. Since it is natural to think that pain just feels intrinsically bad, rather than represents anything as bad, it might seem to support an intrinsic-feeling account of negative valence in particular. (Similar points apply to simple physical pleasures, like the taste of a ripe strawberry.) Indeed, the case of pain is taken by many to present a challenge for representational accounts of conscious experience generally. Chapter 7 will show that these challenges can be met.

Finally, Chapter 8 will examine moral motivation, and the psychological roots of prosociality, through the lens of the theory of valence-based decision-making outlined in previous chapters. The upshot is that human beings are indeed equipped to want to do the right thing for its own sake (some of the time), and to help (some) others for their own sakes. However, the main focus of the chapter will be to argue that some of these motivations are innate or innately channeled. The final two sections then conclude by pulling together the main ideas and arguments of the book.

I should stress that my arguments throughout will be grounded in science, debating how it should best be interpreted. There will be no reliance on the kinds of thought-experiments and appeals to intuition that are the bread-and-butter of most philosophical writing. When it comes to understanding the mind—and understanding the sources of human motivation, in particular—such approaches are worse than useless. They provide an illusion of knowledge and understanding, whereas in fact they just reflect folk theories and common-sense conceptions. It is as if philosophers were to continue to advance claims about the physical world by studying Aristotle (whose views, arguably, capture much of our intuitive folk-physics; Clement 1982; McCloskey 1983; Keleman et al. 2013).

This book will also devote much more space to animal models of motivation than is usual in philosophy. Indeed, many philosophers of mind in the latter half of the last century were suspicious of—not to say contemptuous of—all talk of reward, punishment, and reward-based learning.[3] This was grounded in their rejection of behaviorism, where such language originated, and in their embrace of the cognitive revolution. But the science of evaluative learning has moved on since then. While the language of "reward" and "punishment" is still used, these terms are embedded in sophisticated computational models of conditioning and reward-based learning. In fact, such

---

[3] One of the few philosophers to take the science of affect seriously is Morillo (1995), who is led to endorse motivational hedonism as a result.

models are routinely interpreted realistically, as well, entailing that there are explicit computational and representational processes in the minds of the animals doing the learning. Moreover, while there are, of course, important differences between humans and other animals—resulting especially from gene-culture co-evolution (Henrich 2017)—it is now widely accepted in the affective sciences that the underlying foundations are the same. We ignore them at our peril. As a result, the general approach taken in this book (as in most science) is "bottom-up"—starting with simple mechanisms before building toward an account of more complex cases.

The book will thus devote correspondingly less space to considering philosophical treatments of motivation and decision-making. This is because, as noted above, what most such treatments are really treatments *of* are common-sense theories of motivation, perhaps combined with what people take to be the deliverances of introspection. While it might be fine to take common sense as a starting point if there were no well-developed science in the area, there is now an immense amount of well-established scientific work on the topic. One might wonder, then, what business a philosopher has in addressing these issues at all. Two points can be made in reply. One is that scientific results still need to be interpreted. The other is that scientific work can sometimes be overly narrow. There is a good deal of mileage to be gained from stepping back and looking at the bigger scientific picture in the way that I do here, integrating results across a range of related subdisciplines.

Overall, this book has two main goals. One is to make findings from the new science of affect accessible to a wider academic audience. My hope, in particular, is that many long-standing philosophical debates can be both rejuvenated and illuminated if those engaging in them have more knowledge of the science. The other main goal is to refute motivational hedonism. But in doing so, I take hedonism much more seriously than most other critics have done. In fact, I try to develop the strongest possible form of motivational hedonism *before* showing that it fails. I believe Wittgenstein once said something to the effect that good military generals attack their opponents on their weakest sides, whereas good philosophers attack their opponents on their strongest. For our goal is truth and understanding, not point-scoring or quick victory. Since the resulting kind of argumentative good practice is, in effect, the converse of the well-known straw-man fallacy, it is sometimes referred to using a related name. It can be called "a steel-man argument," "steel-man validity," or, perhaps better, "the steel-man strategy." So my second major goal can be described as an attempt to refute motivational hedonism once-and-for-all through use of the steel-man strategy.

2

The Science of Affect

This chapter sketches the main outlines of our scientific knowledge of affective states in general. Among other things, it demonstrates that there is a distinction between one's stored values, on the one hand—appraisal against which issues in affect—and the valenced output (anticipatory pleasure and displeasure) that provides the basis for subsequent decision making, on the other. Relatedly, the chapter also argues that motivational egoism can only be defensible when cast in the form of motivational hedonism. Chapter 3 will then show how the science of affect can be (and has been) interpreted to support a sophisticated form of motivational hedonism, and Chapter 4 will show how the resulting scientifically informed account can evade all previous philosophical and experimental critiques of hedonism.

There is an immense amount of psychological and neuroscientific research that is relevant to our topic. Although comparatively little work was done on affect and motivation in the early decades of the cognitive revolution in psychology that started in the 1950s, the most recent few decades have seen an explosion of new findings and theoretical models. I cannot hope to do justice to all of this in the scope of a single chapter. Nor, I think, would it be helpful to the reader to pack the text with references. I shall cite judiciously (especially from recent review papers, within which there are multiple references to previous work, for those interested), and will confine myself to well-established findings. Moreover, since this book is aimed at philosophers and a general academic readership, I will skim over most of the underlying neuroscientific technicalities, confining them to footnotes where possible.

Even so, readers who are wholly naïve to the science may find this chapter hard going. My advice is to persevere. Not only is the emerging scientific consensus important for the debate between egoism and pluralism, but it may also impact many other areas of philosophy. These include, for example, distinctions that may need to be drawn in the philosophy of action between intended, intentional-but-not-intended, and reflex actions; distinctions of kind among states that both philosophy and common sense treat as desires; the realization that the contents of felt desires are never wholly propositional in nature (in the way that philosophers generally assume them to be); and

Human Motives: Hedonism, Altruism, and the Science of Affect. Peter Carruthers, Oxford University Press.
© Peter Carruthers 2024. DOI: 10.1093/oso/9780198906131.003.0002

new light that can be thrown on debates between Humean and rationalist theories of motivation generally.

2.1 The Scope of Affect

Affective states constitute a broad class.[1] They include emotions, such as anger, fear, disgust, pride, curiosity, and joy, as well as moods such as sadness and cheerfulness. They also include felt desires such as thirst and hunger, but also felt desires like hoping one has won the lottery or that one's recent social media post will get multiple "likes." They likewise include bodily pleasures and displeasures, such as enjoyment when biting into a ripe strawberry, orgasm, physical exhaustion, and pain, as well as more abstract pleasures and displeasures, such as enjoying or disliking a conversation or a game of chess.

Affective states differ along a number of dimensions. Some, like anger, tend to be short-lived, whereas others, like sadness or cheerfulness can last for weeks or months. Some, like anger, fear, and many felt desires are out-ward looking, whereas exhaustion and pain are focused on the body. And some, again like anger, fear, and desire, have contents that can be described in terms of propositions (one fears *that* the bear will attack, or one's longing has the content, *that I will win the lottery*), whereas others, like orgasm, pain, and pleasure or displeasure in an activity do not. Nevertheless, all affective states share a common underlying structure, as we will see, which is why they are often classified and studied together in affective science and neuroscience.

There are disputes within the field about how real some of the sub-divisions among affective states are—that is, whether they mark out differ-ences between natural kinds in the world (which exist independently of our theories), or whether they are social constructions of some sort. Among emotions, for example, some think that there is a basic set that is pan-human, and which share many of their properties with the emotional states of other mammals (Ekman 1992; Izard 2007; Panksepp & Watt 2011; LeDoux 2012). Others argue that only the dimensions of valence (positive versus negative) and arousal (high versus low) are really real (Russell 2003; Barrett et al. 2007).

---

[1] Not everyone in the field uses the term "affect" to designate this class. Some use "motivational state," reserving "affect" for the evaluative/hedonic component of such states (where I use "valence"); others use "emotion," describing even thirst and orgasm as emotions (Rolls 1999). These are merely terminological differences, not substantive disagreements. On the contrary, there is widespread agreement that the states in question share a common structure. See the discussion that follows.

12 Human Motives

In support of the latter, it does seem that the brain networks underlying emotional experience—and indeed, those underlying affective states more generally—are largely similar.[2]

My own view, however, is that there is now convincing evidence of micro-circuits within these structures that are to some extent type-specific (Adolphs & Anderson 2018; Kohl 2018; Kennedy 2022). Although nothing much hangs on it, this is what I will assume going forward. Moreover, whatever one thinks about emotions, there seems little doubt that there are conserved innate brain-circuits for homeostatic affective states like hunger, thirst, and thermo-regulation, as well as for states of cognitive tiredness, muscular exhaustion, and sensory pain (LeDoux 2012).

Our focus here, however, is on the core properties that all affective states share, about which there is much more consensus. In fact, affective states appear to constitute a natural kind in something like the sense of Boyd (1991, 1999)—they constitute a homeostatic property cluster, comprising a set of properties that not only tend to co-occur together, but do so non-accidentally, in a law-like manner. Or perhaps more accurately, affective states constitute a superordinate natural kind, standing to the various sub-kinds (emotions, moods, and so on) somewhat as the superordinate kind *mammal* stands to the various species of mammals (mice, rats, cats, dolphins, humans, and so on). We will begin our discussion with the causes of affective states before moving on to their characteristic outputs.

2.2 The Input: Appraisals of Value

Most (perhaps all) affective states result from appraisals of the value or personal significance of some property, thing, or event, whether currently perceived, or merely remembered, imagined, anticipated, or thought about (Moors et al. 2013). In some cases (e.g. fear), the appraisal mechanisms take input mostly from the world (e.g. about an approaching bear), whereas in others (e.g. hunger and thirst) they also take input from the current state of the body (calorie depletion or dehydration), and in yet others (e.g. pain) their input is mostly (but not entirely) from the body (Ashar et al. 2017). Even free-floating moods such as sadness and cheerfulness are thought by some to reflect more-general appraisals of the opportunities afforded by the current environment (Eldar et al. 2016). In fact, Eldar et al. (2021) make a

---

[2] These include the amygdala and the ventral striatum among sub-cortical structures; and within the cortex, the anterior insula, anterior cingulate, ventromedial prefrontal, and orbito-frontal cortices.

plausible case that moods are an adaptive part of the computational processes underlying evaluative learning, speeding up the acquisition of positive values (in the case of positive moods) or slowing it down (in the case of negative ones) in response to changing opportunities provided by the local environment.

As should be clear from these examples, appraisal processes need not be judgment-like (let alone conscious). They can be associative in nature, and are sometimes "hard-wired" and uncontrollable (as when fear-responses are initiated by suddenly looming objects, or by oxygen-deprivation; Feinstein et al. 2013). It should also be clear, for the same reason, that my use of the term "appraisal" here is somewhat broader than tends to figure in appraisal theories of emotion specifically, where it is generally confined to judgment-like processes.

What, then, are appraisals? In the most general terms, an appraisal is any mental process (whether associative or judgment-like, whether conscious or unconscious) that links a stimulus (whether real or imagined) to stored personal values (whether innate or acquired), serving to activate them. Some of these values are merely implicit in the "wiring" of innate appraisal mechanisms. This is likely true of the link between oxygen-deprivation and panic (mediated implicitly by the value of survival), or the link between the sensory component of pain (often caused by bodily damage of some sort) and its painfulness. Others are acquired through evaluative learning and are stored in the form of new appraisal-conditions in evaluative memory, as when a rat learns that the onset of a light predicts an electric shock, and comes to disvalue the light itself, responding to it as intrinsically bad (see Section 2.6).

Appraisal processes are not static, of course. While an emotion-related episode or event continues to change and evolve, it will continually be appraised and re-appraised for its personal significance. A glimpse of wriggling motion in the grass (initially appraised as snake-like) may give rise to a fear response; but then closer examination may reveal it to be just a piece of rope being moved by the wind, or perhaps a harmless rat-snake, and one's fear rapidly subsides. And when watching a sporting event involving a team with which one identifies, one's emotions may follow a roller-coaster of joy, anxiety, and sorrow as the fortunes of the team wax and wane. Likewise while one eats a meal when hungry, one's hunger gradually subsides.

Many appraisal processes can be (and often are) highly context sensitive. How much one enjoys a glass of water depends, among other things, on one's current state of dehydration. Similarly, when a rat has previously learned that a cue predicts the availability of a highly aversive salt solution (to the point

14 Human Motives

even of avoiding proximity to the cue), it will immediately—without further learning—find that same cue highly attractive when artificially put into a state of salt-deprivation (Dayan & Berridge 2014). And as is familiar, how much one enjoys eating depends not just on the taste, but also on how hungry one is, and on how much of that food one has already eaten. Moreover, even when replete, one can generally enjoy a food of a completely different type. (This is the phenomenon of sensory-specific satiety.) A caress from one's partner is experienced as pleasant, whereas the very same sensation of touch from a stranger in a crowded metro carriage may be experienced as unpleasant; and the same touch again from one's boss may cause fear. Likewise, stimuli that would be terrifying if real can cause just anxious excitement when seen on the cinema screen. And so on. Some of these contextual cues can be low-level ones, whereas others (like recognition of one's boss as such) can be fully cognitive—a point that will be developed further in Section 2.7 when we discuss how affect can be influenced in a top-down manner.

Appraisals link stimuli to values, then. But what are values, in this context? They are dispositional properties of specialized neural circuits that respond to their inputs with a range of kinds of output (to be explored in later sections, including automatic motor activation, arousal processes, and positive or negative valence that gets used in decision-making and evaluative learning). As already noted, the circuits in question are context-sensitive, adjusting their processing in response to properties of the environment (e.g. open versus enclosed spaces, in the case of fear) as well as properties of one's own body (e.g. calorie depletion or dehydration). What makes it appropriate to describe these dispositions as forms of value is that they have been honed through natural selection to enhance the individual's chances of survival and successful reproduction. LeDoux (2012) calls them "survival circuits," though it might be more appropriate to describe them as "inclusive-fitness circuits." This is because they include dispositions that lead to successful mating and care of offspring (and, in humans, dispositions to care for community members, too, as we will see in Chapter 8). The core (innately determined) values encoded as dispositions of these inclusive-fitness circuits specify a set of primary rewards and primary punishments. These are things that the organism is innately disposed to experience as pleasurable or displeasurable, thereby providing an incentive to pursue them or avoid them. These core values soon become modified and elaborated through evaluative learning and conditioning to issue in new sets of acquired values (often called secondary rewards and punishers), as we will see in Section 2.6.

To illustrate, the circuits involved in thermo-regulation are designed to keep one's body temperature within a fixed range, necessary for normal bodily functioning (and ultimately survival). They receive as inputs signals from thermo-receptors in the skin, as well as from a range of internal bodily organs. They detect when the external temperature is too high or too low, producing a range of automatic behavioral and autonomic responses as a result (sweating, shivering, redirecting blood-flow to the surface or to the core), as well as unpleasant feelings (feeling too hot or too cold), thereby motivating one to take steps to change one's situation—seeking shade and/or removing some clothing when too hot, for example, or seeking shelter and/ or putting on clothes when cold. These same circuits enable the acquisition of novel sets of values, too, leading one to value (seek out and enjoy) a mug of hot chocolate on a cold winter's night, for instance, or a cold beer on a hot day.

Appraisal of the contents of some set of representations as input in relation to stored values is what sets an affective process in motion, issuing in pleasure, a desire, an emotion, or a mood, as we have seen. But what more can be said about the outputs of appraisal processes? What are the effects of appraisal? There are a number of distinct outputs that operate largely in parallel (albeit interacting with one another). In Section 2.3 we focus on behavior, both expressive and instrumental, before moving on to arousal (Section 2.4), valence (Section 2.5), and evaluative learning (Section 2.6).

2.3 Output (1): Behavior

The appraisal component of affective states directly and automatically activates motor-plans of various sorts, depending on the nature of the initial appraisal (Frijda 2010; LeDoux 2012; Adolphs & Anderson 2018). These motor-tendencies will need to be actively suppressed if they are not to be carried through to completion. In the case of emotions, they include motor instructions for facial expressions (the fear-face, the anger-face, the surprise-face, and so on) as well as specific sorts of bodily behavior—approaching or attending more closely, in the case of curiosity; running or freezing, in the case of fear, depending on the affordances of the situation (Pichon et al. 2012). Most felt desires, too, at least initiate basic approach or retreat motor plans, as we can tell from reaction-time studies involving movement forwards or backwards using positive and negative stimuli (van Dantzig et al. 2008). In fact, the urge to get close to a desired thing is triggered automatically, but the mode of action selected to bring about that effect can be flexible,

16 Human Motives

while nevertheless being independent of one's intentions and goals (Krieglmeyer et al. 2010). Likewise, pain will directly activate motor plans for grimacing or crying out (depending on severity), and for nursing and/or protecting the painful part. And even moods issue in characteristic overall bodily postures, muscle tone, and modes of activity (slumped lassitude, in the case of sadness; energetic gait and upright posture, in the case of cheerfulness).

It should be emphasized that these motor-tendencies are produced automatically by the initial appraisal processes, at least in parallel with, and in part causing, the valence-component of affective states (especially when the latter is forward-looking or anticipatory; see Section 2.5). Thus, one effect of evaluative learning is that perception and appraisal of positively valued stimuli issues in two sorts of output (collectively known in the field as "incentive-salience"; Berridge 2009; Smith et al. 2011; Olney et al. 2018)—it directly activates approach motor plans, causing an urge to acquire the stimulus object or event, and at the same time it makes the acquisition of the valued stimulus seem attractive and pleasurable (that is, the stimulus becomes positively valenced). However, this is not to say that valence and action don't interact. On the contrary, valenced feedback will strengthen motor-tendencies over time, issuing in habits; and urges-to-act will create negative valence when suppressed, since self-control is experienced as effortful.

Indeed, stronger still, it seems likely that so-called "sensory forward models" of the appraisal-caused motor plans are themselves appraised for their value, issuing in positive or negative valence. We know that all forms of action-initiation produce, not just changes in the musculature required, but also predictions of the afferent sensory feedback likely to be caused by the action (proprioceptive, visual, and auditory), as well as the latter's immediate consequences (Jeannerod 2006; McNamee & Wolpert 2019). These are used in fine-grained motor control. But it is also likely that they are appraised and evaluated in turn, not just for the physical effort involved (Cos et al. 2014), but also for the consequences of the action itself. Hence when one sees a ripe strawberry on the kitchen counter, an appraisal of it as good to eat might cause one to feel an urge to reach out, grab, and bite into it—actions that are in turn appraised as good and pleasurable in anticipation.

We have already seen enough here to realize that motivational hedonism cannot be universally true, applying to all actions without qualification. For smiling with joy and grimacing with pain are both actions (at least in the sense that both are behaviors caused and controlled by cortical motor systems, not automatic reflexes like an eye-blink or a knee-jerk), but neither is undertaken to insure pleasure or avoid displeasure. This is for the simple reason that emotion-expressive actions aren't generally undertaken to insure *any* outcome, let alone a hedonic one. But then neither do emotion-expressive actions support motivational pluralism, in the sense in which the latter is normally understood. This is because those actions aren't aimed at achieving anything—they have no goal.[3] So it remains a possibility that all actions that are goal-directed and result from decision-making processes among options are hedonically motivated. Indeed, this is just what any defensible form of motivational hedonism should claim.

It is not just expressive behavior that is automatically activated by affective appraisal. Something similar is true of the action-tendencies that are built into some affective systems innately.[4] Thus the impulse to run from a terror-inducing stimulus is directly caused by the appraisal process that produces the fear (Qi et al. 2018). Likewise for the impulse to attack a rage-inducing stimulus, as well as to jerk one's hand away from a pain-inducing one. Although from a common-sense perspective we would describe these actions as goal-directed (to achieve safety; to hurt someone; to avoid pain), in reality they are not. They are activated immediately and directly by the appraisal of the stimulus, and aren't *intended* to achieve anything—at least, not if one thinks of intentions as action-guiding states that result from decision-making processes among options. This is not to say that directly initiated motor-plans can't acquire a goal as the action unfolds, however. As one turns automatically to flee in terror from the approaching predator, for example, one might perceive some locations as affording more safety than others, deciding between them. The one selected then becoming one's goal: something one intends to achieve.

Habitual actions have a somewhat different status. Because habits are generally acquired through affective feedback and learning, one might say that they are undertaken *because of* the hedonic feedback (rewards and punishments) received during the learning process (see Section 2.6). But they are now activated directly by the cue. Here, too, common-sense falsely attributes intentionality or goal-directedness (Wood & Rünger 2016). Consider getting the coffee pot down from the shelf when one first stumbles into the kitchen in the early morning (manifesting a well-established habit, let us suppose). While this may contribute to the achievement of a desirable event

---

[3] Of course one *can* smile strategically, to achieve a goal (albeit less successfully, since the muscles around the eyes aren't under intentional control; Müri 2016). And if one *suppresses* a spontaneous expression of emotion, then that might well be done to achieve some good, among the candidates for which would be hedonic ones (such as a desire to avoid anticipated embarrassment or shame).

[4] By affective *systems* I mean the neural networks that underlie the causation and realization of specific types of affective state (fear, say, or disgust). I will sometimes refer to "the affective system" (singular), intending to designate the entire set of such systems.

18 Human Motives

(drinking coffee), it isn't undertaken with that goal in mind (either consciously or unconsciously). Rather, reaching for the pot is a habitual action initiated by the cue (entering the kitchen in the morning) and then executed automatically. So although one might describe oneself as having reached for the pot *in order to* make coffee, this is actually a mistake—when prompted, one's mentalizing system generates a confabulated interpretation of the behavioral data (Wood & Rünger 2016; Miller et al. 2019). Once again, however, motivational hedonists can (and should) respond by restricting their claims to actions that result from decision-making processes, rather than all actions as such.

Actions that result from a previously formed goal or intention share some (but only some) of the properties of habitual actions. Intentions (especially conditional intentions such as, "When lunch is finished I shall cut the grass") can become activated by internal or environmental cues (in this case, by clearing away the lunch things). When they do they are apt to initiate the intended actions directly, without affectively based decision-making of any sort (Gollwitzer & Sheeran 2006). Goals and intentions belong among the "cold" causes of action in contrast with "hot" (affect-laden, emotional) ones (Metcalfe & Mischel 1999). In effect, they can be thought of as high-level (abstract) motor plans (Carruthers 2015), existing outside of one's affective systems and stored separately in what is generally called "prospective memory" (McDaniel et al., 2013; Momennejad & Haynes 2013).

Nevertheless, intentions are generally caused to exist in the first place as a result of affect-laden decision-making. (Some possible exceptions will be discussed in Chapter 3.) And as we will also see in Chapter 3, future-directed decision-making generally involves prospective rehearsal of the various options and outcomes, responding affectively to each, with estimates of likelihood and value being integrated to select the option with the highest expected value. (For a motivational hedonist, this means selecting the option with the greatest expected positive affective feeling.) As a result, it is correct to say that actions caused by prior intentions are motivated by affect, and not just caused by it. Although the affect in question was experienced when one first formed the intention, it provided the goal-state in the decision-making process that led to the intention. So if the original decision was taken in order to maximize one's hedonic state, as hedonists will claim, then the same can be said of the action that results when the intention is implemented, even if one no longer has pleasure in mind.

In addition to the effects on overt behavior discussed above, evaluative appraisals also have widespread effects on cognition, especially in redirecting attention (which is best construed as action-like; Carruthers 2015)

The Science of Affect   19

and in influencing evaluative judgments. In fact, perceptual systems can be biased toward processing positively or negatively evaluated stimuli even in advance of any re-direction of attention (Barrett & Bar 2009; Persichetti et al. 2015). This can be thought of as a form of low-level appraisal-effect—an initial indicator of danger or reward causes a bias toward processing the perceptual stimulus in question, leading it to be seen or heard in greater detail when attended to. The same set of swift appraisal processes may also serve to attract one's attention, with subsequent ramping up or down of one's emotional response. And mind-wandering, too, is thought to be initiated and controlled by appraisals of associatively activated concepts and memories, when these are deemed sufficiently relevant to one's stored values or salient goals to be worthy of attention (Corbetta et al. 2008; Carruthers 2015). But one's emotion-inducing appraisals can also have differential effects on one's estimates of risk, for example, even in an unrelated choice. Thus incidental anger reduces one's estimates of the riskiness of an option (at least among males), whereas incidental fear increases them (Ferrer et al. 2016). Likewise, there is widespread evidence of the influence of mood and incidental emotion on evaluative judgment (Gasper & Clore 2000; Winkielman et al. 2005; Lerner et al. 2015).

The main take-away from this section, however, is that all forms of affective appraisal directly cause behavioral impulses of one sort or another. These impulses are produced immediately, prior to any evaluative comparison among the options and subsequent decision-making (including any decision to suppress the impulse). There is thus a large class of actions that lack a goal or intended outcome (beyond the performance of the action itself). This includes habitual actions, expressive actions like smiling, and innate or learned instrumental actions like beginning to flee from a looming threat. These actions have causes but lack a motive, in the normal sense of an intended goal. Motivational hedonism, then, if it is to be defensible, needs to be restricted to actions that result from decision-making processes. Hedonists should claim that all actions that result from decision-making aim at maximizing one's own hedonic state, rather than that all actions without qualification do.

2.4 Output (2): Arousal

In addition to directly causing both expressive and instrumental behavior, the appraisals that initiate affective states automatically activate a suite of bodily changes or degrees of "arousal"—including increases or decreases in

20 Human Motives

heart rate and breathing rate, pupil dilation, increased sweating, preparatory release of stress-related chemicals like cortisol and adrenaline into the bloodstream, and so on (Tiemann et al. 2018). Many of these changes are initiated before one even becomes conscious of the stimulus (Adolphs & Anderson 2018), and can be caused subliminally, in the absence of conscious experience (Tamietto & de Gelder 2010; Van den Stock et al. 2011). In fact, most affective states can be organized according to level of arousal, from sadness and contentment at one end (low arousal) to joy, rage, and abject terror at the other (high arousal) (Russell 2003).

Some have thought that the arousal component of affect (on some views when also combined with the automatic behavioral components) constitute the very heart, or essence, of emotion (James 1890; Prinz 2004), and others have thought that it is sensitivity to these bodily changes that drives affective decision-making (Damasio 1994). It is doubtful whether arousal processes have the kind of specificity to be distinctive of individual emotions, however (Siegel et al. 2018). And we now know that while degrees of arousal might signal the importance, or urgency, of the matter to be decided upon, it is the valence component of affect (anticipatory pleasure and displeasure) that plays the main role in decision-making (Storbeck & Clore 2008).

Of course, patterns of arousal cues can come to be positively or negatively valenced in their own right through evaluative learning. Indeed, as we will see in Section 2.6, any cue that is (in context) predictive of something valued or disvalued can come to be positively or negatively valued for its own sake. This is how skydivers can come to enjoy and be exhilarated by the physiological response characteristic of fear, for example—racing heart, heightened alertness, and so on. And it is why some people enjoy watching scary movies. As a result, the arousal component of many affective states can come to make a secondary contribution to the valenced aspect of those states (positive or negative). The arousal component of affective states will play little role in the discussions that follow, however.

2.5 Output (3): Valence

When stimuli are appraised against stored values the result is generally some degree of positive or negative valence, often described in terms of reward and punishment—in effect, pleasure and displeasure by other names, at least when conscious. (We will return to discuss these differences in terminology at the end of this section, treating them as equivalent for now.) When biting into a ripe strawberry, for example, the sweet taste will generally activate a stored positive evaluation of sweet things, giving rise to positive valence (pleasure) that accompanies and is bound into one's overall experience of the taste. In contrast, when biting into a lemon, its sour taste will by default activate a stored negative evaluation of sour things, giving rise to negative valence (displeasure).

As it happens, these are each examples drawn from among the innate settings of one's affective system, serving as primary (unlearned) rewards and punishments, and are common to all mammals. Newborn human infants and rat pups will each exhibit a lip-smacking pleasure response when a few drops of sugar-solution are placed into their mouths, and will exhibit a disgust-like aversive response to lemon juice (Berridge & Kringelbach 2008).[5] But these innate initial settings of the affective system can be altered through subsequent evaluative learning (see Section 2.6), becoming modified through their association with other values. For example, human children can be conditioned to like the bitter taste of broccoli by dipping the food in peanut butter, or by sweetening it (Havermans & Jansen 2007; Yeomans et al. 2008).

Once some degree of affective learning has taken place, stimuli that were previously paired with positive or negative valence will issue in a prediction of reward or punishment, drawing on a weighted average of the degrees of pleasure or displeasure involved in previous pairings. Recognizing a strawberry, and having previously enjoyed their taste, the value system generates an expectation of some degree of pleasure to be derived from eating it. That representation of expected pleasure accompanies one's sight of the strawberry, making the thought of eating it seem attractive. (This is one aspect of so-called "incentive-salience," discussed briefly in Section 2.3 and to be discussed again in Section 2.6.) Expectations of valence of this sort play a critical role in many if not all forms of decision-making, as we will see in Chapter 3. When the strawberry is then eaten, the pleasure derived from it is compared against one's initial expectation. If it is greater than expected a reward-prediction error-signal is created, and the stored value for strawberries (or for strawberries that look like that one) is ratcheted up by some increment; whereas if the strawberry is not yet ripe and not very sweet, the error-signal results in the stored value being ratcheted down. (This is one of

---

[5] Indeed, Peng et al. (2015) show that direct stimulation of sweet-sensitive or bitter-sensitive regions of the mouse gustatory cortex (located in the anterior insula) causes oral pleasure or disgust responses, even in mice that have never previously been exposed to sweet or bitter flavors. Since they also show that the same types of direct stimulation can be used to condition novel place preferences, we can conclude that the stimulation is genuinely rewarding and punishing, and not merely behavior-causing.

the critical roles of valence in affective learning, to be discussed in Section 2.6.)[6]

Although I wrote, in the previous paragraph, of the affective system creating a representation of expected pleasure, what I should really have said is: it creates pleasure in response to a representation of an expected event. For the affective system responds in essentially the same way (only with lesser intensity and vividness when consciously experienced) whether an event (e.g. eating a strawberry) is actually experienced, or is merely anticipated or imagined to be taking place. This is how valence figures into prospection-based, or simulation-based, affective decision-making, as we will see in Chapter 3. One represents the future, responds affectively to that representation with pleasure or displeasure, and then uses one's affective response as a basis for one's decision (Gilbert & Wilson 2007, 2009).

Valence is increasingly thought to be the "common currency" of decision-making, in the sense that valence signals can be compared and traded off across multiple types of reward and punishment (Levy & Glimcher 2012; Chikazoe et al. 2014; Ruff & Fehr 2014; Sescousse et al. 2015). Thus people can trade off electric shocks of some particular likelihood against a chance of monetary compensation, doing so in apparently coherent ways; as well as trading shocks against money combined with a sip of juice, or electric shocks against a chance see beautiful faces or to avoid social exclusion, and so on (Eisenberger et al. 2003; Chib et al. 2009). Moreover, the valence associated with many different properties of a thing or event can be combined into an overall affective evaluation (when experienced or consumed), or into an overall evaluative expectation (when anticipated). Indeed, there are quite general valence-based priming effects (in addition to the emotion-specific ones mentioned earlier). Thus a sunny day can alter one's evaluation of a college campus, and a subliminally perceived happy face or angry face can alter one's subsequent evaluation of a novel beverage upwards or downwards (Gasper & Clore 2000; Winkielman et al. 2005).

In addition, Bromberg-Martin & Hikosaka (2009) show that there are subcortical neurons in the monkey brain (in the ventral striatum) that fire at the mere prospect of *information* about the size of an upcoming liquid

---

[6] It was once thought that dopamine is the neurotransmitter specifically involved in the experience of reward (pleasure or "liking"—the scare quotes here are commonly used to indicate that the experience need not be a conscious one). But the consensus is now that spikes in dopamine networks in the subcortical striatum signal the prediction errors that drive evaluative learning (that is, learning of secondary-reward values as opposed to instrumental learning for existing rewards; Flagel et al. 2011), and that activity in dopamine networks also underlie the motivation to pursue rewards ("wanting" or incentive-salience, including anticipatory pleasure; Berridge & Kringelbach 2015). The role of dopamine in motivation appears to be highly conserved, and is even the mechanism underlying reward-pursuit in honey-bees (Huang et al. 2022).

reward as well as at the prospect of a large reward itself, and that the same neurons also fire on *receipt* of the information that a reward is imminent as well as when that reward itself is experienced. It appears, then, that the brain employs a common neural code for all four of: experienced liquid reward-value and predicted liquid reward-value, as well as experienced information-value and predicted information-value.[7] (See Kobayashi & Hsu [2019] for work with humans to the same effect.)

There is some debate in the field, however, over whether positive and negative valences exist as a genuinely fungible common currency, with a zero-valence midpoint, or rather whether they exist as fully comparable but distinct scales of magnitude (Rolls 2015). There is reason to think that the latter view is preferable, in part because there seem to be cases of mixed emotion—or mixed pleasure and displeasure—attaching to the same thing or event in light of its various properties (Larsen et al. 2004; Shenhav & Buckner 2014). This suggests that positive and negative valences emanating from appraisal of (different aspects of) the same thing don't cancel one another out, but remain distinct. In addition, positive and negative valence are for the most part processed in separate—but overlapping—networks in the brain, again suggesting that the outputs of those networks are representationally distinct.[8]

A comparison with actual currency (money) might help. Go back a few decades or more to a time when money was realized exclusively in valuable physical tokens of some sort (bank notes, for example, or gold coins). One might have a certain quantity of money in one's pocket, or in one's bank account. But at the same time one might have incurred debts. The latter were quite differently realized, not in the form of "negative gold coins" (there were no such things), but rather in the form of promissory notes made out to a specific person or group, or existing as a record in the memories of the people involved. Wealth wasn't organized as a single exchangeable medium around a mid-point (zero money). Rather, one could have a certain amount of positive wealth at the same time as a certain amount of debt. From this one could calculate someone's overall net wealth, of course (which might be

---

[7] In these experiments the animals first saw a cue that either signaled that information would be upcoming, or that it would not. Then after a brief interval of expecting the information (in the informative case) they saw (with 50 percent probability) either a cue indicating that a large reward would be received, or that a small one would. Then after another brief interval of expecting the appropriate reward they received that reward.

[8] Negative valence is processed especially in a network comprising the amygdala and regions of ventral striatum sub-cortically, and cortically within the anterior insula, orbito-frontal cortex, and anterior cingulate. Positive valence, in contrast, is processed in a network involving distinct sub-regions of the ventral striatum, and cortically within orbito-frontal cortex and ventromedial prefrontal cortex.

zero); but that would still leave in place the dollars in one's pocket—the debt doesn't erase the dollars.[9]

There is also some debate about whether and how expected values in the economic sense (which integrate together outcome value and the probability of achieving it) are represented in the brain. For instance, it may be that the expected value of an option is not represented as a cardinal magnitude, but only in comparison with the other salient alternatives. Certainly we know that decisions among options are reached through mutual inhibitory neural processes (Strait et al. 2014). Moreover, it is also possible that expected values are not explicitly represented at all, but rather emerge from competitive interactions among sub-component representations, including outcome values (whether cardinal or comparative), likelihoods, and the anticipated costs of acting (Hunt & Hayden 2017).

On all views, however, positive and negative valence (pleasure and displeasure) are analog-magnitude properties of some sort. Although not sensory-specific, they are like color, length, and size in that they admit of fine-grained discrimination of the magnitudes involved. Something can be more or less pleasurable, or more or less displeasurable. They are also non-conceptual in nature. In order to find an experience pleasurable (rewarding), for example, one need neither possess nor deploy concepts like PLEASURE or ENJOY. But there are different theories concerning what these magnitudes are, as we will see in due course.

We are now in position to discuss the relations among some of the terms that have been employed in this section. There are four pairs: value (positive and negative), valence (positive and negative), pleasure and displeasure, and reward and punishment. On all views, one's affective systems contain stored values (whether innate or individually learned), against which representations of current or anticipated events and stimuli are appraised for significance. On all views, too, one of the outputs of these appraisal processes is positive or negative valence. As for valence itself, it is a form of current or anticipatory reward or punishment. Valence incentivizes pursuit or avoidance when anticipated, and provides feedback to adjust stored values when experienced in the present (see Section 2.6). Moreover, positive and negative valence *could* be equated with pleasure and displeasure. At any rate, anticipatory pleasure and displeasure, too, incentivize pursuit or avoidance; and likewise they impact evaluative learning when experienced. But the terms "pleasure" and "displeasure" carry strong connotations of consciousness,

---

[9] An alternative way of having a net worth of zero, of course, is to possess neither debts nor dollars. And likewise, many kinds of stimuli can be affectively neutral, giving rise to neither positive nor negative valence.

whereas reward and punishment (positive and negative valence) can be unconscious.

Perhaps the clearest cases of unconscious positive valence/reward are the signals that derive from nutrient-sensitive and fat-sensitive neurons in the gut (Li et al. 2022). These can be used to condition, not just food intake outside of one's awareness (Small & DiFeliceantonio 2019; de Araujo et al. 2020), but a range of arbitrary behaviors like place-preferences (Han et al. 2018). In this way the signals act as (primary) reinforcers, just as do many forms of conscious pleasure. But they are deeply unconscious: one cannot be aware of them. Other cases of unconscious valence, in contrast, can be either conscious or unconscious, becoming conscious when attended to. Consider how one will automatically adjust one's bodily posture every so often during the day, shifting in one's seat and responding (unconsciously) to physical discomfort that one might not have been aware of. What one responds to is unconscious negative valence. But when attended to, one experiences it as a feeling of discomfort.

We face a choice. We can either opt to say that pleasure and displeasure should be identified with positive and negative valence (reward and punishment), thereby making room for unconscious pleasures and pains. Or we can say, instead, that pleasure is consciously experienced positive valence whereas displeasure is conscious negative valence. Although the underlying psychological natural kind is valence (it is a signal of the same kind playing the same incentivizing and learning role whether conscious or unconscious), for our purposes I will follow common sense in treating pleasure and displeasure as conscious phenomena. In part this is for ease of comprehension as we proceed, given established habits of semantic interpretation. But in part, too, it is because motivational hedonists have generally had in mind motivation by *felt* (conscious) hedonic states.

Now notice that pleasure and displeasure are kinds of mental state. So if one says that the common currency of conscious decision-making is pleasure and displeasure, with decisions aiming to maximize the one while minimizing the other, then this straight away commits one to motivational hedonism—all such decisions are aimed at producing mental states of certain sorts in oneself. It will thus take some work to reconcile pleasure and displeasure as the common currency of conscious decision-making with motivational pluralism. That will be a task for later chapters.

That brings us, finally, to reward and punishment. On all views, rewarding events are positively valenced and punishing ones negatively valenced, and vice versa. And likewise, to anticipate a rewarding event is to anticipate a positively valenced one, while anticipating a punishing event (one that will make it less likely that one chooses the thing, or does it again) is to anticipate a negatively valenced one. (The same equivalences hold between consciously experienced reward and pleasure, on the one hand, and consciously experienced punishment and displeasure, on the other.)

Notice, though, that there is a major difference between a reward (noun) and something being rewarding (adjective). Rewards are items in the world. One can provide a rat with a food reward, for example, or a liquid one. Here it is the food-pellet itself that is the reward. But the rat will also generally (though not always) find eating the food rewarding—this characterizes the rat's experience, and its role in affective learning. Hence, a statement like, "Creatures pursue rewards and try to avoid punishments" is ambiguous. It can mean, "Creatures pursue rewarding things and avoid punishing ones." This is consistent with a motivational pluralism. Or it can mean, "Creatures pursue rewarding experiences and avoid punishing ones," which entails motivational hedonism. Some care needs to be taken over language in what follows, then.

The main upshot of this section is that valence (pleasure and displeasure when conscious) plays a critical common-currency-like role in decision-making. This will make possible a sophisticated form of motivational hedonism (discussed in Chapter 3), which can evade all of the standard philosophical and experimental arguments that have previously been levied against hedonism (as we will see in Chapter 4). Much will then turn on the question of what valence itself *is*, and exactly *how* it plays the role that it does in decision-making (to be discussed in Chapters 5 and 6).

2.6 Output (4): Affective Learning

As we noted in Section 2.5, valence plays a critical dual role in evaluative learning. One part is anticipatory, the other consummatory. Representations of events that are distal in either space (e.g. a strawberry on the kitchen counter) or time (e.g. continued future eating of the strawberry one has just taken a bite of) can issue in positive valence attaching to the representation of the event, generated from the stored value for events of that kind and modulated by context (such as one's own hunger or satiety, or the taste of the bite one has just taken). Then when the event is experienced (one bites into, or takes a second bite of, the strawberry) the resulting positive valence is compared with that predicted. When the event is more pleasant than expected, an error-signal is sent back to the appraisal system itself, ramping up the stored value for events of that kind (eating a strawberry that has a certain appearance). Something similar happens when the event is less positive than expected, and also in cases when the initial predictions are negatively valenced, or displeasurable (Pfabigan et al. 2011). Importantly, valence doesn't have to be consciously experienced in order for learning to take place (Bunce et al. 1999; Zucco et al. 2009; Greenwald & De Houwer 2017).

Affective learning is often described in terms of an actor-critic model. The actor selects an action in light of its anticipated reward-value; then when the action is executed the critic tells the actor whether its prediction was too high or too low, and by how much. It has been extensively modeled computationally and applied to action-learning problems generally (Sutton & Barto 1998). So-called "temporal difference" models, in particular, can explain how value can get distributed back down the chain of actions or events that led up to a reward being received, issuing in learning of instrumental actions (which can eventually become habitual).[10] Indeed, reward-learning algorithms are built into the heart of many recent artificial intelligence programs, such as those that can successfully beat human experts at chess or Go (Schrittwieser et al. 2020).

Human actors and their critics will often have differing values, of course. But anticipatory and consummatory valence are produced by appraising things against the same sets of values. How is this possible? How can they deliver different verdicts if the values they tap into are the same? The answer is that anticipated and experienced objects and events can differ in their other (non-evaluative) properties, as well as in their contexts of occurrence. Having previously eaten many sweet ripe strawberries, for example, one may have placed a high value on strawberry-eating, leading one to anticipate that the next one will be just as pleasurable. But unexpectedly, it is not so sweet, and the taste is disappointing. The value one attaches to strawberry-eating will then be ratcheted down by some increment, unless some other property of the strawberry makes it stand out (e.g. it is green rather than red). Here the value placed on sweetness is unchanged; what varies are the strawberries (and their sweetness).[11]

The distinction between actor and critic not only receives support through theoretical modelling, but also at the neural level. There is a network of hedonic "hotspots" in sub-cortical regions in particular, direct stimulation of which ramps up the consummatory pleasure associated with a stimulus and

---

[10] Recent modeling and data-collection suggest, however, that instrumental learning is not initially driven by reward predictions, but rather by rewards signaling a retrospective search of memory for predictive cues (Jeong et al. 2022).

[11] Note that even primary reinforcers like sweetness can have their value changed through evaluative learning, however, by becoming connected with other values or disvalues. The innate initial settings of the value systems are just that: initial settings.

inhibition of which depresses it, while there is a distinct network whose stimulation or inhibition alters the "incentive-salience" of a stimulus independently of any change in consummatory pleasure (Berridge & Kringelbach 2008). Thus a rat can be caused to eat much more eagerly and vigorously, but without any sign of increased pleasure. Or if the incentive-salience network is suppressed while the hedonic one is boosted, a rat will respond with intense pleasure when a sugar solution is placed in its mouth, but will make no effort to obtain any more.

As noted earlier, incentive-salience itself is best understood as including two parallel components, one comprising a behavioral urge (e.g. to approach the stimulus, or to chew it, and to do so more energetically) and the other comprising *predicted* or *anticipatory* positive valence. In this respect incentive-salience (desire, or "wanting") conforms to the structure of all distally directed affective states. (Fear involves both an urge to retreat and makes the object of fear seem bad; disgust involves both an urge to avoid the thing and/or retch, while also making the object of disgust seem bad; and so on.) Incentive stimuli energize actions directed at them, while also exerting a magnet-like attractiveness on both attention and decision-making (Nguyen et al. 2021). Indeed, these two sub-components of incentive-salience ("wanting") can be independently modulated and rely upon distinct subcortical networks (Miller et al. 2014).

The two systems ("liking" versus "wanting") seem also to be doubly dissociable in humans. For example, although depression has often been described as involving anhedonia (inability to take pleasure in things), it turns out that the deficit is largely one of incentive-salience (including anticipatory pleasure). In depressed people the pleasure derived from actually consuming a pleasant stimulus is little different from normal; but their motivation to pursue such things is greatly reduced (Dichter et al. 2010; Sherdell et al. 2012). Actions are appraised as unusually effortful, and things that would normally be seen as attractive and interesting appear flat and valueless (Lambie & Marcel 2002). Conversely, incentive-salience can exist in the absence of consummatory pleasure. Long-term drug addicts, for example, may still be strongly motivated to pursue the drug (and drug paraphernalia can prove highly attractive to them), while they experience little or no pleasure from consumption of the drug itself (Berridge & Kringelbach 2008; Olney et al. 2018).[12]

---

[12] Although relief from pain is often experienced as pleasant, some kinds of addictive drug aren't associated with painful withdrawal symptoms. Nevertheless, relief from a hard-to-resist persistent urge to take the drug will be experienced as pleasant, even if the drug itself no long produces a "high."

Berridge and colleagues have sometimes seemed to assert that the incentive-salience of a stimulus can exist in the absence of any *anticipatory* pleasure, too (Berridge & Kringelbach 2008; Holton & Berridge 2013). But in context this is best understood as saying that it can be independent of one's explicit beliefs or conscious expectations, rather than the implicit valence-prediction generated from evaluative appraisal of the stimulus. They point out, for example, that drug addicts may still have a strong urge to take a drug even though they know full well that they are past the point of enjoying the effects of the drug. But note that addicts don't just experience a motoric urge. The drug and drug paraphernalia are also *attractive* to them, attracting their attention and becoming a focus of their thoughts and planning, and in anticipation taking the drug *seems very good* (Lewis 2015; Sripada 2022). This is the positive valence generated automatically by representations of future drug-taking, resulting from the drug having hijacked the addict's affective learning system, despite their explicit knowledge that the effects of the drug will no longer be intrinsically pleasurable.

Berridge & Kringelbach (2015) also point out that states of incentive-salience can themselves be unpleasant. Yet it can still be true that incentive-salience always incorporates anticipatory pleasure. For Berridge & Kringelbach fail to notice here how the objects of appraisal can shift with time and context. While one lines up in the bakery one may be salivating at the sight of the last slice of chocolate cake behind the counter—the thought of eating the cake is strongly incentive-salient (involving, I say, anticipatory pleasure). But then the customer in front of one in line purchases it. Now there is a new object of appraisal. It is that a desired object is unattainable. That produces negative valence (displeasure), since one's desire is frustrated. But still the slice of cake is incentive-salient—it still looks delicious and desirable as it is packaged for the other customer. It is the overall state of mixed emotion that is unpleasant, not the incentive-salience component itself.

Affective learning begins, as it must, with some values that are *un*learned. These are the so-called primary rewards and primary punishers, such as sweet tastes, stroking touch, oxygen deprivation, and physical pain. But these soon become elaborated into a much larger set of secondary rewards and punishers, which are things, properties, events, or actions that are predictive of, or become associated with, other rewards and punishers (whether primary or secondary). This learning can take place through classical—or "Pavlovian"—conditioning, in which no behavior is required for learning to take place. Rather, a cue of some sort (such as the onset of a light) is predictive of the delivery of a reward or punishment (a food pellet, say, or an electric

30 Human Motives

shock). But learning can also take place through instrumental conditioning, in which actions that are often-enough followed by provision of a reward (or prevention of punishment) become valued in their own right.

It is important to emphasize that secondary rewards and punishers are not *just* predictive of primary rewards and punishers. Rather, they become valued/disvalued in themselves. An animal will work to achieve a secondary reward, or avoid a secondary punisher, in the absence of any other reward or punishment. And secondary rewards and punishers can themselves be used to condition yet other rewards and punishers. It is also important to note that classical and instrumental learning will often take place together and in parallel. At the same time as an animal learns that a cue predicts some specific type of reward, leading it to act, it will also learn to attach a value to that cue itself, independent of reward type (Burke et al. 2008).[13]

It is true, however, that the value or disvalue attached to a secondary reward or punisher seems to gradually diminish in the absence of any paired primary reward or punishment, with pursuit or avoidance behavior eventually becoming extinguished altogether. But in fact it has long been known from the animal conditioning literature that extinction effects are best understood as a form of contextual learning, involving top-down inhibition, rather than reflecting an erasure of the conditioned value. Although an animal initially conditioned to fear the onset of a light will gradually lose its fear-response when the light is no longer paired with pain, its fear can be immediately reinstated when the light becomes predictive of pain once again—the negative value of the light doesn't need to be re-learned (Quirk & Mueller 2008). So rather than learning that the light isn't bad (that is, rather than unlearning the negative value of the light), it seems the animal has learned that the-light-in-this-context isn't bad, or something of the kind. It has learned to restrict the negative evaluation of the light to a particular time-period or situation.

Much of the literature in the field uses the language of "model-based" versus "model-free" value learning and decision-making (Gläscher et al. 2010; Doll et al. 2012). In model-based learning the animal acquires beliefs about the cues and actions that will deliver an eventual reward, and responds flexibly in pursuit of the latter. It can often involve simulations of possible future actions and outcomes of the sort described in the literature on prospective reasoning, with important contributions from executive regions of prefrontal cortex (Jones et al. 2012). In model-free learning, in contrast, actions that have previously been rewarded acquire a sort of "cached value," and will be

---

[13] The former predictive sort of learning, but not the latter, seems to be specifically dependent on orbito-frontal/ventromedial prefrontal cortex. Learning of the general (non-specific) value of a cue can take place in a way that relies on the sub-cortical ventral striatum alone (Burke et al. 2008).

The Science of Affect **31**

performed independently of any further reward. At the same time, however, there are predictions made deep within subcortical valuational systems, enabling the cached value in question to be updated over time (Jones et al. 2012; Sadacca et al. 2016). This is, no doubt, how we come to intrinsically value and enjoy many of the activities we do, assigning them with secondary reward value. So one can come to enjoy cooking, independently of the reward value of the food cooked; one can come to enjoy walking, independently of where one walks to; and one can come to enjoy stamp-collecting because it has been paired with some other reward; and so on.

Sometimes the outcome of model-free learning is said to be the creation of a habit. But that is likely a mistake (DiFeliceantonio & Berridge 2016). The term "habit" is best reserved for associatively chained learned action-sequences whose performance is not experienced as rewarding, and for which the initiating cues lack incentive-salience (Wood & Rünger 2016; Miller et al. 2019). Examples include repeating the sequence of letters in the alphabet, as well as automatically reading any word that one attends to. The cues that initiate model-free responding, on the other hand, seem attractive to the individual, and there is an accompanying motor-urge to respond that can be hard to suppress—the classic signature of incentive-salience (Clark et al. 2012; Dayan & Berridge 2014). In contrast, purely habitual procedures like those involved in making one's morning coffee or repeating the alphabet aren't generally experienced as enjoyable, and are easily interrupted. Nor is being able to reach down the coffee-pot something that one will work to achieve for its own sake (for example, when one knows that no coffee is available), in the way that both humans and other animals will work to secure a secondary reward.[14]

There are differences across individuals, too, in the relative weights they assign to learned secondary rewards in contrast to the rewards those cues predict. This has been demonstrated in rats in a Pavlovian learning context where a cue (such as a lighted retractable bar) predicts the delivery of food shortly thereafter at a nearby location. Some of the animals soon seemingly

---

[14] Traditionally it was thought that evaluative responding is controlled by networks centered on the ventral striatum, whereas the shift to habitual responding moved the control of behavior to networks centered on the dorsolateral striatum. But recent findings suggest that the dorsolateral striatum is centrally involved in incentive-salience and secondary reward, rendering conditioned stimuli and conditioned responding attractive in their own right (Balleine et al. 2007; Morales & Berridge 2020). For example, stimulation of the dorsolateral striatum in rats enhances the attractiveness of a conditioned stimulus in ways that suggest enhanced incentive-salience. For the enhanced behavior is flexible, not stereotyped, immediately shifting to a new location when the conditioned stimulus (a retractable lever) is moved; and stimulation of the dorsolateral striatum increases the rats' willingness to work to achieve the appearance of the conditioned stimulus, suggesting that the experimenters' intervention has increased the apparent value of the latter (DiFeliceantonio & Berridge 2016). In contrast, behavioral habits and skills are thought to rely on a network linking the cerebellum, parietal cortex, and primary motor cortex (Galea et al. 2011; Shmuelof & Krakauer 2012).

value the cue for its own sake—they approach it and try to manipulate it, they will work to try to make it appear, and they take longer to retrieve the food—whereas others just treat the cue *as* a cue, and go straight to the location where the food will appear. Animals displaying the former tendency are called "sign trackers" whereas the latter group are described as "goal trackers" (Robinson & Flagel 2009; Morrison et al. 2015; Ahrens et al. 2016). The differences among the two groups are generally a matter of degree, rather than categorical; except that distinct strains of rats have now been bred specifically to accentuate the differences. It is thought that there are related individual differences among humans.[15]

Evaluative learning doesn't just take place through direct experience, but also through social observation. Thus rat pups will learn to fear what their mothers fear, for example (Olsson et al. 2016). And some birds will learn to fear and mob anything feared and mobbed by another member of their species, even a bottle of laundry detergent (Gould & Gould 1994). One of the main mechanisms involved in social learning is emotional mirroring. Sensing their mother's fear, the rat pups experience fear in their own right, and the negative valence component of the latter then becomes associated with whatever cue predicts the mother's fear. The same process takes place among humans, of course, and is one way in which humans rapidly acquire a range of culture-specific values and disvalues.

Notice that we don't have to postulate very much in the way of primary social rewards and punishments among humans for affective conditioning to issue in a range of other-regarding (non-egoistical) values. Suppose, for example, that humans innately value the good-regard or approval of community members and/or innately disvalue their ill-regard or disapproval. (As we will see in Section 2.7, and again in Chapter 8, at least some values of this sort are likely to be innate for group-living humans.) This is initially a value consistent with egoism. What one wants is a benefit for oneself (roughly, social status). But assuming that the community approves of people who act prosocially and/or disapproves of people who act selfishly, then normal affective learning will soon cause one to value prosocial action for its own sake, and to feel negative emotions like guilt at the thought of performing a selfish action. Moreover, these prosocial secondary rewards are unlikely to be subject to extinction effects, for reasons that will emerge in Section 2.7.

Let me stress again that the relationship between primary and secondary rewards and punishments is not an instrumental one. Consider the Garcia

---

[15] While there are differences between humans and other animals in their affective systems, of course (especially in the extent of cortical involvement), the core processes and brain networks involved in evaluative learning are shared (Shechner et al. 2014; Railton 2017; Adolphs & Anderson 2018).

effect, for example. When a mammal has become seriously sick with nausea and vomiting, an appraisal process from a search of memory identifies the most likely cause among items recently eaten. One-shot learning then results in that item evoking disgust (becoming a secondary punisher) for some significant time into the future. This will be familiar to most readers: you wake up vomiting one morning having eaten a chicken salad the night before, and thereafter (often for weeks afterwards) you cannot bear the thought of eating chicken again (although salads themselves are fine), and you would accept a significant cost to avoid doing so. If someone forces you to eat chicken, you are likely to find it extremely unpleasant, feeling nauseated, and perhaps even vomiting again. Yet of course one does not feel nauseous at the thought of eating chicken *in order* not to get sick again. There is no practical reasoning involved. Rather, chicken is an acquired secondary punisher, and is found nauseating in its own right. Likewise, then, for things like lying to others, or helping others in need—they will become appraised negatively or positively in their own right.

It should be obvious, then, that non-hedonist forms of egoism are in deep trouble. Even weak assumptions about one's initial egoistical values and desires will lead, through evaluative learning, to values that are other-regarding. The thought of doing something to help another will produce positive valence, and the thought of not doing so, or of doing something to hurt another, will produce negative valence. Egoism will only be viable as a theory of decision-making, then, if the role of affective states in that process is cast in hedonic form—as, of course, it *can* be. (Whether it should be or needs to be is for subsequent discussion.) One might forebear from hurting someone else's interests, for example, because one anticipates feeling guilty from doing so and one is motivated to avoid that negative feeling (Keltner et al. 2014).

Indeed, even more powerfully, since motivational egoism is a modal doctrine (making claims about what *must* motivate us, as we saw in Section 1.1), we only need to see that it is *possible* for evaluative conditioning to result in secondary other-regarding reward-values for egoism to become untenable—unless, that is, even such values only ever influence decision-making through their output of anticipatory pleasure (from prosocial acts) and/or anticipatory displeasure (from antisocial ones).

In what follows, then, I will be assuming that motivational hedonism is the only scientifically defensible form of motivational egoism. The debate will be about the nature and role of affective valence. If we can be confident that the appraisal mechanisms that issue in valence are (or at least can be) sensitive to other-regarding values, as I have suggested in the present section, and if it turns out that all decision-making depends on valence, then only a hedonic account of valence-based decision-making will be capable of rescuing egoism. As we will see in Chapter 3, many in the field have endorsed just such an interpretation.

It is worth noting that this sort of scientifically informed hedonism must postulate a deep disconnect between what people value and care about, and what actually motivates their decisions. Everyone should now accept that most people have other-regarding values and concerns, I suggest. Good things happening to other people (especially family, friends, and in-group members) is for most of us at least a secondary—learned—reward-value, and will produce pleasure independently of any further effects on oneself or one's situation. Likewise, failure to comply with acquired moral norms is generally a secondary punisher, and will produce displeasure or guilt independently of any further effects on oneself.

Stronger still, as we will see in Chapter 8, there is some reason to think that the foundations of other-regarding values are innate, and so don't need to be learned via affective conditioning. In one way or another, then, most people come to care about (some) others and about morality for their own sakes. But still, when it comes to making decisions, all conscious decisions can be taken so as to maximize one's own pleasure and/or minimize one's own displeasure. So all decision-making can be egoistic, nevertheless. The resulting combination of views can strike one as odd. But that is no argument against them. Science has produced many puzzling and counterintuitive findings.

2.7 Top-Down Influences on Affect

Thus far in our discussion of the science of affect we have mostly been assuming that valence is produced in a "bottom-up" manner, through appraisals of perceived, imagined, or remembered objects and events. But this is mistaken, and mistaken in ways that will prove important in due course. In fact, the valence component of affective states can be influenced (ramped up or down) by evaluative beliefs, concepts, and expectations. Believing something to be good can cause one to experience it *as* good (at least, provided that the experienced qualities don't depart *too* far from one's expectations, resulting in disappointment; Gneezy et al. 2014).

Thus, expecting a wine to taste good (as indicated by its price) can make it taste better (Plassmann et al. 2008; Fernqvist & Ekelund 2014), and expecting what is in fact clean air to smell like body odor (merely labeled as such) can make it smell worse (de Araujo et al. 2005). Moreover, a skin cream that is labeled as "rich moisturizing cream" as opposed to "a basic cream" can be experienced as more pleasant when applied to the skin (McCabe et al. 2008), and a liquid labeled as tasting "rich and delicious" as opposed to "boiled vegetable water" can make it taste better (Grabenhorst et al. 2008). In addition, the effects in each of these cases aren't merely behavioral ones. (Hence they aren't merely *demand effects*, with people saying what they do because they feel that they *ought* to enjoy the stimulus more or less.) Rather, they co-occur with increased activity in known evaluative networks in the brain— that is, they seem to be top-down effects on the experience of pleasure itself (Schmidt et al. 2017).

Likewise, expecting something to be painful can make it more so (a nocebo effect), and expecting something to be less painful can make it less so (a placebo effect)—again, with discernable changes in components of the known negative-valence network in the brain (Ashar et al. 2017; Petrie & Rief 2019). Scientific medicine depends crucially on the use of placebos (inactive substances) for testing new drugs, of course. This is because placebo effects on medical outcomes can be so large (by some estimates, contributing up to 50 percent of the benefits of many real medicines). Placebos have their largest and most direct effects on affective forms of illness, as one might expect (including chronic pain, depression, and anxiety disorder; but also, oddly, Parkinson's, which is a motor disease). Their benefits for other forms of illness most likely result from reductions in the patient's anxiety and stress. For these are apt to cause inflammation that can impede healing (Nathan & Ding 2010; Liu et al. 2017).

In connection with depression, a meta-analysis by Cuijpers et al. (2012) found that simply listening sympathetically to patients and their concerns (which can be considered a form of placebo treatment) accounts for most of the benefit that can be provided by any specific psychotherapy. (They also found that the apparent added benefits of specific therapies might be attributable to experimenter bias.) Likewise, a meta-analysis by Khan et al. (2012) found that both drug-treatments and psychotherapy are only moderately more effective than placebo pills in treating depression, at least when the clinicians rating the outcomes are blind to the condition. There was a 46 percent improvement from drugs, for example, as opposed to 38 percent from placebo pills. (Note that since placebo effects are incorporated within any drug effects, this means that the drugs themselves are responsible for only around one fifth or sixth of the improvement in symptoms.) Khan et al. also found no significant differences between drug treatments and psychotherapy treatments.

36 Human Motives

In connection with anxiety disorders (panic disorder, generalized anxiety disorder, and social phobia), an extensive meta-analysis by Bandelow et al. (2015) found a statistically large beneficial effect from the use of placebo pills (albeit not as large as that provided by most drug treatments, but equivalent to that produced by psychotherapies, suggesting that the latter are entirely placebo-based).

Importantly, beneficial effects from placebos don't require one to *believe* that one has taken a real medicine, nor that it is likely to be effective. This should be obvious from the structure of clinical trials, where patients are fully informed that there is a 50 percent chance that they have been assigned to the placebo condition. But it has also been established experimentally. Conditioning (by administering lower levels of pain) can cause a placebo skin-cream to reduce participants' experienced pain, even when they are fully informed that the cream in question is an inert substance (Schafer et al. 2015). As a result, the mere sight of stimuli associated with healing (like people wearing white physician's coats) can be enough to issue in a benefit. Moreover, conditioning can result in reduced pain experience even when the stimuli used in the conditioning process are unconscious ones (Jensen et al. 2012, 2015).

In addition, forming the belief that one prefers one thing to another can alter one's evaluative processing of those things, with effects detectable both behaviorally and in evaluative brain networks up to three years later (Sharot et al. 2009, 2012), and implicit evaluations of a group of people induced by reading a single short narrative can survive many rounds of affective counter-conditioning (Gregg et al. 2006). It seems that evaluative attitudes, once formed, are hard to get rid of—indeed, as we noted in Section 2.6, even extinction effects are really a kind of contextual learning, leaving the original values in place.

It is thus a mistake to think of affective processing as entirely "bottom-up." On the contrary, although bottom-up appraisals of a stimulus or memory-image will initiate down-stream effects on arousal, behavior, and valence swiftly and automatically, background beliefs, expectations and associations can modulate those effects. For example, the experience of falling from an airplane can be terrifying or exhilarating, depending on one's belief that one is wearing an effective parachute.

One important source of top-down influence on affect comes from previously created goals and intentions. Although the latter are, in themselves, "cool" rather than "hot" states (Metcalfe & Mischel 1999), and are apt to issue in action when triggered without requiring any contribution from one's affective systems, indications of progress toward achieving a goal are experienced as rewarding (pleasant), and things that impede or frustrate a goal are experienced as just that: frustrating (negatively valenced) (Juechems & Summerfield 2019). Moreover, as Schroeder (2004) points out, sudden and unexpected goal-achievement is likely be experienced as especially pleasant.[16]

In addition, later processes of conceptualization and reappraisal can (and often do) modify or modulate the outputs of affective processing. There has been extensive work done on the various ways in which people can intentionally modify their emotional states in ways that are beneficial or adaptive (Gross 2015). And it has long been known that self-affirmation (reminding oneself of one's value or one's strengths) can have significant effects on mood and optimism (Cohen & Sherman 2014). Indeed, self-talk protocols are widely used in cognitive-behavioral therapy, and are increasingly seen as protective against depression and PTSD for those who undergo a traumatic event (Bonnano 2021). And distanced ("third-person") self-talk may be especially effective in this regard (Orvell et al. 2021). But top-down modulation of affect doesn't have to be conscious or intentional. It can also be associative and/or habitual (Martin Braunstein et al. 2017).

It is easy to find puzzling the extent and power of these top-down effects of implicit and explicit expectations on one's affective responses and stored values. Why are they so robust? After all, one might think that it is just as important to reliably recognize the adaptive values and dangers that exist in the environment as it is to recognize shape, color, and movement. But although top-down effects within the visual system are real (Ogilvie & Carruthers 2016), they are miniscule in comparison to these top-down effects within affective systems. The answer to this puzzle, however, likely lies in the adaptive benefits of cultural learning. This point is worth elaborating.

Recent theorizing, combined with anthropological findings and theoretical modeling, have made it increasingly clear how deeply cultural the human species is (Henrich 2017). It is cultural evolution and cultural learning that enabled ancestral humans to successfully colonize nearly every corner of the planet, from grasslands, to tropical jungles, to deserts, to high altitudes, to remote tropical islands, and even to the frozen arctic itself. All of this was made possible through cultural adaptations to local ecological demands, fueled partly by happenstance and partly through incremental innovations, and then stabilized and sustained through learning and imitation (Muthukrishna & Henrich 2016). Moreover, humans—more than any other

---

[16] Unfortunately, much of Schroeder's (2004) discussion of pleasure and desire conflates goal-states—which are intention-like—with affective, or "felt," desires.

38 Human Motives

species except perhaps eusocial insects like termites—depend critically on the support and cooperation of community members for survival and reproductive success. But (unlike termites) much of this support comes from non-relatives and strangers. In fact, there is every reason to think that humans have become deeply adapted for culture and cultural learning through processes of gene-culture co-evolution (Henrich 2017).

The most basic task for any human child, then, is one of cultural learning. This involves learning the local language, of course, as well as learning the skills and knowledge needed to become a productive member of the group. But it also involves learning the local norms and values, as well as the group's religious beliefs and practices. From the perspective of our own diverse and culturally liberal culture, it is easy to lose sight of the importance of cultural conformity among traditional peoples. Failures to adopt the shared beliefs and practices of the group would generally be punished informally through gossip, ostracization, or withdrawal of opportunities for cooperation; and in extreme cases they could be punished more formally through exile that would likely result in death.

Now notice that much of what a human child needs to learn can be characterized as value learning. Members of a culture need to learn what is locally adaptive to eat, of course, which means coming to find rewarding the consumption of the cultural cuisine. But it also means internalizing the culture's norms and related values. Merely knowing *of* the norms and strategically attempting to comply with them out of self-interest is likely to prove unreliable, and is apt to be recognized by others as inauthentic. It is thus quite risky. One would expect gene-culture co-evolution to produce a faculty for both learning and producing intrinsic motivation to comply with one's culture's norms, whatever those norms happen to be (Sripada & Stich 2006). And indeed, this appears to be the case (Chudek & Henrich 2011).

Top-down influences on affect and value, then, are plausibly explained as adaptations for cultural learning. If people in your group tell you that something is good to eat, then that is likely part of the culturally evolved local wisdom, and you would do well to encode (and thus feel) the value of eating it yourself as swiftly as possible. And if people in your group tell you that something is good to do, or bad not to do, you should internalize that as a source of motivation for the self as well. Likewise, too, for indirect cues to the values of the group, such as widely observed practices, even in the absence of overt evaluation (perhaps utilizing a "common is moral" heuristic; Lindström et al. 2018).

It is important to note that these ubiquitous effects of top-down belief and expectation on affect will likely mean that prosocial values acquired through evaluative conditioning, in the manner outlined in Section 2.6, are exempt from normal extinction effects. Any other-regarding, prosocial, value that is acquired through its association with the approval or disapproval of other people will continue to exist thereafter in the absence of any further primary rewards, sustained by the person's top-down belief that the type of action in question is a good one to perform, or the belief that not performing it would be bad. Indeed, this point has implications for the philosophical debate over the question whether moral beliefs are themselves motivating, in the absence of any accompanying desire (a view generally known as "moral internalism"). For we can now see that a belief about what is right or good can be sufficient, by itself, to *create* an affective/motivational state directed at the action in question (a view defended on other grounds by May 2018). So moral beliefs can motivate action in the absence of any pre-existing desire, but only by serving to create such a desire in the sort of top-down manner discussed here.

2.8 Conclusion

This chapter has laid the foundations for what follows. One crucial distinction has been left mostly implicit in the structure of the chapter, but will prove important later. This is the distinction between the processes that issue in affective states, on the one hand (that is, appraisals of stimuli and other forms of content against stored values), and the outputs of those processes, on the other (including motor-activation, arousal or de-arousal, and positive or negative valence). The former are generally directed at the world or body, rather than being experience-directed. That is to say, the contents that get appraised to issue in affective states generally concern extra-mental objects or events. The valence that gets created as part of the output of appraisal processes, in contrast (pleasure or displeasure, when conscious), can be seen as an intrinsic property of one's own experience, in which case valence-based decision-making can be all about maximizing experiences of a certain sort.

Chapter 3 will elaborate and defend the role of valence in decision-making. What will emerge is that all, or almost all, decisions seemingly depend on computations designed to maximize the balance of positive over negative valence. Then if valence should be equated with pleasure and displeasure, at least when conscious (as we have seen here), it is easy to see why so many psychologists have been drawn to motivational hedonism. Deploying the steel-man strategy, Chapter 3 will attempt to develop the strongest possible view of this sort.

3
The New Hedonism

This chapter will show how the science of affect can be used to support a new and more sophisticated form of motivational hedonism—albeit one whose main outlines were anticipated by Morillo (1995). It discusses the role of valence in decision-making, and considers whether there are forms of decision-making that don't rely upon valence. (Although not its main focus, this chapter also shows how the science of affect vindicates a form of Humeanism about human motivation.) Chapter 4 will then show that the resulting theory evades all extant critiques of hedonism. Throughout the present chapter I propose to treat valence (pleasure and displeasure) as intrinsic feelings that attach to experiences—a sort of "hedonic gloss" on those experiences. My goal, here, is to use the steel-man strategy, building the strongest hedonist theory possible. Other views of the nature of valence will be considered in due course.

3.1 Prospective Decision-Making

When bound into the contents of perception, imagination, or memory, valence plays a critical role in conscious decision-making. In prospective reasoning, especially, people imaginatively envisage alternative actions and outcomes, responding affectively to each. In the absence of any conflict with existing goals (and assuming likelihoods are equated), the alternative that ranks highest in overall positive valence is generally chosen (Gilbert & Wilson 2007, 2009; Seligman et al. 2013; Benoit et al. 2014). Indeed, valence is now thought by many to be the "common currency" of all decision-making processes, as we saw in Section 2.5—or if not a common currency, at least that it can be quantified and compared on a common scale. And even when there *is* a conflict with existing goals, valence still plays a central role. This is because goal achievement, or indications of progress toward a goal, will issue in positive valence, whereas goal frustration, or indications of obstacles to achievement, will issue in negative valence (Juechems & Summerfield 2019).

Prospection is now widely accepted as an account of conscious value-based decision-making. (Other forms of decision-making will be considered

Human Motives: Hedonism, Altruism, and the Science of Affect. Peter Carruthers, Oxford University Press.
© Peter Carruthers 2024. DOI: 10.1093/oso/9780198906131.003.0003

The New Hedonism   **41**

in due course.) And the social psychologists who have defended it have mostly interpreted it in hedonic terms. It is said that when one imagines a future event one "pre-feels" one's likely future affective reaction to that event, and makes one's choice in order to secure or avoid feelings of that sort. Consider these excerpts drawn from Gilbert & Wilson (2007):

> All animals are on a voyage through time, navigating toward futures that promote their survival and away from futures that threaten it. Pleasure and pain are the stars by which they steer....Humans have this ability too [to learn via conditioning the cues that predict future pleasures and pains]. But they also have another ability that extends their powers of foresight far beyond those of any other animal....People mentally simulate future events...[They] use their immediate hedonic reactions to simulations as predictors of the hedonic reactions they are likely to have when the events they are simulating actually come about....Simulations allow people to "preview" events and to "pre-feel" the pleasures and pains those events will produce.
>
> (pp. 1351 and 1352; parentheses added)

Since pleasures and pains are mental states, not items, events, or properties in the external world, the implication is that all actions steer toward one sort of mental state (pleasure) and away from another (pain or displeasure). This makes decision-making all about oneself and one's feelings. And the suggestion is that we take our decisions because we believe that our actions will secure (or avoid) such feelings in the future. We use the "pre-felt" valence we experience when simulating a future event as a predictor of what we can expect to feel were that event to occur; and that feeling is what we aim to achieve (or avoid). Plainly, this is a form of motivational hedonism.

If the "pre-feels" one undergoes when envisaging a rewarding future option are a genuine form of pleasure, however, then one might wonder why anyone ever bothers to do anything. If all decision-making is about achieving pleasure (and avoiding displeasure), and the feelings evoked by imagining a rewarding outcome are themselves experiences of pleasure, then what could motivate us to act? For one already has those feelings. In reply, hedonists will point out that the pleasures of imagination are generally a pale shadow of the real thing. In part this is because imagination is generally much less rich and vivid than real experience; so the responses of one's value systems to appraisals of mere imagery are likely to be correspondingly diminished. And indeed, enhancing visual imagery of future goods tends to make those options seem more attractive, reducing the extent of people's delay discounting of the future (Peters & Büchel 2011; Benoit et al. 2014).

42   Human Motives

In addition, affective responses to the options one is currently considering are likely to be competitive in nature, as we saw in Section 2.5. So pleasure responses in considering a choice between a pair of alternatives will inhibit one another. What matters for choice is the ordinal ranking of the options, not the cardinal values.[1]

Prospection that relies on hedonic responding may provide a good model of reflective, slowed-down, evaluative decision-making. It seems less obviously good as an account of the sorts of speeded decisions one often makes about options with little conscious thought or imagination. And indeed, the scientists who model this sort of decision-making and study its implementation in the brain for the most part use different language (Huys et al. 2011; Orsini et al. 2015; O'Doherty et al. 2017). They talk mostly about unconscious processes that integrate outcome values with likelihoods and estimates of effort to compute an overall expected value, in the economist's sense. (In fact, this branch of cognitive science often goes under the label of "neuroeconomics.") But it is easy to provide such models with a hedonic interpretation. We just have to realize that outcome values are signaled by the valence component of the incentive-salience directed at the options (and that effort-estimates will be signaled by negative valence), and to equate valence in these circumstances (where the options are consciously represented) with pleasure and displeasure. We then get an account of decision-making according to which people generally select the option that delivers the greatest expected balance of pleasure over displeasure (allowing, as usual, for neural noise and other factors that can interfere with normal outcomes—recall from Section 1.1 that special-science laws always incorporate an "other things being equal" clause).

Whether one is using action-simulation and conscious forms of imaginative reflection about the future, or taking decisions unreflectively for the here-and-now, it seems that quantities of valence (pleasure and displeasure) and estimates of outcome likelihood are the main determinates of choice. So vast swathes of human action, at least, can be given a hedonist construal (Knutson & Greer 2008; possible exceptions will be considered in Section 3.5). However, there is reason to doubt that the form of hedonism

---

[1] Evaluative learning, in contrast, seems likely to involve a comparison between the valence generated during consumption with that predicted moments before, creating an error signal through direct comparison of the two. (Otherwise evaluative learning would require episodic memory of the valence experienced during earlier prospective decision-making, at the same time adjusting for its lesser intensity.) This process is likely to involve comparison of signals buried deep within subcortical evaluation systems, however, rather than as part of one's conscious experience. It might still be the case, though, that the comparison process automatically adjusts for the lesser effects of predicted over experienced stimuli prior to generating an error-signal.

developed by Gilbert & Wilson (2007) and others is the best available. This is where we go next.

3.2 How Valence Works

Gilbert & Wilson (2007) assume that prospection-based decision-making requires one to have beliefs about the feelings one will undergo in the future if the prospected event takes place, or if the action one is rehearsing is successful. But that is not the only possible model of the role of valence in decision-making. As suggested by Morillo (1995), an alternative possibility is that positive valence attaching to a representation of a future action or outcome influences its selection or pursuit directly (in competition with others), without requiring any further beliefs (beyond beliefs about probabilities of *the event* occurring). In particular, one does not have to believe that if the future action or outcome occurs, then one will experience a similar level of valence. This kind of direct-influence account should seem much the more likely of the two when placed in the context of known decision-making capacities of non-human animals. Or so I propose to argue shortly.

Humans might *sometimes* take decisions as a result of explicitly predicting that the outcome will bring them pleasure or displeasure, of course. Sometimes humans can have explicit hedonic goals, as when one selects a dish from the menu because one believes one will enjoy it. And presumably people who are hedonists in the colloquial sense ("pleasure lovers") take many of their decisions because they believe they will enjoy the results. But this is not the basic, most fundamental, way in which decisions are taken, either in humans or other animals.

It seems that many species of primate and bird are capable of simple forms of prospection: simulating possible actions and their outcomes, and responding affectively to those simulations before making a choice. At any rate, we know that the attentional networks that control entry into working memory are at least partly homologous among birds, other mammals, and humans; as is working memory itself (Mysore & Knudsen 2013). We also know that working memory in humans, monkeys, and birds is subject to the same limit of three to four items (Buschman et al. 2011), and it seems that this limit results from the same underlying neurological constraints (Pinotsis et al. 2019; Hahn et al. 2021). So it should not be surprising if these creatures could use their working-memory capacities to simulate future outcomes, as humans do.

44 Human Motives

Moreover, both apes and birds can solve problems that humans would use future-simulation to solve. For example, both groups can solve the "floating peanut problem," and can do so by insight (on a first trial) rather than by trial and error (Mendes et al. 2007; Bird & Emery 2009; Hanus et al. 2011). In these experiments, animals (and human children) are confronted with the problem of reaching a peanut contained in a fixed upright Perspex tube. (In the experiments with rooks, a floating worm is used instead.) The tube is too narrow, and the peanut too deep, to be reached by hand or by beak. In the version of the problem faced by the birds, the worm is already floating, and the solution is to drop some nearby stones into the tube to raise the water level sufficiently for the worm to be retrieved. In the version of the problem faced by the apes, in contrast, the tube is dry, but there is a bucket of water nearby. The solution is to spit water into the tube until the peanut floats within reach. Humans would solve these problems by imagining what one could do with the materials available, predicting and responding affectively to the results.

Likewise, crows have been shown to engage in multi-step planning to achieve a reward, again without using overt (as opposed to simulative) trial and error (Taylor et al. 2010; von Bayern et al. 2018). Moreover, they can do so without ever having experienced some of the steps involved. For example, birds have been confronted with an apparatus in which they need to figure out that they should pull up some string to retrieve the short stick attached to it, which can then be used to retrieve a longer stick from behind some bars, which can in turn be used to retrieve some meat from the end of a horizontal Perspex tube. Strikingly, one of the birds observed the set-up for nearly two minutes before seamlessly executing the whole sequence on the first trial. Another bird studied the situation for a little over 40 seconds. It then started to pull up the string, but dropped it again before studying the set-up for a further 40 seconds. Then it, too, smoothly executed the entire sequence. It is hard to resist the inference that the birds were imaginatively simulating various actions and sequences of action suggested by the affordances of the situation until they hit upon a workable plan.

Gruber et al. (2019) provide an especially convincing demonstration of simulative planning in crows. Across a number of different experiments the crows had to select one tool to obtain a second one from an apparatus (ignoring a distractor apparatus), and then use the second tool to extract a reward from a container. But each stage was done out of sight of the next, so we know the crows were not just perceiving the affordances of the situation presented to them. On the contrary, they had to bear in mind (imagine) what they were expecting at the next stage when choosing what to do at the current one.

It is no less plausible, in principle, that crows should be motivational hedonists than that humans are. That is, it is not implausible that when they simulate a sequence of action that would finish with the retrieval of some meat, the positive affective response they feel at the thought of the latter is sufficient to issue in a decision to execute the sequence. What *is* implausible is that crows should be relying on the belief that when they retrieve the meat they will feel what they are currently feeling while they *imagine* retrieving the meat. That would require the animals to be thinking about their own current and future experiences. (Remember, for a hedonist, pleasure is a property of experience; so in order to believe that doing something will produce a certain amount of pleasure in oneself one has to be capable of thinking about future experiences.) Although it is possible that birds can do this, there is little evidence that they can;[2] and we should in any case prefer a simpler explanation if one is available, such as the belief-free "direct effect" model sketched earlier.

The case is strengthened still further—indeed, it becomes orders of magnitude stronger—when we remember that motivational hedonists need to be capable of explaining speeded unreflective choice in addition to choices that result from conscious prospective reasoning. Almost all living creatures are capable of making valence-based choices. Indeed, even bumblebees can adaptively trade off differing concentrations of sucrose solution against varying degrees of noxious heat (Gibbons et al. 2022). And even snails and ants are capable of affect and affective learning (Kobayashi et al. 1998; Cammaerts 2004). So it seems that almost all creatures are capable of learning which actions produce positive valence (pleasure), and then selecting those actions again in future when an appropriate situation arises, anticipating positive valence as a result. For remember, in the absence of anticipated valence, there can be no error signals created at the consummatory stage, and hence no evaluative learning either.

This point is worth elaborating further. Recall from Section 2.6 that evaluative learning requires predictive positive or negative valence (signals of future reward and punishment) to be compared with the actual amount of valence experienced at the consummatory stage, generating an error signal. The latter then causes the stored value for events of that sort to be ramped up or down by some increment, thus altering the degrees of predictive valence that will be created in situations of that sort in the future. So without predictively generated valence there can be no evaluative learning. And recall, too,

---

[2] Some have reported evidence that corvids can take account of the visual perspective of another bird, at least, when trying to avoid food-pilfering (Legg & Clayton 2014; Legg et al. 2016). But this claim has now been seriously undermined (Amodio et al. 2021). In any case, it is one thing to be capable of thinking about another's visual *perspective*, and quite another to think about one's own visual *experiences*.

that action-selection is a function of the comparative incentive-salience of the available options, one component of which is predictive valence. So any creature capable of conditioned behavior will be utilizing a simple form of valence anticipation. And that includes invertebrates, as we noted in the previous paragraph.

In light of this ancient ancestry, it is simply unbelievable that the role of valence in decision-making should depend on any sort of explicit belief that positive or negative valence will result from actually achieving the goal of the decision. Rather, valence (positive or negative), when attaching to a future-directed representation, must automatically influence decision-making in favor of or against the object or action represented. One might say that the valence attaching to a future-directed representation of an action or outcome *tacitly* predicts what one will feel when that action or outcome occurs. Indeed, this accurately describes its role in affective learning. But there need be no explicit representation or belief that those feelings will occur.

Nor is it believable that the role of valence in decision-making should be radically different in humans than in other animals. Humans are continuous with other animals, and must share core aspects of their psychology. And as we noted in Section 2.6, it is known that the core processes and brain networks involved in evaluative learning and simple forms of decision-making are shared across species (Shechner et al. 2014; Railton 2017; Adolphs & Anderson 2018). Moreover, it is (to say the least) quite unlikely that as humans evolved away from other primates, the basic principles of evaluative learning and decision-making should have changed to become less reliable (because dependent on beliefs about the valenced experiences one expects to result from one's decisions)—for Gilbert & Wilson (2007, 2009) show that people are quite bad at predicting their future hedonic experiences when asked to do so explicitly.

Recall that when Gilbert & Wilson develop their hedonic account of prospective decision-making, they say that people decide as they do because they believe that their pre-feels (caused by pre-viewing the events) are a good indication of what they are likely to feel when the event actually takes place. And people take their decisions in order to achieve or avoid the latter. We can now see that although humans might sometimes take decisions in this manner, it is both unnecessary and unlikely that this should be the general case. When conscious prospection is placed alongside forms of valence-anticipation common to almost all creatures, a better account is as follows. When one pre-views a future event, this engages one's affective appraisal systems, resulting in positive or negative valence attaching to the representation of that future event. This immediately causes the event to seem worthy of being achieved or avoided, and influences one's decision-making accordingly. In particular, positive valence attaching to a future-directed representation pulls one toward choosing the event represented—it provides it with incentive-salience—whereas negative valence makes it seem repulsive.

The upshot of this section is that it is a mistake for motivational hedonists to present their model of decision-making as requiring one to have beliefs about the degrees of pleasure or displeasure that are likely to result from the actions one is considering. Rather, they should say that simulations of possible future actions or events are received as input by one's affective systems and appraised against one's stored values, resulting in some degree of pleasure or displeasure attaching to those future-directed representations. These can then influence choice directly, modulated by one's estimates of the likelihood of achieving the envisaged outcomes, of course, but without requiring any beliefs about one's likely future hedonic states were those outcomes to occur. Chapter 4 will show that once framed in these terms, motivational hedonism is immune to all of the standard attempts at refutation, whether philosophical or experimental.

3.3 Future-Directed Pleasure

One might worry whether the form of motivational hedonism to emerge over the previous two sections is genuinely worthy of the name—that is, whether it is really a form of hedonism. For the pleasure that is produced by appraisals of simulated or anticipated future events is felt in the present. (I will focus on pleasure throughout this section for simplicity. The same points hold—appropriately modified—for the role of anticipatory displeasure in decision-making.) In which case, even if we grant (as the evidence reviewed above shows we should) that these presently experienced anticipatory pleasures are what determine choice (modulated by estimates of likelihood), it would seem that the resulting decisions are made *because of pleasure* rather than *for the sake of* pleasure. The pleasure that one currently feels when simulating future events or outcomes might be what causes one to pursue the latter. But it doesn't follow that in pursuing those events or outcomes one is pursuing pleasure—nor acting for the sake of pleasure, nor in order to achieve pleasure. But this is surely what motivational hedonism requires. Hedonists think that the pursuit of pleasure and avoidance of displeasure are our only goals. In contrast, it might seem that what has emerged from

48 Human Motives

Section 3.2 is that experiencing pleasure and avoiding displeasure aren't really goals at all, but mere causes of choice.[3]

The distinction between cause and goal is surely important; indeed, it is of vital importance for our topic. And it really does apply to the stored values, appraisal against which results in affect and anticipatory valence. We choose as we do because of those values, but not for the sake of those values, nor in order to secure those values. At any rate, this is surely true given an intrinsic-feeling account of valence (pleasure and displeasure) of the sort under discussion in the present chapter. One's values enter into appraisals of outcomes to cause feelings of pleasure, which in turn determine choice; and if all goes well, one's actions will end up satisfying or matching those initial value-representations, to some greater or lesser degree. But there is no sense in which one's actions *aim at* satisfying those values. This is because they fail to play a direct role in the decision-making processes that lead to the selection of one over another goal (on the contrary, this is the role played by pleasure and displeasure).

It would be a mistake to claim that pleasure is merely the cause of our choices, however. Granted, the pleasure is felt in the present, albeit resulting from evaluative appraisal of a future-directed representation. But then so, too, does the imagining of the future event occur in the present. And more importantly, the pleasure one feels is not a separate thing, independent of the representation that initially causes it. It doesn't "float free" of the imagined future. Rather, it gets bound into the content of the future-directed representation itself. In so doing, it becomes a component in a future-directed representation, thereby becoming future-directed itself. When one imagines a future outcome, positively evaluates it, and feels pleasure, it is the anticipated future outcome that feels pleasant. In effect, the representation becomes a representation of a pleasant future event. And in choosing that outcome because of the pleasure one feels when one represents it, one *is* then choosing *for the sake of* a represented future pleasure. This is hedonism in more than just name.

Why should we think that valence (pleasure and displeasure) gets bound into the content of future-directed representations, however, rather than merely existing ("floating free") alongside them? In part, this is because it is just what we would expect from what we know about sensory processing generally (Carruthers 2015). And it is because we also know that perception

---

[3] Note that the objection to hedonism sketched here is distinct from Butler's (1726) famous critique. Butler points out that we generally only feel pleasure as an *effect* of achieving things we antecedently desired; in which case those desires were not desires for pleasure. The current critique, in contrast, is that anticipatory pleasure felt in the present is a *cause* of choice rather than its object.

and imagery share the same mechanisms and processes—albeit with one caused by external stimuli, the other caused by internally generated representations produced in a top-down manner (Kosslyn et al. 2006; Albers et al. 2013; Vetter et al. 2014). In each case attended-to stimuli result initially in the formation of object-files or event-files, with increasingly abstract information being built into the file as processing proceeds. So one doesn't just see a gray shape moving along, one sees a mouse running towards the wall. And one doesn't just hear the pitch and timbre of a voice, one hears someone welcoming visitors to their home, or asking the way to the church (Carruthers 2015). So when one experiences an event—eating a ripe strawberry, say— whose processing produces a positive evaluation, one doesn't just feel pleasure alongside the taste. On the contrary, one experiences the taste of the strawberry itself as pleasant. And likewise, then, when an imagined future event is processed and evaluated positively, exactly what we should expect is that the resulting pleasure gets attached to the event-file itself. So that event-file gets pleasure built into it, becoming the imagining of a pleasant future event. It thereby becomes incentive-salient and motivates choice.

Suppose that one is choosing between a slice of chocolate cake and the fruit-cup. One imagines eating each. Appraisal of the predicted taste of the chocolate cake produces more pleasure (in the present) than the predicted taste of the fruit. That pleasure is bound into (becomes a component of) the imagined future eating of the cake. So the action of eating the cake seems more pleasant to one, leading one to choose it. (I am setting aside other considerations that might enter into the choice, such as one's health.) One selects the represented future action *in order to* secure the pleasure that is its central evaluative component. And if all decision-making ultimately conforms to this pattern, then it follows that all decisions are taken in order to achieve pleasure (and/or avoid displeasure). This is a full-blown form of motivational hedonism. But notice that it doesn't depend on, nor need it involve, any belief that if one eats the cake it will be pleasant. Rather, the future-pleasantness of eating the cake is built into the representation of the future event itself.

3.4 Concerns about Consciousness

Motivational hedonism is partly grounded in the phenomenology of choice—that is, in what it is like, introspectively, to make a decision (Mercer 2001). When one imagines performing various actions, or imagines their outcomes, one is often conscious of feeling pleasure or displeasure as a result.

50 Human Motives

When one imagines leaping from an airplane with the ground laid out thousands of feet below, one experiences fear—or else a thrill of excitement, as the case may be. (People differ in their emotional reactions to the thought of sky-diving, of course.) As a result, the choice seems aversive or attractive. When one imagines winning the lottery, or getting an article accepted by a top journal, one feels pleased, motivating one to buy a ticket or submit the paper, whereas when one imagines losing one's home in a flood one feels sad and afraid, motivating one to purchase flood insurance.[4]

When developed from this starting point, motivational hedonism seems to entail that valence comprises two distinctive kinds of phenomenal property—or qualia—attaching to the experiences or images in question. When one imagines the loss of one's home it is the negative—bad—way the content of one's imagining feels that motivates preventative action. And when one imagines winning the lottery, it is the positive—good—feeling that attaches to one's imagining that motivates purchasing a ticket. Likewise, when such outcomes actually occur, one generally feels good or feels bad when experiencing them. Motivational hedonism thus claims that pleasure and displeasure are distinctive kinds of conscious feeling, and that choices are taken, tacitly, to secure or to avoid such feelings.

Do intrinsic-feeling accounts of pleasure and displeasure then commit one to claiming that hedonic qualia are extremely widespread across the animal kingdom? Since we know that ants and snails are capable of affective learning and decision-making (Kobayashi et al. 1998; Cammaerts 2004), motivational hedonists might seem to be committed to the claim that such creatures are phenomenally conscious. Some philosophers have claimed just this (Godfrey-Smith 2016), and it could be true (although I myself have argued that there is no fact of the matter; Carruthers 2019). But it is a strong commitment to make, as well as one that many will be unwilling to endorse without argument. Moreover, it is one for which we lack independent evidence.

The best way for motivational hedonists to reply is by accepting the claim made in Section 2.5 that it is valence (which can be conscious or unconscious) that does the real work in decision-making and evaluative learning. They can then embrace some sort of physicalist identity-theory or physicalist multiple-realization account of the phenomenology of pleasure and displeasure, while claiming that the causal work in determining choice actually

---

[4] Philosophers who have endorsed an intrinsic-feeling view of the evaluative component of emotions, at least, include Goldstein (2002), Whiting (2011), and Shargel (2015). Those who have endorsed a hedonic-feeling account of pleasure and displeasure more generally include Moore (1903), Mendola (2006), Smuts (2011), and Labukt (2012), among many others. Morillo (1995), too, endorses an intrinsic-feeling account of pleasure and displeasure, and uses it to ground a form of motivational hedonism similar to the one outlined here.

takes place at the lower physical level. (Although strictly, if it is an identity-claim that is made, then there aren't really two "levels," and phenomenal feelings can be causally efficacious because identical to the physicalist base.)

Thus it might be that an affective appraisal of a thing or event results in a distinctive kind of intrinsic physical tag or symbol becoming attached to the experience or imagining of that thing or event. These tags would be analog physical magnitudes of some sort (admitting of degrees), and they would come in two varieties: with a positive causal role in decision-making (motivating selection) or a negative one (motivating rejection). When these tags are attached to representations that occur in whatever way renders experiences or images conscious (for example, by being "globally broadcast" and entering active forms of working memory; Dehaene 2014), then the result is the felt conscious phenomenology of pleasure or displeasure. But when those representations are active outside of consciousness, the tags in question would still influence choice and evaluative learning in essentially the same manner. Likewise when the creature in question is incapable of consciousness altogether.

Making this move is theoretically well-motivated. For as we saw in Section 2.5 conscious and unconscious valence belong to the same psychological natural kind—they are instances of the same kind of thing (only one occurring consciously, the other unconsciously). It also has the benefit of putting hedonists in a position to reply to an additional objection to the generality of their view. Their claim is that all actions that result from decision-making processes aim at pleasure and/or avoidance of displeasure. But prospective imagining, too, is an intentional action. And yet one surely does not first consciously appraise whether and what to imagine before one engages in prospection of the future. So it looks like hedonists might need to restrict their claims to overt forms of (bodily) action. And then the resulting theory would begin to look arbitrary and unprincipled. Why should hedonism only be true of what motivates overt actions, leaving mental actions to be motivated differently?

In reply, hedonists can now deploy the intrinsic-tag proposal about how valence in general is realized. They can say that when unconscious decisions are taken to imagine one overt action rather than another, or one outcome rather than another, it is the valence-tags that determine choice. So all decisions are taken in order to maximize positive valence. But only in the case of conscious decision-making (whether among consciously simulated outcomes or among perceptually presented options) are decisions taken to maximize pleasure as such. Nevertheless, it is the same intrinsic analog-magnitude tags that do the work in each case.

52 Human Motives

The resulting account is actually not implausible. For we know that there is an unconsciously operating saliency network (although I prefer to call it the "relevance network"; Carruthers 2015) that continually evaluates unconsciously activated memories and motor plans, competing for the resources of top-down attention (Corbetta et al. 2008; Menon & Uddin 2010; Sestieri et al. 2010). Indeed, we know that action-production, likewise, involves evaluative comparison of alternatives, at multiple levels of implementation (Cos et al. 2014). When an unconscious motor plan is deemed relevant enough (being appraised locally as good-enough-to-be-attended to and becoming positively valenced), then attention shifts, and the result is a consciously rehearsed simulation. This can then be globally broadcast to one's affective systems in their entirety and evaluated "in the round," issuing in a conscious decision of some sort.

A worry of a quite different sort is that conscious pleasures and displeasures are too heterogeneous to have anything in common phenomenologically (Korsgaard 1996; Feldman 1997), thus potentially undermining the claim that they can form the common-currency of conscious decision-making. Think of the differences between enjoying a taste, enjoying someone's touch, enjoying a sunset, enjoying a concert, enjoying a run, enjoying a conversation with a friend, enjoying a crossword puzzle, and so on. The objection is that the experiences involved are so different from one another that it is doubtful whether there can be any single feeling that they have in common. Likewise for displeasures: think of the differences between pain, disgust, fear, grief, boredom, exhaustion, and so on. In fact, this heterogeneity provides one of the main motivations philosophers have had for advancing desire-theories of pleasure and displeasure (Heathwood 2007; Labukt 2012). Pleasant experiences are said to be ones that one wants to have, on this latter view, whereas displeasures are experiences that one wants to avoid.[5]

Motivational hedonists should make a pair of replies, I think. The first is to emphasize the scientific evidence that valence (described as pleasure and displeasure when conscious) provides the common currency for decision-making. So desire needs to be explained in terms of valence rather than the other way around. It is valence that is psychologically basic, not

---

[5] I myself once endorsed just such an account of the painfulness of pain, claiming that painful pains are pain sensations that one wants to be rid of (Carruthers 1999). Desire-theories of pleasure and displeasure have been quite popular among philosophers. Those endorsing them include Brandt (1979), Korsgaard (1996), Feldman (2004), Heathwood (2007), and Parfit (2011), as well as many others. However, desire-theories of pleasure confront the same problem as imperative-theories, to be discussed in Chapter 6. This is that consummatory pleasure is present-tensed, directed at something actually occurring, whereas desires are, by their nature, distally directed—either toward the future, or to the past (if wishing is a kind of desire), or toward counterfactual events when mind-wandering.

desire. In which case, the best account of desire is that it is a representation of a distal (non-actual) event with positive valence attached. Indeed, this is the best account of affective forms of desire (in contrast with goals and intentions, which are often described as desires) whatever one's view of the nature of valence might be.

The second reply is to point out that the phenomenology of valence is quite unlike the phenomenology of experience and sensation, and much less salient. So all of the striking variation among different kinds of pleasant experiences can be put down to differences in the non-hedonic components of the experiences involved. (Taste is very different from touch, which is very different from sight; chatting with a friend is very different from listening to a favorite piece of music, and so on.) There can still be a phenomenological thread linking them all, which is easily missed and not easy to describe (Labukt 2012).

It can be quite hard to distinguish, introspectively, between feelings of pleasure and the other components of a pleasurable experience.[6] In part, this is because it is rarely the case that one has the same sensory or other experiences side-by-side or immediately following one another, where one is enjoyed and the other not. For instance, a conversation one enjoys will generally differ in innumerable respects from one that one does not. But consider sensory-specific satiety. Compare the first bite one takes from a huge slice of one's favorite chocolate cake with the last. The flavors stay the same. But the first bite is wonderful, whereas the last is so-so or mildly unpleasant. Even here, however, it can be hard to separate out the contribution that consummatory pleasure makes to one's phenomenal experience from that provided by incentive-salience—that is, whether or not the next bite seems attractive and pleasurable, and whether or not one feels an urge to eat more. Moreover, one's salivary glands will be working overtime at the outset (this is one aspect of the arousal component of hunger), whereas the final bite of cake may cloy in one's mouth and be less easy to swallow.

What valence has in common with experiences and sensations is that it is an analog-magnitude property (or pair of such properties: positive and negative). But unlike them it is abstract and amodal—or non-sensory—in nature. It may be helpful to compare valence to numerosity, in this connection. Many creatures besides humans (as well as human infants) can perceive approximate numbers or set-sizes (Barth et al. 2003; Jordan et al. 2008; Izard

---

[6] The same is true of the displeasurable (painful) component of pain. It took a quite lot of work before philosophers could become convinced that pain sensations are not intrinsically painful. Rather, the two components are separable, with the painfulness of pain resulting from an evaluative appraisal of the sensation in its context. See Chapter 7.

et al. 2009). They can discriminate and respond to the approximate number of items present, controlling for all other properties of the items (size, density, and so on), and they can even do so cross-modally (e.g. equating four sequentially presented tones to four dots on a screen rather than seven). Moreover, they can use those numerical perceptions in down-stream computations over numerosities, as when an animal calculates the rate of return from a food source (Gallistel et al. 2001)—for a rate of return is the number of items received per unit of time. But what it is *like* to see or hear an approximate number of things is quite subtle.

Imagine looking briefly at 30 dots flashed up on a screen. You would have a rough sense of "how many," and you could probably tell the difference if 40 differently arranged dots were flashed up thereafter (but not if 35 were—numerosity discrimination is only approximate). If you had to guess, your guesses would tend to center around 30, plus-or-minus a few. But numerosity perception seems genuinely perceptual or perception-like, not a matter of down-stream judgment. It is computed in interactions among sensory areas of the brain spontaneously, even when task-irrelevant, as well as prior to the occurrence of anything concept-like or judgment-like (Cicchini et al. 2016). Hence it is available even in new-born human infants (Izard et al. 2009).

Is there something it is like to see 30 dots rather than 40? One's nonconceptual impression of number will differ between the two cases. One will have an impression of *more dots* in the latter case when compared with the former, which one might naturally express in those terms. And it does seem that there is something genuinely deserving the label "phenomenology" here (Carruthers & Veillet 2017). But it is quite subtle. And one can easily imagine someone claiming that there isn't any phenomenology in common between seeing 30 dots, on the one hand, and hearing or feeling 30 taps, on the other. Likewise, then, for valence. A motivational hedonist should insist (I think rightly) that there is a subtle commonality between a pleasurable taste and a pleasurable conversation, or between a disgusting taste and a boring lecture. That is what enables one to trade them off against one another when one does so consciously.

3.5 Other Forms of Decision-Making

As we have seen, valence seems to operate as the common currency of prospection-based decision-making. In prospection, people imagine performing an action or achieving an outcome and respond affectively to those simulated contents. Something similar seems to happen in cases where we aren't conscious of imagining anything, such as deciding whether to ask for the chocolate cake displayed on the dessert trolley. This is because predictive processing is arguably ubiquitous in cognition, and is known to routinely anticipate future events from current conditions (Clark 2013; Seligman et al. 2013). So as one examines the various items on the dessert trolley, one anticipates (unconsciously) what it would be like to eat each, responds with some degree of positive or negative valence, and (other things being equal) selects the one that "feels best" or "looks the most attractive." (This is the one that generates the greatest positive valence bound into the content of its representation.)

Other things are often *not* equal, of course. One may have standing goals that conflict with some choices more than others. The goal of losing weight might favor the fruit bowl over the chocolate cake. Or one might have evaluative beliefs that favor some choices over others. One might believe, for example, that fruit contains vitamin C, and is healthy. But we saw in Section 2.7 how such factors can have an impact, consistent with the centrality of valence in decision-making. For evaluative beliefs can impact one's appraisal of the options, altering one's affective response. And appraising an option as conflicting with a goal will result in negative valence (Juechems & Summerfield 2019). So the final decision about what to choose can still result from computations involving valence, but resulting not just from appraisals made in light of stored values but also from evaluative beliefs that influence those values, as well as from previously formed goals that were themselves formed in light of other stored values.

What of cases where there is nothing to compete with the implementation of a previously formed goal or intention? Surely here a decision to act can be taken without any affective contribution? Since goals and intentions are best thought of as high-level—abstract—stored motor plans, as we suggested in Section 2.3, it would seem that once activated they produce a direct motor urge. These might be guided in their implementation by the affordances of the current environment (into which computations of relative effort might figure; Cisek & Kalaska 2010; Cos et al. 2014), but the initiation of the action itself needs no contribution from affective states. This is especially likely to be so in connection with intentions that are stored in conditional form and become activated when one recognizes the truth of the antecedent. Recall from Section 2.3 the intention, "Once lunch is finished I shall cut the grass." Here the trigger contained in one's awareness of putting away the lunch things may activate an intention to cut the grass *now*. Something can, of course lead one to reconsider one's intention (such as awareness that it has started to rain), but the default will be action so long as the intention becomes activated unopposed (Bratman 1987, 1999).

56   Human Motives

In contrast, intentions that don't specify an implementation condition are ripe for procrastination (Gollwitzer 1999). If one's intention is just, "I shall cut the grass today," then each time it is recalled one has to take a further decision: should I cut the grass now or later? One is then thrown back into a situation in which other forms of affect (current laziness, other things one would like to do now) can compete with the intention for control. The result is often that by the last time in the day when the intention gets recalled, it is too late (it is now dark).

Consider, then, the case of an unopposed goal, like "I shall cut the grass now." Surely this, when activated, leads to a decision that is affect-independent? There need be no anticipations of future affect, and no computation of expected values. Two points should be made in reply. The first is that it is unclear that any decision needs to be made here at all, any more than there needs to be a decision to get down the habitual coffee pot when entering the kitchen in the morning. The intention will lead to action by itself once activated, unless it is inhibited. (There may be situations in which one takes a decision *not* to inhibit it. But this seems unlikely in a case of this sort.) The second point is that the intention is actually an instrumental one. Why is one cutting the grass? The answer will appeal to the various affective factors that went into the original decision, even if they are now forgotten (love of a neat-looking lawn, embarrassment at what the neighbors would say if it went uncut any longer). So although no affect need be felt "in the moment," the ultimate goal of one's action is set by the affective values that factored into one's initial decision-making. And these can, of course, be cast in hedonic form.

Consider, now, decisions that that result from discursive, verbally based, reasoning processes. Can these be affect-independent? Much language-involving decision-making involves a back-and-forth between verbal statements or questions (whether in inner or outer speech) and affective responding to their contents (often tacitly elaborated in imagery). One says, "I could go to the gym; or I could go for a run; or I could get down to work." Each possibility is elaborated in imagination and affectively appraised as one speaks, producing a hedonic response. But sometimes it seems a decision can be reached through processes that are purely discursive. If so, this might be thought more problematic for the claim that all decision-making is hedonically based.

Reflect, first, on the processes that generate verbal premises. There is extensive evidence that these generally result from affective decision-making, just as do most other actions. Speech, after all, is an action; and the same is true of inner speech. And there is plenty of reason to think that the processes that produce speech actions of either sort are subject to affective influences, at least (Carruthers 2011, 2018a, 2018b). Even simple reports of the contents of semantic memory (e.g. "Paris is the capital of France") are unlikely to be affect free. As with any other action, there will be competition among alternatives (in this case, with other things one might say). Appraisal against the norm of truth-telling is likely to lead to a swift resolution of the competition in this sort of case; but the decision will still be valence-based. And as soon as we turn to speech actions that have evaluative significance, whether direct or indirect, the picture becomes even clearer. We know that expressions of evaluative attitudes, or attitudes with evaluative significance (such as the assertion of a believed stereotype about a group) are influenced by swift appraisals of the likely consequences for one's audience and how those might reflect back on the self. So in cases where speech is being generated with a view to making a decision about something, there will be appraisals of the evaluative significance of the various things one might say, either weakening, strengthening, or inhibiting the relevant action plans to issue in a decision.

Inferential transitions *among* sentences, and between premises and conclusion, are another matter. Some of the dispositions involved might be innate or innately channeled, especially for simple forms of logical inference (Mercier & Sperber 2017). Others will have a habit-like quality, acquired over time by reward-related feedback. This will be true of many inferential heuristics, for example, of the sort studied in the "simple heuristics" and "heuristics and biases" literatures (Gigerenzer et al. 1999; Kahneman 2011). But they might also result from explicit training. Consider someone who is well-versed in economic theory, for instance, and is familiar with the (reasonable, overall effective) temporal discount rates imposed by businesses on future-oriented investment decisions. When placed into one of the experimental frameworks designed to discover people's intuitive (personality-like) discount rates, this person might eschew reliance on intuition, instead doing a swift approximate calculation of how the economic discount rate applies in the case in hand, combining that with the outcome value (often expressed monetarily as a number, in such experiments) to result in a comparison of expected utility among the two options. Nothing evaluative need be involved here at all, nor in expressing the resulting answer. Even here, however, there is an affectively formed evaluative goal in the background of such a procedure: one has to have come to value maximizing long-term economic values, or to think it right that decisions should be taken that way; and one has to positively evaluate truth-telling.

Now, how does one transition from the sentential conclusion of a piece of verbal decision-making to an actual decision? (Assuming that the various inferential procedures—whether logical or heuristic—are formal ones, then

58 Human Motives

the final sentence in the sequence won't express a decision that has already been made.) So how does one get from a sentence of the form, "I shall do X" or of the form "Doing X is the best of the options available" (whether expressed in inner or outer speech), to the formation of an intention or goal of doing X? There are two options, each of which is likely to be true on at least some occasions, and which can be used singly or in combination (Carruthers 2015).

One possibility is that comprehension of the decision-like sentence, once extracted in context by the language faculty, is affectively appraised for acceptance, giving rise to the corresponding intention provided the appraisal is positive. Compare the case of receiving an instruction from another person who says, "You will do X." There needs to be a swift (generally unconscious) appraisal of the benefits and costs of complying, often issuing in the formation of an intention to do X. So hearing oneself say at the conclusion of a piece of verbal reasoning, "I shall do X," and appraising its content positively, causes one to form a nonverbal intention to do just that, thereafter encoded in prospective memory. (This is memory for what one is going to do, which only partially overlaps with other forms of memory; McDaniel et al. 2013; Momennejad & Haynes 2013.) On this account the intention that gets created following the conclusion of a verbalized piece of reasoning results from an affective appraisal of the latter's content.

The second possibility is that comprehension of the decision-like sentence causes, not a decision as such (although it might do, operating in parallel with the idea to be suggested here), but rather a *belief* that one has made a *commitment* to perform a specific future action, or else a belief that one has formed the *intention* to perform that action. Hearing oneself say, "I shall do X" (especially, perhaps, when said aloud in the presence of other people) one comes to believe that one is committed to doing X; or else one might hear it *as* the formation of an intention. This is stored in episodic memory rather than prospective memory. Note that both beliefs are meta-representational in character: one belief represents oneself has having performed a particular mental act—making a commitment—whereas the other represents oneself as having formed an intention. Then later when either belief becomes activated in the context appropriate for doing X, one feels that one *ought* to do X. This might be underwritten by one's evaluative self-conception as a strong-willed person, or out of a desire to be self-consistent (Frankish 2004, 2009; Carruthers 2015).

The second possibility is thus that the causation underlying the decision to act can resemble one of the following inferences: (1) I have committed myself to doing X/I have decided to do X; (2) I would feel bad if I didn't execute my commitments/didn't do what I have decided; with the two premises then creating (3) an occurrent first-order goal of doing X. This renders the decision-making process an affective one, of course. And from a hedonist perspective, it can be said that one acts as one does in order to feel good, or in order not to feel bad.

It is worth noting in passing that verbal articulation of one's reasons for action can lead one to make commitments that are out of line with one's actual values. This is because when people are asked to state reasons for choice in advance of making a decision, they naturally focus on factors that are easy to articulate in language, overlooking factors that are *not* so easy to articulate. And then having stated those reasons, they feel committed to making their decision in accordance with them. The result can be choices that people are less satisfied with later, or judgments that are less reliable predictors of long-term satisfaction (Wilson et al. 1989, 1993; Wilson & Schooler 1991).

For example, Wilson et al. (1984) had steady couples come into the lab to rate the quality of their relationship (doing so separately). But one group were asked to give their rating having first listed the reasons for their judgment, whereas the other group just reported how they felt about the relationship. The output measure was whether or not the couples were still together some months later. There was less consistency between the initial ratings and the outcomes in couples who had analyzed their reasons for liking each other—so couples who had rated their relationship as rather poor might still be together, whereas those who had expressed high satisfaction might not be. This is probably because it can often be quite hard (especially early on in a relationship; the participants were undergrads) to know what the relevant factors are, and how much weight they should be given. The reasons-giving participants would likely have focused on obvious and easy-to-articulate factors; and having listed them, they then felt constrained to rate the relationship accordingly. In contrast, those who just considered their feelings without offering reasons would have been accessing a sort of affective summary of all the factors in the relationship, whether easy to describe or not. So although philosophers are apt to assume that one's capacity to articulate reasons is the gold-standard for rational decision-making, this seems not to be the case. Sometimes, at least, it is better to just go with one's "gut feeling."

The upshot of this section is that we have found nothing to challenge the claim that all decision-making is affectively based. At the very least we have established that *almost* all decision-making results from comparisons of anticipatory positive and negative valence, often integrated with estimates of the likelihood of achieving the outcomes in question. So if valence-based

60 Human Motives

decision-making is well described by the sort of motivational hedonism sketched in Sections 3.2 and 3.3, then we can conclude that hedonism is either universally true or pretty close to being so.

3.6 Difficult Decisions

Some decisions are easy, some are hard. Some are hard for the mundane reason that the options in question are too close to one another in value to be easily separated. Others are hard because there are too many options (think of 50 different varieties of toothbrush lined up on the supermarket shelf). In such cases we employ a variety of strategies to avoid decisional paralysis. Sometimes one might employ a metacognitive appraisal of the likely benefits of engaging in further deliberation. If the benefits are too minor, one might decide at random (flipping a coin or selecting whichever comes first to hand). Or one might outsource the decision to someone else ("Why don't you choose something from the menu for me?"). In other cases one might employ heuristics to narrow down the options (considering only recognized brands, or choosing based on mere color-preference, or always choosing the cheapest). Although decisions taken in these sorts of ways don't obviously support a hedonic common-currency model, they are surely consistent with it. For in adopting such heuristics it appears that what one is doing is weighing the mental and/or physical effort involved in attempting a direct choice (as well as the value of the extra time likely to be needed to reach such a decision) against any marginal gains that can be achieved from an optimal choice.

Other decisions are hard because the underlying judgments are difficult. Consider someone recruited to take part in a psychophysical experiment, perhaps involving color-categorization under differing conditions of illumination, where it is sometimes hard to say what the correct answer is. Each individual decision (e.g. to say "red" in response to a particular stimulus), although hard, may well be affect-free. But responding to the stimulus at all (continuing to participate in the experiment) will be driven by a sense of obligation, even when it gets quite boring—having agreed to participate, one would feel guilty or embarrassed to stop. So *what* one judges may be affect-free, but judging anything at all is not.

Additionally, some decisions are hard because the choices on offer are so different. Indeed, some decisions can be so hard that they lead philosophers to suggest they involve incommensurable or incomparable values.[7] A

---

[7] Although writers often use the term "incommensurable"—which strictly implies lack of a single cardinal scale of value—most of the discussions in the field only really require incomparability (Hsieh & Andersson 2021).

frequent example in the literature concerns someone who is faced with a choice between two successful careers—either as a lawyer or as a clarinetist (Raz 1986). One can feel that neither choice is definitely better or worse than the other, without thereby judging that they are of equal value. Indeed, given that one's life would be so different in multiple respects in the two careers, and that the choice seems so momentous, one can feel paralyzed when it comes to selecting between them.

It might seem that the existence of incomparable options like this causes a problem for the claim that valence is the common currency for decision-making. But it does not. On the contrary, the common-currency idea, combined with well-known facts about cognition, actually *predicts* that there will be cases where choices seem incomparable. For recall what one does in prospection: one imaginatively simulates one outcome, responding to it with positive or negative valence, and then imaginatively simulates the other, comparing the affective response one has to that. But many real-life decisions are complex, comprising many distinct facets. These cannot all be simulated at once, resulting from well-known limits on the contents of working memory. (This is now thought to be limited to just three or four items in the absence of strategies for rehearsal or chunking; Cowan 2001.) For example, one can try to imagine how one's day might be filled as a lawyer (meeting with clients and researching case-law) and compare that with a day filled with musical practice. But one then has to compare the benefits and drawbacks of a rooted occupation (law) against those of an itinerant life-style (a musician). And then there are the comparisons of likely earnings, and what one might do with them, as well as how family and friends might respond to one's choice, and so on.[8]

As will be familiar to many readers, what one does in real cases of this sort is cycle back and forth between the options, often over the course of many days or weeks. Not only is it impossible to prospect each future option in its entirety at once, but one will constantly be coming across new sources of uncertainty—how much vacation time might a lawyer normally enjoy? Do orchestras provide pension plans and health insurance? These complicate one's choice still further, even assuming one can find determinate answers. In the end, people will often rely on just one or a few significant factors to determine their choice—such as that a career as a lawyer is more consistent with family life—or will draw on some aspect of their self-conception that can help them discriminate between the two ("I've always seen myself as a creative sort of person").

---

[8] Moreover, the limits on simultaneous evaluation probably don't only result from working-memory limits. Even if the latter were unconstrained, there are probably quite severe restrictions on how many items or properties can be received by one's affective systems and appraised at once.

62 Human Motives

Especially difficult are choices that will transform one into a different kind of person, with different values and concerns (Paul 2014). In trying to decide whether or not to have a child, for example, one should know that becoming a parent is apt to radically restructure one's values and priorities. On one level this is no more difficult than trying to decide between a career as a lawyer or a clarinetist. One will go back and forth considering different factors and possible outcomes, responding affectively to each. In doing so, of course, one is drawing on one's current values. But most of us also have at least some concern for our future happiness and well-being as such, wanting to live in accordance with our future values and satisfy our future desires whatever they turn out to be. Here simulation of the future is of no help. One will be responding affectively to scenarios as appraised against one's current values, not one's future ones. It is one's affective system as it is now that responds with positive or negative valence, making the choices seem good or bad. But it is the structure of that system itself that will be transformed on the other side of the decision to become a parent.

There is nothing in the idea of a transformative decision that conflicts with a common-currency view of valence, however, nor with the centrality of prospection in most forms of conscious decision-making. What it does mean is that in such cases one may have to rely on other resources to help one reach a decision. This might involve utilizing the testimony of others to predict the likely structure of one's future concerns if the decision is taken, for example—responding affectively to what one is told—or taking a meta-level decision to leave the outcome to chance.

3.7 Conclusion

It seems that most (if not all) actions that result from decision-making depend on affective appraisal of the options and are valence-based. Hence, all such actions are grounded in one way or another in "the passions," scientifically vindicating a form of Humeanism about motivation. (We will return to complicate this conclusion somewhat in Chapter 8.) Actions that result from conscious forms of imaginative prospection depend on computations of pleasure and displeasure, as do actions that result from swift appraisal and choice among consciously experienced options. Unconsciously made choices, too, aim to maximize the balance of positive over negative valence (which can be thought of as unconscious forms of pleasure and displeasure). Even those actions that result from applying some decision-making heuristic often do so only because valence-based decision-making is too hard in the circumstances (in which case choosing itself becomes negatively valenced), and yet a decision has to be made somehow. So although the final choice might not be made on the basis of valence, the ensuing action is nevertheless motivated by valence. Likewise, although actions that implement a previously formed intention might not implicate valence at the time of acting, they crucially depend on it at the time when the intention is formed or decided upon.

We can conclude, then, that all (or almost all) actions that result from decision-making processes are motivated by valence, and are aimed at securing an optimal balance of positive over negative valence. Moreover, all actions that result from *conscious* decision-making processes involve future-directed pleasure or displeasure (conscious positive or negative valence), with the balance of the one over the other automatically determining choice when integrated with likelihoods and compared with other options. So if pleasure and displeasure are intrinsic felt properties of one's experiences, it follows that all conscious decisions aim at achieving good feelings for oneself, or avoiding bad ones. As a result, motivational hedonism will be true of vast swathes of human action. And, most importantly for our purposes (as we saw in Section 3.3), the way in which prospective valence influences choice needn't depend on the belief that one will undergo similar hedonic experiences in the future when the chosen event takes place.

The resulting account would not apply directly to all actions, as we noted in Section 2.3. In particular, it would fail to apply to habitual actions, as well as to spontaneous affect-caused actions that are expressive or immediately instrumental. But such actions lack any mentally represented goal, in which case motivational hedonism can—and should—be formulated as saying that one's own hedonic states provide the goal of all actions that have any overt goal at all, or else all actions that result from decision-making.

Chapter 4 will show that the form of motivational hedonism outlined here—which is made possible by the science of affect—is immune to all of the main arguments mounted against hedonism previously, by both philosophers and experimental psychologists.

4
Traditional Critiques Critiqued

The present chapter will show that the scientifically informed version of motivational hedonism that emerged from our discussion in Chapter 3 is impervious to all the main arguments that have been advanced previously against hedonism and in support of pluralism, by both philosophers and psychologists. Thereafter the chapter will briefly show that similar considerations render an alternative form of hedonist account similarly invulnerable (framed in terms of experience-directed imperatives, to be discussed in Chapter 6).

4.1 Evolutionary Arguments

There was a good deal of debate in the second half of the twentieth century over the question whether it is possible for altruism to evolve. This is because natural selection operates on the basis of inclusive fitness—that is, on how many descendants or copies of one's genes one contributes to the future gene-pool of the species. It proved important, however, to distinguish between two rather different notions of altruism: evolutionary and psychological (Sober & Wilson 1998). *Evolutionary* altruism would be an innate disposition to act to benefit others at the cost of one's own inclusive fitness. Plainly, no such disposition could evolve, except via some form of group-selection (which remains controversial). This is because the genes of those whose inclusive fitness one sacrifices oneself to benefit would come to dominate the gene-pool, rather than one's own. Hence evolutionary altruism, even if it were to emerge, would be selected against and would soon disappear. *Psychological* or *motivational* altruism, in contrast, would be a matter of people having a desire to benefit others as an intrinsic or non-instrumental goal. It is obvious that desires of this sort could evolve. For example, desires to benefit one's children and other relatives are likely to improve one's inclusive fitness, and so could be selected for.

It might be thought, though, that evolutionary considerations place tight restrictions on the scope of psychological altruism. Plainly, it can allow for altruism towards kin, through processes of kin-selection (Hamilton 1963;

Human Motives: Hedonism, Altruism, and the Science of Affect. Peter Carruthers, Oxford University Press.
© Peter Carruthers 2024. DOI: 10.1093/oso/9780198906131.003.0004

Maynard Smith 1964). This would produce degrees of altruistic motivation in proportion to genetic relatedness. And it can allow for the evolution of intrinsic motivations to benefit others in collaborative species given cues of likely reciprocity (Trivers 1973). As we now know, however, among humans, processes of gene-culture coevolution can, in principle, produce all manner of innate prosocial motivations (Richerson & Boyd 2004; Henrich 2017). For example, if cultures reliably punish or exclude antisocial individuals, then that would create powerful selection pressure towards innate prosociality. (Although this is possible in principle, it remains an open question, of course, whether it has actually occurred and, if so, which innate prosocial motivations humans in fact possess. We will return to these questions in Chapter 8.)

Notice, however, that what has been at stake in these discussions is the question whether, and to what extent, psychological altruism is innate. But as we saw in Section 2.6, a negative answer to this question would by no means entail motivational egoism. This is because the debate between motivational egoism and motivational pluralism (including motivational altruism) is about what people are in fact motivated to do for its own sake, not what they are motivated to do innately. And as we also saw in that chapter, among highly social—especially cultural—beings such as humans, affective conditioning can give rise to new intrinsic values of many kinds. These can include altruistic and moral-norm-based ones. Even if the only innate motivations are egoistic ones, it can still be true that many of us are motivational pluralists and motivational altruists, resulting from processes of affective conditioning and affective learning.

As also emerged from our discussion in Chapters 2 and 3, however, even if people in fact have multiple types of other-regarding intrinsic values, this still doesn't entail motivational pluralism or altruism. This is because motivational *hedonism* remains a possibility. Even if one's affective systems respond to the suffering of another with compassion and sympathy, or if the thought of transgressing a moral norm produces guilt, the way in which these affective states motivate decision-making can still be a hedonist (and hence egoist) one. In acting out of sympathy, for example, one might be attempting to reduce negative feelings in oneself or to secure the good feelings that would result from successful helping. And in choosing to act morally, likewise, one might just be aiming to avoid feeling guilty, or in order to feel the subsequent glow of righteous satisfaction.

Sober & Wilson (1998) recognize these possibilities, but nevertheless attempt to construct an evolutionary argument against hedonism. They take as their central example human parents' motivations to care for, protect, and

66 Human Motives

provide for the needs of their children. There is no doubt that kin selection has produced such motivations in humans, just as it has done in all female mammals, at least. But there are two different ways in which such motivations could work. One is by creating intrinsic (non-instrumental) desires for the welfare of one's offspring. This would be a form of motivational altruism. The other would be via the positive and negative feelings produced by one's affective system at the prospect of good or bad things happening to those offspring, leading one to act to secure the good feelings and avoid the bad— the means to which would be helping one's children to do well. The upshot would, of course, be a form of motivational hedonism.

Each of these options, to be adaptive, would require people to form reliable-enough beliefs about how to secure the welfare of offspring, of course. Sometimes this might not happen, and children will end up dying— thereby creating significant selection pressure for reliable belief-formation in this domain. But no belief-formation process can be completely reliable. Hence sometimes when parents act on their child-directed altruistic values they will fail. But Sober & Wilson (1998) claim that the hedonist option requires people to have, not only these beliefs, but an additional set as well. They need, in particular, to reliably acquire either the belief that securing the welfare of their children will make them feel good, or the belief that failing to help their children will make them feel bad, or both. This introduces an additional form of vulnerability.

Suppose, first, that the beliefs in question are empirically acquired. Then at least sometimes one would predict that the learning process or its evidential basis would go awry, and people fail to form these beliefs—with negative consequences for their inclusive fitness. And even if the beliefs in question are innate or innately channeled, people would still be potentially vulnerable, for they might acquire beliefs that conflict with, or override, those beliefs, with similar effects on their fitness. Hence one would expect evolution to select for the altruistic form of motivation rather than the hedonist one, Sober & Wilson claim, for since altruistic motivations for the welfare of one's children aren't dependent on these sorts of belief, they will lack these additional sources of vulnerability.

In criticism of this argument, Stich et al. (2010) make the point that not all beliefs and belief-like states are empirically acquired and/or vulnerable to change or disruption from other things one might come to believe. Some, in contrast, are "sticky." They may be inaccessible to normal processes of inference and belief-revision (Stich and colleagues refer to them as "sub-doxastic") and they may form an innate component of the human and/or mammalian reproductive system. Although this criticism is a good one, and shows that

Sober & Wilson (1998) have failed to establish their conclusion, it lacks any independent motivation. There is no particular reason for thinking that people should actually have such "sticky" beliefs about the relationship between their children's welfare and their own affective feelings. In contrast, the science of affect gives us a better way to make a similar point, or so I shall now argue.

Recall from Chapter 3 that valence is the common currency of decision-making. And let us suppose, with the hedonist, that valence is comprised of intrinsic feelings (pleasure and displeasure) that attach to currently experienced actions and events (providing a learning-signal), as well as becoming attached to representations of anticipated future actions and events. In the latter case, how does valence do its work in influencing decision-making? There are two possibilities, as we noted in Section 3.2: direct and indirect. One possibility is that positive valence attaching to a representation of a future action or outcome influences its selection directly (in competition with others), without requiring any further beliefs (beyond beliefs about the likelihood of achieving the outcome). The other possibility is the one assumed by Sober & Wilson (1998) in their critique of hedonism (as well as by Gilbert & Wilson 2007). This is that positive valence attaching to a future-directed representation needs to be paired with a belief that successful performance of the action or successful achievement of the outcome would result in a similar extent of pleasure to that currently felt in anticipation. We saw in Section 3.2, however, that the direct-influence account is much more plausible when placed in the context of evaluative learning and decision-making across a wide range of non-human animals. And this then gives motivational hedonists all that they need to rebut Sober & Wilson's (1998) evolutionary argument against them.

Consider what a motivational hedonist should say about supposed altruistic motivations towards kin (specifically one's own children). When one imagines one's child giggling with pleasure when tickled, for example, this is positively appraised in light of the stored value attaching to the child's welfare, and one experiences positive valence (pleasure) as a component of that future-directed representation itself. Then, contrary to what Sober & Wilson claim, in the absence of competing motivations, this may be sufficient to initiate tickling. No belief that one will enjoy tickling the child is required. Likewise, when one's child has fallen and begins to cry, mental rehearsal of the kiss-it-better routine may lead to a prediction of reduced pain. This is appraised positively, making the execution of that action-routine seem attractive and pleasurable, and directly influencing the decision to act accordingly. One doesn't have to believe, on any level, that getting the child

68 Human Motives

to stop crying will make one feel good in order for this to work as described. But the mechanism is still a hedonist one: one's goal is to achieve or avoid events that are represented as pleasant or unpleasant.

Notice that on this way of construing hedonism, actions are not selected in order to secure pleasure and avoid displeasure in the ordinary sense that would require instrumental beliefs about one's future hedonic states. Nevertheless, as we saw in Section 3.3, actions are selected or avoided because representations of their future implementation have pleasure or displeasure bound into their contents. So one selects pleasant-seeming future actions and rejects unpleasant-seeming ones; and one's goal is thus to achieve hedonically optimal outcomes. Moreover, (in the positive case) one's evaluative systems then measure the success of the action by matching the pleasure subsequently experienced against the pleasure generated in immediately prior anticipation, issuing in an error signal that increases or decreases the stored value attaching to actions of that sort. So in this way, too, it is appropriate to think of hedonic goals as being implicit in the choice procedure, and of choice as being implicitly designed to secure pleasure and avoid pain. The system is set up in such a way that pleasure attaching to future-directed representations of action renders the execution of those actions attractive and choice-worthy; and successful actions will in turn be apt to issue in pleasure and avoidance of displeasure, influencing one's stored values accordingly.

When motivational hedonism is seen in terms of mechanisms of affective learning and decision-making that we share with many other animals—as it surely should be, if one is to be a hedonist at all—then the worry Sober & Wilson (1998) raise about the vulnerability of our inclusive fitness from false or inappropriately formed beliefs about future pleasures and displeasures simply dissipates. Their argument against motivational hedonism fails accordingly. No such beliefs are needed. But still it is the positive or negative valence (pleasure or displeasure) attached to future-directed representations of events and anticipations of action that makes those events and actions choice-worthy or repulsive.

4.2 Self-Sacrifice: Spontaneous and Reflective

One argument often advanced against motivational hedonism (and against motivational egoism more generally) is that it cannot make sense of cases where people sacrifice their lives for a cause. (I previously used this argument myself in Carruthers 2018c.) Consider the soldier who throws himself onto a live grenade, in full knowledge of what an exploding grenade will do to a human body. Or consider the political protester who sets fire to herself in a public square in order to start a revolt against an oppressive regime. Surely neither of these people is acting to secure good feelings for themselves, nor to avoid bad ones, for the results of their actions are inevitably just pain and death, and we can suppose that they know this. (The soldier doesn't irrationally believe that the grenade will do him no harm, for example.) And we can stipulate, moreover, that neither person is religious, nor believes in an afterlife. So the acts aren't done to secure hedonic benefits after they are dead, either.

There is a relevant difference between our two examples, however: one is spontaneous, done on the spur of the moment, without reflection; the other may be done after extended thinking and planning. Consider the former first. Some cases of this sort could well belong among actions of the kind that aren't really done with any goal in mind (discussed in Section 2.3), like fleeing in terror from a predator. This can sound odd. It is certainly counterintuitive. Surely the person in question *aims* to cover the grenade with his body, and by absorbing the explosion to save his comrades? In one sense that might be true, but not necessarily in a way that involves decision-making, whether affectively based or otherwise. In fact, given pre-existing, already encoded, values of comradeship and mutual-aid among soldiers, the sequence might unfold as follows. Seeing a live grenade drop into the foxhole, and judging that there is no time to pick it up and throw it back out, the soldier's appraisal of the situation is one of extreme danger to his comrades. This produces an intense affectively caused motor-urge to save them, comparable to the urge to get away from a predator. The only affordance for action he can perceive in the circumstances is to fall on the grenade himself; so that is what he does. Here there need be no decision-making at all, although of course there can be (for instance, the soldier may take a swift decision not to inhibit the motor impulse). The soldier may merely fail to inhibit an affectively caused motoric urge (without taking any decision to do so), that is then guided in execution by the affordances of the situation.

Would this account make the soldier's actions any less heroic and worthy of praise and admiration? Not necessarily. For an intense in-the-moment urge to save his comrades, of the sort just envisaged, must reflect his strong valuation of them and their lives. Those are the values against which affective appraisal of the situation takes place. So his action, although unplanned and un-premeditated, both reflects (expresses) and provides good evidence of values that we can admire. (Whether his action should qualify as courageous, however, is another matter. Perhaps not, if courage involves overcoming

70   Human Motives

fear.) But this would seem to be a form of consequentialist evaluation of character, similar to our evaluations of people made in other cases that lack intent, such as someone whose spontaneous action displays a racial bias.

Of course, not every instance of in-the-moment self-sacrifice need fit this mold. Many might not be truly spontaneous, but involve swift comparison among the alternative options that results in a decision. Such cases will then belong with instances of reflective self-sacrifice, like the person who—after many fruitless protests—decides that the only way to spark a rebellion is by self-immolation. These are the kinds of case we discuss next.

There are at least a couple of explanations a hedonist can offer for reflective forms of self-sacrifice. Both build on the account of the role of valence in decision-making laid out in Sections 3.2 and 3.3. First, suppose that when our intending revolutionary reflects on her failures to spark protests against the regime, and perhaps having reviewed evidence of successful cases in the past, she comes to think that self-immolation, and only self-immolation, is likely to do the job. (For present purposes we can suppose that she is right.) When she imagines pouring paraffin over herself and striking the match, she knows there will be a minute or two of intense pain. She appraises that as bad, and the pain she feels in imagination produces fear and an urge not to do it. But then she imagines the protests that she predicts will follow, and an evil regime starting to crumble, and she appraises that as very good. This produces intense pleasure as she considers it, perhaps mixed with pride at the thought that she herself would be the one to start things off. This outweighs the pain, causing a decision: she makes up her mind to do it.

Notice that for this to make sense, and provide a successful explanation, the revolutionary agent doesn't have to believe that she will experience intense pleasure in the future, after she is dead. She may be an atheist, and know full well that her final moments of pain will be her final moments. So she is not using the joy she feels in anticipation of the effects of her action as predictive of what she can expect to feel if she takes that action, as Gilbert & Wilson (2007) would claim. But such beliefs aren't needed, as we saw in Sections 3.2 and 3.3. Rather, the way in which valence influences decision-making is immediate, and independent of belief. The pleasure she experiences when imagining the fall of the regime gets bound into the content of her future-directed imagining, making that future seem especially pleasant and attractive; and this outweighs the displeasure that gets bound into the content of imagined self-immolation; so she decides to bring about the former despite the latter. (I am ignoring the role of likelihoods; we can assume for present purposes that she is equally certain of each outcome.)

A different way in which a case of this kind might unfold is that, having come to believe that only self-immolation will be successful in sparking the needed protests, she considers the possibility of *not* doing it, but instead continuing the fruitless attempts she has already been making. This produces in her intense feelings of guilt and/or shame, outweighing the displeasure she anticipates feeling from the act itself. Again this can cause the decision directly. She doesn't have to believe—irrationally—that the guilt she would feel would be permanent, and prevent her from living a worthwhile life if she fails to act. No, the intense guilt makes the thought of failing to act seem highly aversive, worse than a painful death. And in fact, given her values, that might be right. In taking a hedonically motivated decision, she can in fact be taking a decision that appropriately reflects the strength of her underlying values, appraisal against which issues in those hedonic feelings.

The general framework outlined here can be used to explain all other cases in which people take decisions in full knowledge that they will never get to experience (nor take pleasure or displeasure in) the results. There are people who write their wills secretly, for example, leaving their money anonymously to valued institutions or people. Such decisions plainly aren't taken for the pleasures of social status or gratitude during their life-times, since their actions are anonymous. And they might know full well that they will feel no pleasure in what they have done when they are dead. But still, when they imagine the institution, or the people, flourishing in the future, that gets appraised as very good, and they feel intense pleasure while they imagine it—making that outcome seem highly attractive. The pleasure, when unopposed, can lead directly to a decision, without needing support from predictions of future enjoyment. Again, the pleasure they feel when considering the outcome might be an appropriate expression of the underlying values against which the outcome is appraised. But the decision is hedonically motivated nevertheless.

Should we admire such a person? And should we admire the self-immolator (assuming that the regime is indeed repressive and that the action will in fact be successful)? We can admire their values, and the strength of those values; and we can be glad of the consequences of their actions. But if motivational hedonism is correct, those actions are undertaken for the sake of the pleasure that attaches to the thought of performing them—they are hedonically motivated. The people in question are choosing the most pleasant-seeming option (or avoiding the most unpleasant-seeming one) because of its represented pleasantness. Most of us will think that this is the wrong kind of reason to underlie a morally good action. So it seems one can admire the self-sacrificer's values, but one should not admire the action that results.

72 Human Motives

4.3 Desire and Satisfaction

One long-standing philosophical argument against motivational hedonism is that pleasure is generally a result of satisfying a desire for something *other* than pleasure, such as food, wealth, or the success of one's children; in which case not all actions can result from desires for pleasure (Butler 1726; Broad 1952; Nagel 1970; Feinberg 1984). But this argument fails to separate the appraisal component of desire from the valence aspect. It is true that many desires are felt in response to properties or events in one's own body or in the world, such as calorie-depletion, in the case of hunger, or a financial offer, in the case of a desire for wealth. That is, there is an appraisal of a need and/or opportunity for food or for money that issues in an affective state. But the output of that process is positive valence attached to the thought of eating, or to the thought of becoming rich. And it is this valence-component that makes the outcome seem worthy of choice, and that influences one's decision-making. Everything then turns on the nature of valence itself. If it is an intrinsic feeling that decision-making processes implicitly seek to maximize, for example, then hedonism is supported: one decides to eat in order to secure a future outcome that is represented as positively valenced (pleasurable).

Often, the only concepts that figure in one's verbal expression of a desire are non-hedonic ones, of course. One says simply, "I want to be rich," not, "I want to feel the pleasure of being rich." And likewise, the only instrumental beliefs that guide one's actions can be ones that make no mention of pleasure. The way one would describe one's decision-making can just look like this: "I want to be rich; I believe that investing in Meta will make me rich; so I decided to buy some shares." But if valence is the common-currency of decision-making, as was argued in Chapters 2 and 3, then what really happened ("under the hood," as it were) is that one came to believe that buying Meta stock would make one rich; one envisaged becoming rich, which caused one to experience positive valence (pleasure); the resulting pleasure was bound into the representation of future riches, making it seem attractive; so one decided to make the purchase. Here the pleasure produced by appraisal of one's future riches was not only the proximal cause of the decision, but the goal of the decision. (Again, I am ignoring the role of likelihoods, for simplicity.)

Recall, too, that the success-condition for action, from the point of view of evaluative learning, is that the pleasure one experiences on completion of the action matches or exceeds the pleasure evoked just previously in anticipation. If the pleasure received either exceeds or falls below what was expected (strictly: is greater or lesser than that attached to an earlier future-directed representation of goal-achievement), then an error-signal causes the stored evaluation of outcomes of that sort to be ratcheted upwards or downwards by some increment. So pleasure in anticipation is not a *mere* cause of action; it also sets the crucial success-condition for evaluative learning.

Moreover, since it is the pleasure one experiences in anticipation of the goal-outcome that motivates one's decision to pursue it, it seems right to say that the goal-outcome in question is—tacitly—really an instrumental one. Becoming rich is selected because its appraisal is pleasure-giving. Indeed, since pleasure is a component of the resulting future-directed representation, then it, too, is future-directed. Tacitly, then, one aims at riches in order to achieve pleasure. Although one need not *believe* that achieving the goal will cause one pleasure, and although one need not believe that one pursues it for that reason, this is, in fact, the underlying mechanism.

A natural objection to make at this point is that pleasure, even when experienced as a component of a future-directed representation, is not the right kind of thing to motivate either decision or action. Feelings in themselves can't motivate. Only desires can do that. It is only if pleasure is *wanted*, someone might say, that it can play any explanatory or causal role in decision-making. And indeed, this is probably the right thing to say from the perspective of common-sense psychology. The latter treats desire (sometimes generalized by philosophers to "pro-attitudes" so as to encompass goals, hopes, wishes, and so on) as the basic motivator. Pleasure only motivates to the extent that it is desired. And likewise, displeasures like pain only motivate to the extent that one wants to avoid them, or wants them to cease.

It turns out, however, that in this respect common-sense psychology is mistaken (just as it is in many others; Carruthers 2025). It makes sense that the latter's explanatory structure should have the shape that it has, though, for two reasons. First, if pleasure plays a ubiquitous role in conscious forms of decision-making then it can go unmentioned. Descriptions of any given desire will just focus on what is specific to that desire. What all conscious desires have in common (anticipatory pleasure) doesn't need to be mentioned. And second, positive and negative valence (pleasure and displeasure) are often not phenomenologically salient—indeed, they can be wholly unconscious and still do their work in forms of unreflective decision-making.

In fact, then, the efficacy of desire needs to be explained in terms of the causal efficacy of valence, and not the other way around. To have a currently felt desire for something (as opposed to a goal one has formed previously, which is more intention-like, and as opposed to the standing values appraisal against which issue in occurrent desires) is to be in a state in which a representation of a future event is causing positive valence (pleasure) that gets bound into the representation of the event, motivating a decision to pursue it. It is the pleasure caused in anticipation that influences choice. "Desire" is just the name for the overall state, encompassing both a representation of a future event or outcome, together with the pleasure that the representation in question causes and incorporates.

Is this a revisionary theory of desire? In a number of respects, yes, it is. Philosophers tend to characterize desires as states that are apt to bring about the desired state of affairs (common sense probably does as well). On the view presented here, however, the impact of the affective component of desire (as opposed to desire's automatic motor-urge component; see Section 2.3) on the world is indirect, not just in the sense that desires require guidance from belief, but because their only direct influence is on decision-making processes (which then in turn result in intentions, which *are* apt to cause the desired state of affairs). Moreover, both philosophy and common sense think of feelings of desire as having as their content just the desired state-of-affairs. In contrast, we have seen that pleasure attaching to a representation of the desired state-of-affairs is a crucial component of desire. Roughly, the content of desire always has the form *such and such would be pleasurable*. And finally, standard views of desire fail to distinguish between the automatic motoric components of desire (urges to act, directly caused by appraisal processes) and the valenced output that plays a central role in decision-making.

4.4 The Experience Machine

Another widely influential argument against hedonism derives from the *experience machine* thought-experiment (Nozick 1974). One is asked to consider living out one's life in a machine that would simulate, in complete detail, any sequence of experiences one wishes. (These would be selected in advance, in outline at least.) But at the same time it will cause one to forget that one is in the machine, and hence that the experiences don't derive from real events. Many have the intuition that life in the machine is not really a good one. And likewise, it is said that people would resist getting into the machine, despite the fact that it could insure an ideal hedonic future.[1] The claim, then, is that since one would reject an ideal hedonic future in

---

[1] In fact, many undergraduate students say they *would* get into the machine (Weijers 2014). This might indicate the pervasiveness of hedonist theories in popular culture, or else the extent to which many students are hedonists in the colloquial sense.

circumstances of this sort, motivational hedonism must be false. And for the same reason, the fact that one would reject such a future seems to support a non-hedonic account of desire: what one wants is real success and real loving interactions, not the pleasure that experiences of success and love can bring.

Once again, however, if one keeps separate the appraisals that generate affective states from the valence that results, then these intuitions can be readily explained, consistent with the truth of motivational hedonism. For one's own appraisal mechanisms are largely activated by perceived or imagined real-world contents (worldly items or events), not by experiences represented as such. But when one imagines life in the machine, one is *only* imagining sequences of experience. Small wonder, then, that one's own appraisal mechanisms should fail to respond positively. In contrast, when one imagines stepping into the machine, one appraises the loss of everything that one's appraisal mechanisms normally evaluate positively, issuing in negative valence.

Many of the values against which events get appraised are world-focused, of course. One values success in one's profession, the respect of one's colleagues, time spent with loved ones, the welfare of one's children, and so on. Admittedly, all of the appraisal processes that issue in affectively based decision-making must proceed via one's experience (or memory, or imagination) of the events in question. It is only when one sees (or hears) the approaching bear, or imagines a bear in the dark forest around one, that one becomes afraid, for example. But it is the bear (and the threat that it poses) that one is afraid of, not one's own experience or imagination. Likewise, it is only when one becomes aware that one's child is in need of help that processes of appraisal can issue in an affective desire to assist. But it is one's child's welfare against which the perceived situation is being appraised. Although affective appraisal must proceed *via* one's awareness (understood broadly, to include unconscious forms of representation), it is not the states of awareness themselves that are being appraised. Rather, it is their contents: what in the world they represent.

So when one imagines, and evaluatively appraises, a successful career, resulting in motivation to pursue one, it is the actual career that is being appraised (albeit via one's imaginative representation of it). When one imagines stepping into the experience machine, in contrast, and having all the experiences distinctive of a successful career, the stored value that one attaches to one's career and/or one's social standing will fail to become activated at all. One might *also* value happiness and pleasant feelings, and appraisal of the high likelihood of achieving those in the machine might issue in at least some motivation to enter it. But provided that these are not

76 Human Motives

all that one values, then entering the machine will inevitably be appraised as bringing losses, too. If one also values success in one's career, as well as time actually spent with loved ones, then appraisal of what happens when one enters the machine will issue in negative affect; for those things will inevitably be lost.

How one responds to the experience-machine thought-experiment, then, may partly depend on whether one is a hedonist in the colloquial sense of the term—that is, how much one just values having good experiences and good feelings. But even those who are hedonists in this weaker sense generally have some world-directed values that will issue in negative appraisals of getting into the machine. Hedonists who just like hanging out with their friends, for example, seem to want more than just *seeming* to hang out with their friends (which is all they will get in the experience machine). When they consider entering the machine, they should realize that they will never *actually* see their friends again, and that will produce a negative appraisal, and issue in at least some motivation for declining.

4.5 Experimental Evidence

Experimental psychologists have done a great deal of empirical work attempting to undermine egoism and motivational hedonism. Batson (1991, 2019), in particular, has methodically attempted to test every proposed hedonic explanation of seemingly altruistic helping behavior. These include the suggestion that people help to avoid feeling guilty, as well as that they help to obtain feelings of pride for having helped, or to feel pleasure at someone's relief from suffering. All of these experiments take as their starting point that people help because they feel empathy for the situation of the target person. The question at stake is whether empathy's role is that of a hedonic motivator, or whether it involves an intrinsic desire to benefit another person for its own sake.

Batson's work builds on an extensive body of evidence that feelings of empathy can be manipulated. For example, one can ask people to imagine what the target person is feeling (as opposed to considering their situation objectively), or one can emphasize similarities (as opposed to dissimilarities) between the person participating in the experiment and the target. And likewise, there is extensive evidence that such manipulations generally succeed in increasing rates of helping—empathy does cause helping behavior (Eisenberg & Miller 1987). In each of Batson's experiments empathy is manipulated so that he can test the effects of manipulating some other variable when empathy is felt (is high). But the experiments also generally manipulate people's beliefs about the situation in ways designed to test specific motivational-hedonist proposals.

For instance, in order to test whether people are motivated to help because they will feel proud of themselves if they do, Batson et al. (1988) set up a high-empathy/low-empathy experiment in which some participants had the opportunity to work to prevent electric shocks (reportedly) being delivered to another person, whereas others didn't. In addition, some participants learned later that the other person would in fact be enrolled in the receive-shocks condition, whereas others learned that she would be receiving no shocks in any case. Changes in mood were measured before and after learning these things. The pride hypothesis predicts an increase in positive mood only among people who had actually performed the task in the situation where the other person was in the receive-shocks condition. (Since the task was an easy one, participants in this condition could be confident that they had prevented the person from receiving all or most of the shocks.) In contrast with this prediction, there were no mood-change differences in the two conditions where participants actually performed the task (whether preventing shocks or not). But in cases where participants ended up not performing the task, their mood got worse in the receive-shocks condition (presumably because they could do nothing to prevent them), but significantly improved on learning that the other participant would not be receiving shocks anyway (presumably reflecting relief, since there was nothing they could have done to help).

The proposal that people who act out of empathy for another do so because they anticipate feeling proud is probably not the most plausible hedonist construal of prosocial behavior. But rather than discuss all of the alternatives (and Batson's attempts to refute them), I propose to stake out the strongest case for motivational hedonism by granting as much as possible to the opposition. In particular, let us suppose that human affective systems (whether innately or as a result of affective learning) attach intrinsic value to the welfare of others (especially close others) and attach intrinsic disvalue to things that cause harm to others (especially to in-group others).

Then when one appraises something as improving someone's welfare (bringing relief from harm, for example), this should produce positive valence (whether or not that thing is one's own action); and when one appraises something as causing an in-group member harm, this should produce negative valence. In cases where one can do something to help, positive valence (anticipatory pleasure) should motivate one to do it; and when one sees that what one is doing will cause harm to another, negative valence

78 Human Motives

(anticipatory displeasure) should motivate one to forebear from action. But what one feels should be independent of one's capacity for action (contrary to the anticipatory-pride hypothesis and the anticipatory-guilt hypothesis).

The version of hedonism just sketched closely resembles what Batson (2019) calls the "empathic joy" version of motivational hedonism. The idea is that when feeling empathy for someone's situation, people are motivated to help because they anticipate feeling good if they succeed—for just as one feels bad when someone one identifies with is pained, so one will feel good when someone one identifies with is pleased. Batson et al. (1991) set out to test this hypothesis, employing, as usual, a low-empathy/high-empathy experimental induction. The crucial manipulation was whether or not participants could expect to receive feedback on the results of their help. The reasoning was that if participations are only motivated to help because they anticipate feeling good when the other person's situation improves, then they should be disinclined to help if they know they won't ever learn of the outcome.

Participants were told about a (fictional) student, Katie, whose parents had just died in an accident, and who was in danger of having to drop out of school to take care of her younger brother and sister. Participants had the option of volunteering to stuff and address envelopes to raise money to pay for child-care for the younger children, so that Katie could continue her studies. (Degrees of empathy were manipulated—successfully—by either asking participants to remain objective about Katie's situation, or asking them to imagine what she must be feeling.) The main experimental manipulation was that some participants were told that Katie would be providing volunteers with feed-back on the results of their efforts, whereas others were told that they would never learn anything about the results. The main finding was that high-empathy participants still volunteered to help Katie at very high rates even in the no-feedback condition. This was taken to refute the "empathic joy" version of motivational hedonism.

Notice, however, that the version of hedonism tested here is thought to depend on an explicit belief or expectation about the conditions under which empathic joy will be felt in the future. Indeed, it is just these beliefs that get manipulated—one group of participants is led to believe that they will experience empathic joy by helping, whereas the other group is led to believe that they will not. Although this is the version of hedonism similar to that assumed by Sober & Wilson (1998) and Gilbert & Wilson (2007), we saw in Sections 3.2 and 3.3 that it is by no means the most plausible. Rather, the pleasure experienced as a component of one's anticipation of acting motivates one to perform the action directly, independent of one's beliefs (or lack thereof) about future pleasure.

So consider someone in the high-empathy plus no-feedback condition of the experiment described above. Feeling empathy for Katie, and imagining the possibility of helping to raise money for child-care (which they predict will help), participants will experience positive valence (pleasure). This makes the act of helping seem attractive (pleasurable), and directly motivates a decision to act. It makes no difference whether or not they will ever learn of Katie's improved situation, for they are not acting because they want, explicitly, to feel good in future. Rather, feeling good now, as they rehearse the possibility of future acting, they are motivated to act. It is the seeming-pleasantness of future helping that motivates them to do it.

A similar error underlies Batson's attempt to refute what one might regard as the inverse of the "empathic joy" version of hedonism. This is the suggestion that empathy motivates people to help because they want to get rid of the displeasure they feel at the thought of the other person's suffering. So people help because they are aware that, if they don't, they will likely remember and continue to feel bad about the person's situation. This was tested in Batson's lab using a version of the Katie scenario by manipulating whether participants believe that they will, or will not, remember Katie's plight in the future (Stocks et al. 2009). Participants were convinced that there was a new memory-training/memory-wiping procedure that would insure that recent memories would either be retained or lost; and they were told which condition they were participating in. Then they were presented with Katie's situation, and given the opportunity to volunteer to help. If people in the high-empathy condition are only motivated by the fear that they will continue to feel bad for Katie if they choose not to help, then the memory-wiping manipulation should greatly reduce offers to assist. But it did not.

Again, note the dependence here on an explicit-belief version of motivational hedonism, of the sort we rejected in Sections 3.2 and 3.3. In contrast, the direct-effect version of hedonism readily predicts these findings. When participants in the high-empathy condition are considering Katie's plight, they might mentally rehearse choosing not to assist. That predicts an increased likelihood that Katie will be unable to continue her studies, and will be distressed as a result. This outcome is appraised negatively in light of the stored negative value the affective system attaches to the suffering of (in-group/like-me) others, giving rise to negative valence (displeasure). That displeasure gets bound into the representation of the do-nothing option,

80   Human Motives

making it seem aversive. And that then directly motivates avoiding it, and results in a decision to help Katie instead. The belief that one will, or will not, remember participating in the experiment is simply irrelevant to the choice process.

It is worth considering just one other experimental paradigm from Batson's lab, both because it doesn't manipulate people's beliefs (as do those discussed above) and because it carries important morals for how one should think about prospective decision-making. Batson et al. (1988) used a version of the so-called "Stroop Test" to try to get at what high-empathy participants are thinking about while they reflect on Katie's situation and decide whether or not to help. The Stroop is a reaction-time test. People have to report the colors of printed words as quickly and accurately as they can. This should be inhibited (slower) if the underlying concepts are easily accessible, and facilitated (faster) for concepts that are not. (This is because word-reading is an over-learned habit, and people have a strong disposition to read the word rather than state its color, especially when the word is familiar or accessible.) The test used four positive-hedonic words ("nice," "proud," "honor," "praise") and four negative ones ("duty," "guilt," "shame," "oblige"), as well as four need-relevant words ("loss," "needy," "adopt," "tragic"), and four neutral words. Batson's prediction was that if high-empathy participants had been thinking about their own future moralistic emotions—whether positive (from helping Katie) or negative (from declining to help)—they should be slower to name the colors of the related words. If they had just been thinking about Katie's miserable situation, in contrast, there should be a reaction-time effect for the need-related words (and only those words). The latter is what Batson et al. (1988) found, taking this to support motivational altruism over hedonism.

It is one thing to say that people decide as they do because when they think about Katie's tragic situation they feel anticipatory pride or guilt, however, and quite another to say that they must therefore be thinking *about* pride or guilt, and activating those concepts. One can feel proud without being aware of oneself as proud, of course—just feeling good as one considers one's own achievements. And likewise, one can feel guilty without activating the concept GUILT, merely feeling bad as one thinks about having done something that breaches a moral norm. So participants considering Katie's plight, and empathizing with (and thinking about) her tragic situation, may feel good when they anticipate being able to help, or bad when they consider not helping. These feelings attaching to the future-directed rehearsal of an action influence the decision to perform it directly, a hedonist should say, without participants needing to conceptualize themselves *as* feeling good, or proud, or bad, or guilty.[2]

4.6 Two Forms of Hedonism

The preceding discussion has assumed an intrinsic-feeling account of valence (pleasure and displeasure). On this view, positive valence is a good intrinsic feeling attaching to experiences, caused by appraisals of the value of the events that those experiences represent. When bound into future-directed representations of events these feelings directly motivate or influence decisions to pursue those events. Likewise, negative valence is a distinct (bad) sort of intrinsic feeling that motivates decisions to avoid the represented future events. This is the account of valence that will be discussed and critiqued at length in Chapter 5. But there is another theory of valence that also entails motivational hedonism. On this view, pleasure and displeasure are experience-directed imperatives, *more of this!* and, *less of this!* (Barlassina & Hayward 2019a, 2019b), where the "this" in each case refers to the type of experience within which the imperative is embedded. Such views will be discussed and critiqued in some detail in Chapter 6. But it is worth pausing, here, to show that they, too, can escape the standard critiques of hedonism. With the groundwork already laid, our discussion can be quite brisk and selective.

One crucial point is that imperativism can be developed in such a way as to not require explicit beliefs that the decided-upon actions will actually issue in experiences of the type one wants to have or to avoid (that is, at which an imperative is directed). The motivation for developing experience-directed imperativism in this way is essentially the same as was offered on behalf of intrinsic-feeling accounts of valence in Sections 3.2 and 3.3. Given how widespread valence-based decision-making is in the animal kingdom, it is highly implausible that the mechanisms underlying it should need to rely on explicit beliefs about one's likely future pleasures and displeasures, nor beliefs about

---

[2] Recall that motivational hedonism needs to apply to non-human animal decision-making as well as to ourselves. That is what motivates the direct-effect version of hedonism over one that requires beliefs about future hedonic states, as we saw in Section 3.2. In Chapter 5 we will note that some emotion-theorists hold that in order to experience an emotion one has to conceptualize oneself as feeling that very emotion (Barrett et al. 2007; LeDoux 2012). The claim is ill-motivated. But in any case, even if true, it may be that empathizing subjects don't feel full-blown emotions of pride or guilt (thus described), but merely positive or negative valence when they consider helping or not helping someone in need (together with some degree of arousal and a related motor-urge, perhaps).

82 Human Motives

one's likely future experiences. This can, rather, be left implicit in the normal reliable connection between one causing events of a certain sort via one's actions and one undergoing experiences of those events as a result.

Here is how the account should go. When deciding among possible alternatives one simulates the outcomes in imagination, causing one's affective systems to respond with an imperative directed at the imaginative experience one is undergoing—in a positive case, with the imperative, *more of this!*, where "this" refers to one's future-tensed experience. If that imperative wins out in the competition with others, then it motivates actions that are expected to bring about the future event that is the represented *content* of the episode of imagining. Normally, when that happens, one will experience it, thus satisfying or matching the original imperative.

To see how this works out in practice, consider first a simple every-day case. One is deciding whether to have the fruit-cup or the chocolate cake for dessert. To do so, one anticipates eating each. Representing in imagination the event of eating the cake, one's affective system responds with the imperative, *more of this!* embedded in (and directed at) the experience of imagined eating. Supposing that this imperative is stronger than the one that gets generated from imagining eating the fruit, the result is an urge to perform the represented action (eating the cake). One doesn't have to *believe* that eating the cake will issue in a similar strength of imperative directed at the experience of actually eating the cake (that is, one doesn't have to believe that eating the cake will produce that degree of pleasure). But such a prediction is tacit in the way that evaluative learning works. If the experienced imperative is lesser than the one felt in imagination, for example, then that produces an error-signal, and one's future appraisal of cake-eating of that sort will be ratcheted downwards.

Now apply this framework to a case of reflective self-sacrifice. When our would-be revolutionary imagines setting fire to herself in the public square, this generates anticipatory pain, issuing in the imperative, *less of this [imagined sensory experience]!* That provides some motivation not to do it. But when she imagines the oppressive regime starting to crumble as a result of her action, that generates a much stronger imperative, *more of this [imagined seeing/hearing about the fall of the regime]!* The force of the imperative content is transferred back to the initial event (setting fire to herself) that predicts it, and so that is what she decides to do. Notice that, for this to work, she doesn't have to *believe* that she will ever have the experience of seeing or hearing about the political consequences of her action. Rather, the imperative embedded in, and directed at, her current imagining of setting fire to herself and bringing down the regime directly motivates the action represented.

Since experience-directed imperativism is best developed in a way that avoids any need for decision-makers to reason via a belief that the actions they are considering will bring about a similar experience-directed imperative if the actions are successful, it can sidestep any of the philosophical and empirical critiques that presuppose such a belief (as we have just illustrated). But experience-directed imperativism can also evade the critiques that fail to take note of the distinction between the appraisals that issue in an affective state and the valence that results. It can, for example, explain why many people are reluctant to enter the experience machine, for the appraisals that issue in experience-directed imperatives are generally focused on real-world events. So the thought of stepping into the machine will fail to activate many of one's values, and will thus fail to issue in an imperative directed at the experience of entering the machine. Indeed, stepping into the machine will be appraised as frustrating many of one's values (e.g. for the respect of one's colleagues), and will thus issue in an imperative directed *against* the experience of entering the machine.

It appears, then, that both varieties of scientifically informed motivational hedonism—whether an intrinsic-feeling account or an experience-directed imperatival one—can readily escape the standard philosophical and empirical arguments that have been offered against more traditional kinds of hedonism.

4.7 Conclusion

The kind of motivational hedonism we arrived at in Chapter 3, grounded in the science of affect outlined in Chapter 2, is immune to all of the well-known philosophical and experimental critiques. Two points are especially relevant. One is the distinction between the input and the output of affective processing. The input always comprises an appraisal of the content of some kind of representational signal (whether from perception, imagination, or memory) against one's stored values. So it is generally external objects and events (including events that are happening to one's own body) that are evaluated positively or negatively. Moreover, normal processes of affective conditioning and evaluative learning are likely to ensure that some of these values are prosocial ones, as we have seen. People learn to positively evaluate good things happening to at least some others, and negatively evaluate bad things happening to them. But the output of these appraisal processes includes positive or negative valence (anticipatory pleasure or displeasure), which plays the determining role in subsequent decision-making. So on any view of

84 Human Motives

valence that sees pleasure and displeasure as intrinsically good or bad feelings (good or bad components of experience), or as experience-directed imperatives (*more of this!* or *less of this!*), a form of motivational hedonism results. And this is despite the outward-focused, prosocial, nature of the underlying stored values.

The second point to emphasize is that motivational hedonism, to be scientifically plausible, should claim that valence attaching to future-directed representations influences decision-making directly. The pleasure or displeasure that one's affective system creates when one rehearses a potential future action, or otherwise anticipates some future event, makes those actions and events seem either attractive and choice-worthy (pleasant) or aversive and to be avoided (unpleasant). Since the valenced output of one's appraisal processes is a component of a future-directed representation it is implicitly predictive of what one might experience were that future event to take place. But no beliefs of that sort are required. Other things being equal, the option that gets selected for implementation is the one whose anticipation creates the greatest balance of pleasure over displeasure. Explicit beliefs about future pleasure or displeasure need play no role (although they can do, of course).[3]

If traditional critiques fail in light of these points, then how is the dispute between motivational hedonism and motivational pluralism to be resolved? How else might one defend the truth of pluralism and altruism? Everything depends on the best scientifically informed account of what valence is, I suggest, and of what pleasure and displeasure actually are. Put differently, motivational hedonism only avoids the familiar philosophical and empirical critiques if certain views of the nature of valence are assumed. Valence either needs to be comprised of good and bad intrinsic properties of experience (as we have been assuming through most of this and the previous chapter), or it needs to be constituted by experience-directed imperatives (as we have just now been discussing in Section 4.6). But these are not the only possible accounts of the nature of valence, nor of pleasure and displeasure more specifically. One competing view—and the view I ultimately proposed to defend—is that valence is a representation of adaptive value or disvalue. As we will see, this value-representing view provides the best overall account of the scientific evidence, while also vindicating motivational pluralism. We will embark on this discussion in Chapter 5.

---

[3] While positive valence (pleasure) bound into a future-directed representation normally makes pursuit of the represented option seem attractive, and is apt to cause a decision to pursue it, people can also come to believe, explicitly, that achieving the future event would be pleasant. But that in turn will generally be appraised positively (given the secondary value one attaches to pleasant experiences), issuing in positive valence. The belief that one will feel pleasure in the future, too, is then apt to produce positive valence (pleasure) bound into the representation of that future, influencing decision-making accordingly.

5

Feelings Versus Representations of Value

This chapter will compare and contrast two competing accounts of the nature of valence. One sees pleasure and displeasure as intrinsic feelings that attach to our experiences, resulting from evaluative appraisals of the contents of the latter. These feelings can be thought to motivate choice directly. The upshot is then motivational hedonism. The other account sees pleasure and displeasure as representations of value. Pleasure represents the event or activity that occasions it as good, and displeasure represents it as bad. The chapter argues in favor of the value-representing view, the upshot of which is motivational pluralism. Chapter 6 will then compare the value-representing account with a different representational theory of valence, according to which valence has imperative content.

5.1 Valence as Feeling: An Initial Concern

Chapter 3 attempted to develop the strongest possible form of "hedonic gloss" or "intrinsic feeling" version of motivational hedonism; and Chapter 4 showed how the resulting account can evade all previous critiques of hedonism, whether provided by philosophers or experimental psychologists. One concern raised in Section 3.4, however, was about how a feeling-based account could accommodate unconscious forms of valence. In response, it was suggested that motivational hedonists should postulate a brute identity between conscious feelings of valence and the physical "tags" that play the decision-influencing and evaluative-learning roles, whether conscious or unconscious. That suggestion will be compared (unfavorably) with what can be said from the perspective of a value-representing account of valence in Section 5.3 of the present chapter.

A different sort of worry for motivational hedonism concerns the radical disconnect that it postulates between the input and the output of one's affective systems, noted briefly in Section 2.6. The input concerns representations of worldly objects and events, which are appraised against innate or learned

Human Motives: Hedonism, Altruism, and the Science of Affect. Peter Carruthers, Oxford University Press.
© Peter Carruthers 2024. DOI: 10.1093/oso/9780198906131.003.0005

86 Human Motives

stored values for the properties possessed by those kinds of object or event. But the output (or the output relevant for our present discussion) is an intrinsic feeling attaching to one's own experiences. So although the system works to evaluate and learn the relative importance of worldly (and bodily) things, one's down-stream decision-making is all about securing good experiences and avoiding bad ones. The underlying values are about the world (and body), whereas the outputs are about one's own feelings and experiences. Why so different? Why isn't the output also about the world?

This is by no means a knock-down argument, for as we noted in Section 2.6, psychology has made many surprising discoveries about the mind, and this might be one of them. But what *is* puzzling is why such a system should (or could) have evolved, for natural selection couldn't care less whether people feel happy or not. (At least, this is true to a first approximation; there are down-stream effects of happiness and sadness on stress, for example, with impacts on long-term health; see Gianaros & Wager 2015. But momentary small valences will have no such effects. And stress-reduction is just one adaptive property among many.) What matters is inclusive fitness. So what matters in decision-making, from the point of view of evolution, is that one selects options that will maximize one's inclusive fitness. It is then puzzling that instead of computing over such values directly, human and animal decision-making systems should have evolved to compute over subjective feelings instead. And indeed, the contrasting view to be discussed and elaborated through the remainder of this chapter holds that pleasure and displeasure are representations of the underlying values that produce them.

5.2 Valence as Representation of Value

The account of the nature of valence to be elaborated here is that positive and negative valences are fine-grained, analog-magnitude, perception-like signals that represent degrees of value or disvalue attaching to the appraised objects or events. (Another—imperative-like—pair of accounts will be considered in Chapter 6.)[1] Pleasure represents (nonconceptually) the appraised

---

[1] Yet another representational account of pleasure and displeasure is offered by Schroeder (2004). He claims that pleasure represents a net increase in desire-satisfaction relative to one's implicit expectations. This is plainly wrong. First, because it is inward-looking rather than outward-looking. When one enjoys something, it is the event itself that is experienced as pleasant, not the changes taking place in one's own mind. This is better captured by the view being defended here, that pleasure is a nonconceptual representation of value. Second, as we saw in Sections 3.2 and 4.3, pleasure is actually a component of states of desire (recall: to desire something is to have pleasure built into one's representation of that thing). So desire needs to be explained in terms of pleasure rather than pleasure being explicable in terms of desire, as Schroeder would have it. And then third, Schroeder's account seems more appropriate as a description

object or event as good (without categorizing it as such); whereas displeasure represents it (nonconceptually) as bad (again, without categorical judgment). And because these representations are analog-magnitude/nonconceptual ones, they can in principle be found in any creature that is capable of representation at all, even if it lacks anything resembling thought. So there need be no difficulty, here, in explaining how ants and other invertebrates are capable of affective learning and decision-making.

Enjoying an event or activity is not the same as *thinking* that it is good, of course; and disliking an event or activity is not the same as thinking it bad. Those are down-stream conceptual or concept-like judgments, whereas valence is more experience-like, and is a component of the current experience itself. When one enjoys biting into a ripe strawberry, for example, the taste is experienced, nonconceptually, as good, to some greater or lesser degree; and likewise when one enjoys a conversation with a friend, it is the conversation itself (as revealed in one's experience of it, of course) that seems nonconceptually good. Parallel points hold for experienced events and activities that one finds unpleasant.

Note that there is a significant resemblance between this account of valence and perceptual theories of desire advanced by philosophers like Stampe (1987) and Oddie (2005). These hold that to desire something is to perceive it as good. However, the perceptual theory fails to distinguish between conceptual and nonconceptual representations of goodness (indeed, it is framed in terms of the former), whereas on the account proposed here, desires only need to include the latter. And the account being advanced here applies equally to the valence component of all affective states, not just desires.

Note, too, that on this account there is a nice match between the appraisal processes that give rise to affective states and their valenced outputs. Inputs (either perceptual representations, or imagined or remembered ones) are appraised against one's stored values, whether innate or previously learned. And the outputs are then contextually sensitive representations of the value of the perceived or imagined events. This makes it easy to see how valence can play a dual role in both prospective decision-making and affective learning, for it is the very same mental-state type (an analog-magnitude representation of value) that is created when future-directed representations are appraised, on the one hand, and when the events themselves are experienced in the present, on the other. These can then be compared directly, issuing in

---

of the error signal that results from comparing current with expected pleasure (issuing in evaluative learning) than as an account of pleasure itself.

an error signal, and the stored value for events of that type can be ratcheted up or down accordingly.

For a similar reason, there need be no difficulty in seeing (at least in outline) why and how such an arrangement might have evolved. All animals need to evaluate things that might happen to them (some to be avoided, some to be sought out). And all animals capable of learning need to be able to compare the values of things that actually do happen to them to their stored expectations, altering the latter where necessary. So the awkwardness that arises for the intrinsic-feeling account of valence simply does not emerge here. (Recall: "why should evolution care whether organisms *feel* good or bad, or whether they undergo good or bad *feelings*?") Although feelings are involved, what matters for decision-making are the values that those feelings represent. And it is the underlying values that natural selection selects for, together with reliable-enough mechanisms for learning new ones on the basis of old.

Another significant advantage of the value-representing account of valence is that it comports nicely with the outward focus of most emotions, as well as of affective episodes more generally. When confronted with an approaching grizzly bear in the forest, the fear one feels is directed entirely at the bear itself. Granted, the negative-valence component of one's fear of the bear gets bound into one's perception of its approach (Fulkerson 2020), but it is the approaching bear that seems bad and displeasurable, not one's *experience* of the bear. (Not in the first instance, at any rate; of course one *can* turn one's attention to one's own experiences at the time, and those will likely strike one as bad too. But who will start introspecting on their own experience in such circumstances?) If one expresses one's fear verbally, saying, "Oh, this is bad!" the word "this" refers to the approaching bear, not to one's experience of it.

Likewise, when one is longing to visit an old friend, it is conversing with the friend that seems attractive and (nonconceptually) good, not (in the first instance) one's experience of conversing with the friend. Of course, normal processes of associative conditioning can lead the experience itself to become positively valenced. It is not uncommon for grieving people to seek out videos or recordings of the dead loved one, for example. Although they can no longer see or hear that person for real, they can sometimes derive comfort (pleasure) from the *experience* of seeing or hearing them. But this is a secondary pleasure, caused by its previous reliable association with *actually* seeing and interacting with the loved person. It is the seeming-goodness/pleasurableness of the latter that normally plays the main role in decision-making and evaluative learning.

In addition, since explanatory appeals to representation are rife within cognitive science, no matter whether the processes involved are conscious or unconscious, there need be no awkwardness in saying that it is the very same kind of representation of value that plays a role in conscious forms of prospective reasoning and in swift kinds of unreflective—and even unconscious—decision-making and evaluative learning. Nor is there any problem in supposing that it is the same type of representation that guides the decision-making of snails, ants, humans, and all other creatures capable of evaluative learning. Indeed, the resulting account meshes smoothly with the extensive neuroeconomics literature, too, in which it is assumed that decisions result from computations (often unconscious) over outcome-values, likelihoods, and estimates of the negative value of effortful action. These issue in an overall expected-value for each option, which can then be compared with the expected value of the others to issue in choice (Botvinick et al. 2009; Levy & Glimcher 2012; Winstanley & Floresco 2016).

The value-representing account of valence seems to lead directly to motivational pluralism. When one engages in prospective decision-making and imagines engaging in some future activity, the pleasure or displeasure produced by one's imagining of that activity represents it—the activity itself—as nonconceptually good or bad. So one's motivation for deciding to eat a strawberry is that, in anticipation, eating the strawberry seems good; and one's motivation for deciding to visit friends is that the anticipated activity of sharing time with them seems good; and so on for anything else that one might be motivated to do. Valence is the common representational currency of decision-making across such cases, enabling them to be mapped onto a common scale of value. (One can weigh up staying home to eat fresh strawberries against going out to meet with a friend, for example.) And it is the values we attach to the options that motivate our decisions, not the phenomenal-feelings involved in pleasure and displeasure themselves.

Moreover, many of the so-called "prospection errors" identified by Gilbert & Wilson (2007, 2009) in their studies of affective forecasting and decision-making are only really errors given a hedonist construal of valence. (This is an additional piece of evidence that they intend their account to support motivational hedonism.) One source of alleged error is most people's ignorance of their likely resilience in the face of tragedy (Bonnano 2021). For example, consider an athlete who rejects an important operation because of the risk that it might cause permanent paralysis, and because when she envisages becoming paralyzed this makes her feel terrible. Since she, like most people, would probably soon adapt to a paralyzed state, Gilbert & Wilson might be committed to claiming that she is making a mistaken decision (depending on the extent of her affective forecasting error and the likelihoods involved). But this would only be an error if what people are trying to do in prospection is maximize their own hedonic happiness in the long run. If, on the contrary, the severity of the athlete's anticipatory misery represents the value that mobility has for her—how much mobility now matters—then there is no error. Becoming paralyzed could be very bad from the perspective of one's personal values, whether or not one's day-to-day levels of happiness would bounce back to normal within a few months afterwards.

Consider a different sort of example. Moller (2011) argues that it is a mistake to take a decision on the basis of anticipated future guilt, because normal processes of confabulation and self-justification will in fact see to it that one's guilt is short-lived. But this is only an error if one is taking the decision to avoid what one anticipates to be a long-run negative feeling, which is a hedonist construal of the role of valence in prospection. On an account that sees valence as a representation of value, there is no error here, either. The guilt one feels when one anticipates having performed the action represents the action (nonconceptually) as bad; and in doing so it reflects and expresses one's stored personal values. There is no error in avoiding an action because it would be bad.

Now consider the way in which the value-representing view handles the case of the person who sacrifices her life for a cause, contrasting it with the hedonic-feeling account discussed in Section 4.2. Recall the woman who sets light to herself in a public place in an attempt to spark a revolt against an oppressive regime. On both views it is the pleasure she feels when she anticipates the success of her action (and/or the negative-valence component of the shame she feels when she imagines not doing it) that motivates her choice. But for the hedonist it is the feeling of pleasure itself (and/or the feeling of displeasure) that directly influences choice. According to the value-representing view, in contrast, the pleasure she feels when she contemplates success nonconceptually represents that outcome as good; and the shame she feels when she imagines just continuing life as normal nonconceptually represents that option as bad. And it is these quasi-perceptual appearances of goodness and badness that determine choice (along with estimates of likelihood, of course). Note that both accounts can say that the woman's action is motivated by pleasure and/or displeasure. But the hedonic view interprets this to mean that decisions are all about securing good and avoiding bad mental states in oneself (at least tacitly); whereas the value-representing view will say that they are about securing good and avoiding bad states of the world, as represented by the way one feels when considering them.

The value-representing view is committed to claiming that valence has an indicative or descriptive (albeit nonconceptual) content. It has correctness-conditions, just as do other forms of analog-magnitude representation. Just as a representation of approximate number (numerosity) is correct to the extent that it accurately matches the number of items present, so valence-representations are correct to the extent that they accurately match the degree of goodness or badness of the action or event in question. We will return to consider some surprising implications of this view in Sections 5.5 and 5.6. But it is worth replying at this point to an objection raised by Barlassina & Hayward (2019a). Like many philosophers, they assume a form of Humean account of motivation according to which only imperative-like states can motivate actions; belief-like (indicative) states cannot. They therefore claim that indicative, world-describing, representations of value are the wrong *kind* of representation to motivate action; and this is said to support their own imperative theory of valence instead.

A number of points should be made about this argument. One is that affective appraisals do, indeed, give rise to imperative-like representations directly, as part of their output. But these are the motor-urges that all affective states cause, both expressive and instrumental. And as we saw in Section 2.3, they are distinct from the valence output. Secondly, valence doesn't motivate action *directly*, in any case; rather, it influences decision-making (in interaction with estimates of likelihood). Decisions issue in intentions or goals, and it is these that then motivate action directly (and have an imperative-like role). Valence only causes motivation indirectly, via its effects on decision-making. As a result, a value-representing theorist about valence can happily agree with Humeans that motivation requires some sort of action-motivating state, and that these states (especially goals and intentions) have imperative-like roles. But there is no reason to insist that the valence-output of appraisals must itself be imperative-like or directly motivating. It can still play a central explanatory role among the processes that cause actions, via its effects on decision-making.

Moreover, recall that valence is a basic category of affective science. So theories of valence aren't beholden to folk-psychological or philosophical intuitions. And the best account of valence that fits all the scientific facts is the value-indicating one; or so I am arguing in this book. In which case occurrent affective desires (as opposed to stored goals and intentions that result from previous decisions) turn out to have a pair of indicative contents: a representation of some future action or event, and a nonconceptual representation of that action or event as good. The fact that philosophers have intuitions that conflict with this account should carry no weight. We are doing psychology here, not folk psychology.

The value-representing theory of valence entails motivational pluralism, as noted earlier. But in addition (and as was remarked briefly in Section 2.5), it won't take much in the way of innate social rewards and/or punishments for normal evaluative learning to give rise to a range of altruistic and norm-based motivations among humans. Provided that human societies reward people who are prosocial and/or punish those who are not; and provided that some similar set of rewards and/or punishments are used to enforce whatever norms have taken hold in a given society; then people will soon come to value, for its own sake, acting for the benefit of at least some other community members; and they will soon internalize and value compliance with whatever moral norms they have acquired. So when someone then acts to benefit another, it will be because doing so seems nonconceptually good to them (at least in part; people can have mixed motives, of course). Likewise, when someone forebears from breaking a moral norm because they feel guilt when they anticipate doing so, the resulting decision is taken because the negative valence component of guilt represents performance of that action as being nonconceptually bad (again, at least in part; they might also have self-interested reasons for not performing the action).

At this point there are some good reasons to prefer the value-representing account of valence over the intrinsic-feeling one; but nothing so far is probative. Section 5.3 will argue that the representational account gains some further support from the general reasons we have for accepting a representational theory of consciousness (which are overwhelming powerful in my view, while nevertheless still being controversial; see Carruthers 2019). And then Section 5.4 will argue that even the intrinsic-feeling account of valence is forced to accept that these feelings are *also* representations of value. That section will at the same time confront an important challenge to the value-representing view. This is that science in general, and scientific psychology in particular, can only traffic in natural—real-world—properties. But *value* seems not to be such a property. Surely, it might be said, there are no real values out there in the natural world. So the challenge to be addressed in Section 5.4 is to show, not just that valence represents values, but that those values can in turn be cashed-out in terms of naturalistic properties.

5.3 Valence and Consciousness

The intrinsic-feeling account of valence seems committed to a non-reductive theory of consciousness. It need not be committed to qualia in the strong dualist sense; so it need not claim that qualia are nonphysical properties. But it is at least committed to properties (feelings) that are brute-identical to certain physical ones. For instance, the suggestion made on the account's behalf in Section 3.4 was that conscious positive and negative valences are identical to physical analog-magnitude tags attaching to experiential states that occupy the consciousness-constituting role (such as figuring in working memory), whereas unconscious valence is identical with those tags themselves, outside of the consciousness-making role. But it would remain unexplained why valence-tags in working memory should feel like anything, or have any distinctive phenomenology at all.

The best-known, and widely endorsed, competing account of phenomenal consciousness is reductive representationalism (Tye 1995, 2000; Prinz 2012; Carruthers 2019). On this view, consciousness is constituted by nonconceptual—fine-grained—representations of the world and body that play a certain specific functional role (e.g. when those representations are "globally broadcast" and figure in working memory). There is no extra property over and above the representations of redness, greenness, timbre, loudness, and so on. And the reason why these representations seem so philosophically puzzling when they are made globally available is just that we can then think about them in a distinctive kind of way, employing so-called "phenomenal concepts." On the view defended by Prinz (2012) and Carruthers (2019), the latter are acquaintance-based indexicals, of the sort that might figure in thoughts like, "There could be a creature exactly like me in all physical and functional respects [a zombie] which nevertheless lacks *this* [experience of red]." That there is felt to be a problem of consciousness is a philosophical illusion, created by philosophers' thought-experiments that deploy phenomenal concepts.[2]

There are general benefits of reductive explanation for anyone with naturalist and physicalist sympathies. But an additional consideration supporting a representational account of consciousness is the so-called "transparency" of experience (Tye 2002). When one attends introspectively to any of one's experiences, what does one find? Arguably, just the properties in the world or body that those experiences are *of*, or that they represent. Look at a ripe red tomato, for example, and focus on your experience of its red color. What you end up doing, it seems, is just focusing more closely on the redness experienced (while at the same time being aware that you are experiencing it, no

---

[2] The resulting account is closely related to what Frankish (2016) calls "illusionism" about phenomenal consciousness, except that I treat the illusion as a cognitive—and distinctively philosophical—one, whereas Frankish thinks of it as more perception-like.

doubt). There seem to be no properties—no qualia—attaching to one's experiences other than the represented properties.

Similar considerations seem to show that valence, too, is transparent to introspection, supporting the representational account of its nature. Suppose you are enjoying a sunset. Attend carefully to your experience to see if you can find the intrinsic feeling attaching to the experience that makes it pleasant. What happens? It seems that you focus ever more intently on the sunset itself, which still strikes you as good and attractive (note: these are properties of the sunset, not of your experience). No extra property of experience—the "feeling of pleasure"—seems to emerge. Admittedly, one does feel pleased as one looks at the sunset. But there seems to be nothing to this feeling over-and-above the goodness one's experience attributes to the sunset itself. Expressed in words, one might naturally say, "Wow! That's really good." Here "that" refers to the sunset, and not to one's experience.

Bodily feelings can also be evaluatively appraised and enjoyed, of course. Looking at the sunset might make one feel calm and relaxed, and this, too, might be positively appraised. "I love how peaceful I feel sitting here watching this," one might say. But here it is the bodily feelings involved in relaxation that seem nonconceptually good. Focusing more intently on them, as well, will issue in nothing more than greater awareness of them and their seeming-goodness.

Anyone who is sympathetic towards a representational account of consciousness (whether or not they endorse the specific proposals put forward by Carruthers and/or others) has a reason to accept a representational theory of valence. By accepting that the two valences are analog-magnitude representations of value (or, alternatively, by accepting that they are imperative representations of future outcomes; see Chapter 6), one can then explain, fully, the conscious status of pleasure and displeasure. If one rejects any such account of valence, in contrast, then one is committed to placing limits on the scope of the representational theory of consciousness. For there will then be some conscious states that the representational theory cannot account for. And in fact, a number of authors have made just this kind of case: arguing that affective valence is the counter-example that demonstrates the falsity of reductive representational theories of consciousness (Aydede & Fulkerson 2014; Kind 2013). The strongest set of arguments of this sort has been developed for sensory forms of pleasure and—especially—physical pain. These will be examined at length as a test-case for the value-representing theory of valence in Chapter 7.

5.4 Theories of Representation

A number of questions will be addressed in this section. One is: what reason is there to think that the two valences (pleasure and displeasure) are representations of anything? Then, supposing that valence is representational, how do we figure out *what* it represents? And finally, supposing that there is reason to think that valence is a nonconceptual representation of value, can a naturalistic account be provided of the values represented? In the background of all these questions is the issue of what mental representations *are*. So we first need to ask: what account should be given of mental representation in general, which can then be applied to the case of valence? We begin here.

All, or almost all, naturalistic theories of representation are built around the notion of *information* (Millikan 1984, 1989; Papineau 1987; Dretske 1988, 1995; Fodor 1990; Neander 2017; Rupert 2018; Shea 2018). When one type of thing causes, or is apt to cause, another, the latter event carries information about the former. Roughly speaking, knowing the latter, one can deduce, with some degree of confidence, that the former event has occurred. So when events in the mind/brain are caused by properties or events in the world or body, the mind/brain events carry information about the world or body. But this is not enough, as yet, for them to qualify as representational. Someone's blistering skin carries the information that their skin has been exposed to the sun for a significant amount of time, but the blisters don't *represent* previous sun exposure. And spiking melatonin levels carry information about the onset of evening, but they don't *represent* the time of day. For that, there has to be some down-stream consuming system or process that can make use of that information—that is, one that responds to, uses, or computes with the information-carrying state in a manner that is somehow appropriate for, or dependent on, the information carried.

As a first approximation, one can say that information-carrying states of the mind/brain qualify as representations provided that they cause down-stream effects (whether other mind/brain events or overt behavior) that are sensitive to the information carried. This means that, in one way or another, those down-stream effects occur as they do *because of* the distal cause of the state. Teleological theories cash this out in terms of evolution by natural selection (Millikan 1984; Papineau 1987; Neander 2017). The down-stream effects occur as they do because they are an adaptive response to the distal cause, selected through evolutionary processes. But other approaches can instead (or better, also) emphasize learning as the process that gives rise to adaptive responses (Dretske 1988; Shea 2018).

96 Human Motives

Any representational state will carry much more information than is actually represented, of course. Consider the state caused by perceiving a cat. In addition to carrying information about the presence of a cat, it carries information about a complex (disjunctive) pattern of stimulation on the retina, about light passing through the intervening space, as well as about the fact that a cat-mating event and a kitten-birthing event occurred sometime in the past (in that temporal order). But it *represents* none of the latter set of things. In addition, a cat-representing perceptual state can be caused by a raccoon seen at twilight, when one mistakes a raccoon for a cat. But it doesn't represent the disjunctive property cat-or-racoon-at-twilight, either (Fodor 1990). On the contrary, if one takes the raccoon to be a cat, that is a *mis*representation, and is false or incorrect.

What, then, picks out the *represented* information from among the total set of causes and possible causes of the state in question? Many of the writers cited above offer detailed and subtly different answers to this question. Those details won't matter for our purposes. Here I propose to follow the account provided by Shea (2018), which is designed specifically to explain the notion of representation employed in cognitive science. He argues that what makes it the case that something is a representation is that it is an information-carrying state that plays a computational/functional role in some cognitive process. And what fixes the content (or correctness condition) for a representation from among all the information it carries, is what causally *stabilized* the role of that representation in the computations that it enters into, either through natural selection, or through learning, or through its contribution to individual survival. The content of the representation is the information carried that we need to appeal to in explaining the role that the representation plays in determining the behavior of the organism.[3]

Applied to the case of visually representing a cat, this account delivers the right answers. What explains the evolution of animate-object perception in general is the proximal stimulus-object (e.g. a cat), for it is this that underlies the success of subsequent actions (such as approaching or avoiding the creature in question). Carrying information about temporally distal events

---

[3] It is worth noting that Shea (2018) actually defends what he calls "varitel semantics," which includes *two* basic kinds of representing-relation. One is informational, with an internal symbol causally co-varying (in the right circumstances and in the right way) with the represented property or thing. The other is a form of structural mapping, with the relations among a set of internal symbols mirroring the relations among a set of external entities in a map-like manner. It is only the first of these sorts of representing-relation that is relevant here. Note, too, that Shea's account is specifically designed to apply to low-level nonconceptual representations. There might be other constraints on conceptual content and thought.

(e.g. an earlier cat mating) played no role in stabilizing the success of the system, nor did the patterns of stimulation on the retina (except insofar as they carry information about the distal object). And when perceptual learning leads one to distinguish cats from other living creatures, it is the presence of cats (and only cats) that explains the successful accumulation of knowledge about cats in the resulting animate-object kind-file.

Turning now to valence, it is obvious that it carries information about the underlying values against which the stimulus event is appraised. But does it represent those values? It surely does. For if we ask what stabilized the role of valence in decision-making, the answer is clear: that happened because anticipatory valence is caused by (and carries information about) one's underlying evaluation of the thing, and the magnitude of the valenced response (the extent of one's anticipatory pleasure or displeasure) scales with the contextually sensitive stored value attaching to things of that sort. If decisions are taken to maximize valence, then they serve to maximize fulfillment of one's values. So valence *is* a representation of value, and the role that it plays in decision-making is explained by the values that it represents. Although valence can sometimes be a conscious feeling, it is not *only* a feeling, let alone an intrinsic one. On the contrary, it is relational in the way that representations generally are, having a causal role that is explained by, and scales with, the information about value that it carries.

But what is it to carry information about value? What are these values, appraisal against which issues in anticipatory or consummatory pleasure and displeasure? Recall from Section 2.6 that affective states are produced by the presence of, or in anticipation of, both primary and secondary rewards and punishers. Primary rewards and punishers are things whose adaptive value or disvalue have been fixed through natural selection. Primary rewards include such things as eating when hungry, drinking when thirsty, orgasm, and (in humans, quite probably) indications of liking or admiration from community members. Primary punishers include pain, nausea, signs of immediate physical danger, and (among humans, again probably) indications of hatred or disrespect from community members. All primary rewards and punishers have played a critical role in the inclusive fitness of individual humans and ancestral organisms over significant stretches of evolutionary time, and their default value or disvalue is now innately fixed (albeit modifiable through subsequent learning). So valence produced by primary rewards and punishers carries information about the adaptive value or disvalue of the things and events in question; and the fact that it carries such information explains the role of valence in decision-making. So it *represents* adaptive value or disvalue.

98   Human Motives

Secondary rewards and punishers, in contrast, are things that can be merely associated with, or are predictive of, primary rewards and punishments. Thus Pavlovian conditioning can lead a rat to dislike the sound of a particular tone intrinsically, and not just (or not only) because it predicts pain. Similarly, sign-tracking rats will take pleasure in the appearance of a lighted bar, and will work to obtain it, even if this means less time harvesting food. These are products of individual learning, not evolutionary processes. So is the correctness-condition for secondary forms of valence simply *associated with adaptive value/disvalue*? I suggest not. For the affective-learning mechanisms themselves have been honed by natural selection to be adaptive. So it must be adaptive, on the whole, to come to intrinsically value or disvalue things or events learned about in this manner. And indeed, under natural conditions (when not misled by human experimenters), most animals will make decisions that are adaptive—foraging near-optimally, or making near-optimal trade-offs between food-gathering and information-gathering (Pyke et al. 1977; Vasconcelos et al. 2015).

This suggests that the values and disvalues that positive and negative valence carry information about, and represent, are all of them *adaptive* values and disvalues. The initial innate settings of the affective systems have been established by natural selection to maximize inclusive fitness. And likewise the affective-learning system itself that updates those values by context and adds new ones that are associated with or predictive of those already existing has been shaped by natural selection to maximize inclusive fitness. So the common currency that human and animal decision-making trades in is adaptive value and disvalue. Pleasure is a representation of positive adaptive value (whether in anticipation or in consumption), and displeasure is a representation of adaptive disvalue, or of inclusive *unfitness*. It is the fact that states of the affective systems carry information about these properties that explains how the initial settings and learning rules of the affective systems were caused, stabilized, and sustained.

All animals have to make trade-offs, of course, somehow comparing the benefits of foraging against the risks of predation (Fanselow et al. 1988); or the benefits of foraging in the heat of the day against the costs of hyperthermia; or comparing the benefits of foraging against the costs and benefits of defending territory; or deciding whether to stay in a current foraging patch or begin searching for another; and so on. All of these choices have implications for the animal's health, survival, and reproductive fitness. But of course animals cannot think in terms of inclusive fitness as such; that concept simply isn't available to them, and they would lack the information needed to make judgments about it even if it were. Instead, they employ proxies for inclusive fitness: pleasure and displeasure. And this is the way in which the common-currency idea has been understood and modeled in much of the animal literature, too (McNamara & Houston 1986; Shizgal & Conover 1996; Montague & Berns 2002).[4]

Pleasure when eating carries information about the nutritive value of the food eaten, of course; and pains carry information about bodily damage or risk of damage. So, might one then claim that pleasure and displeasure are comprised of *multiple* representational kinds, with distinct contents in the differing domains in which they occur? But if food-pleasure represents nutritive value and painfulness represents bodily harm, then how could an animal trade them off against one another adaptively? Affective systems have evolved precisely to solve this trade-off problem, setting weights (intensities) to pleasure-signals and displeasure-signals modulated by bodily state (e.g. hunger) and context (e.g. the source of the pain, the availability of social support) so that, on the whole, the organism's fitness is enhanced. But then what does the explaining, here, is not nutritive value and bodily harm specifically, but rather inclusive fitness, which has shaped the mechanisms that set and modulate the evaluative weights and trade-offs, as well the affective-learning mechanisms that alter those weights as needed thereafter.

Adaptive values are, of course, fully naturalistic properties. There is no mystery about their existence in a physical world. They are also fully objective, without needing to exist outside of the natural order or in some sort of Platonic heaven.[5] They can be cashed out in terms of likelihoods of one's survival and reproduction, and of one's descendants' and relatives' survival and reproduction. Neither, then, is there any mystery attaching to the idea that components of human and animal minds (specifically pleasure and displeasure) might represent such values. The default settings of human affective systems will have been set by past adaptiveness, of course, through processes of human and animal evolution. But when the valence output produced by those systems is bound into a future-directed representation of an action or outcome in the course of decision-making it becomes, in effect, a prediction of future adaptive value.

---

[4] Consider this quote from Shizgal & Conover (1996) in describing their common-currency model of decision-making: "The relative utility of two different goal objects will depend not only on their abundance but also on the physiological state of the consumer and the ecological context in which the goal objects are embedded. In effect, we treat utility as a subjective estimate of the potential contribution of a goal object to fitness" (p. 37).

[5] This is not to deny that there can be other forms of objective value that are nevertheless naturalistically acceptable. For example, some forms of constructivist account of moral value might have this character (Scanlon 1982, 1998; Milo 1995; Carruthers & James 2008). But it is not these values (even when internalized by an agent) that explain the stabilized role of valence in moral decision-making, but rather the adaptive values that those valences also carry information about.

Humans are deeply cultural creatures. And as we will see, many of the values (and subsequent pleasures and displeasures) that humans acquire through evaluative learning are obtained from their culture or sub-culture. As a result, many people today decide not to have children in order to pursue their careers, regularly use contraception when having sex, and take other actions that almost certainly do not contribute to their inclusive fitness. Many of their values thus qualify, not just as representations, but as *mis*representations—misrepresenting the relative adaptive value of the options. While strictly correct from a scientific standpoint (since it is adaptive value and disvalue that explain the default settings and learning rules of human evaluative systems), this upshot is of little practical significance. Indeed, for everyday purposes of prediction and explanation, it is more helpful to think of consummatory and anticipatory pleasures and displeasures as being representations of *the individual's* values—which are, of course, highly varied and variable. They result from individual differences in the relative weights assigned to the initial innate values people possess, together with their unique affective-learning histories.

The upshot of this section amounts to a powerful argument against the intrinsic-feeling account of pleasure and displeasure, for all, or almost all, naturalistic accounts of representation entail that these feelings are *also* representations of value, at least. And what explains the role of pleasure and displeasure in decision-making is not their felt qualities, as such, but rather the values that they signal. So valence is best understood, not as an intrinsic feeling that attaches to our experiences, but rather as a representation of the value or disvalue of what those experiences represent. This is not yet to say that the value-representing account of valence is best overall, however; for we have yet to compare it with imperative accounts of valence. That will happen in Chapter 6.

5.5 Erroneous Emotions

If the valences (pleasure and displeasure, when conscious) are representations of value, then they have correctness conditions. And if the valences are analog-magnitude representations of adaptive value and disvalue then they can be erroneous to greater or lesser degrees. Compare analog-magnitude representations of number. When one looks at a set of blobs on a screen, or listens to a quick sequence of taps (too quick to count), one will have a rough impression of number. With training, children and animals become increasingly good at discriminating approximate numbers (Odic et al. 2013). So if a young child equates five dots on a screen to nine taps on the arm, that is to some degree mistaken (as well as to some degree accurate), whereas if an older child can distinguish five dots from nine taps, that is correct. But that child may still fail to distinguish seven dots from nine taps—erroneous, but to a lesser degree. Likewise, then, pleasure and displeasure (whether felt in consumption or in anticipation) will represent the adaptive value and disvalue of the events in question more or less accurately. One significant difference between valence and numerosity, however, is that the only way approximate-number representations can be completely erroneous is when there are literally zero items present, but the system nevertheless represents a plurality, whereas events can presumably be represented as having positive adaptive value when they are actually maladaptive, and vice versa.

We do not normally think of pleasures and displeasures as being accurate or erroneous, correct or incorrect. Of course, we are familiar with the idea that people can take pleasure in things that are actually harmful (e.g. smoking); and we all know that people can find to be unpleasant things that are actually beneficial, as are many medical procedures. But we don't normally describe such cases by saying that someone's enjoyment of smoking misrepresents the value of the activity, nor that the pain someone feels during a prostate exam misrepresents what is happening as bad. On the other hand, there is an established tradition in philosophy of ascribing correctness conditions to emotional states. Some emotional episodes are said to "fit" their objects, whereas others are said to fail to fit them. For example, it is appropriate or fitting to feel fear at an approaching grizzly bear, whereas fear at a harmless spider is unfitting or incorrect. We will discuss the sense in which emotions have correctness conditions first, before returning to the less-familiar case of erroneous pleasures and displeasures in Section 5.6.

Many philosophical theories of emotion allow emotions to be incorrect, mistaken, or unfitting. Some do so because they maintain that emotions are a form of, or embed, judgments (Solomon 1976; Nussbaum 2001). On this view, to feel fear at a harmless spider is to judge that the spider is fearful or dangerous, which is false. Others think that emotions embed, not judgments, but rather mere thoughts about (Greenspan 1988) or evaluative construals of (Roberts 2003) their objects. So to fear the spider involves thinking of it as dangerous (without necessarily judging it to be so) or construing it to be dangerous. All such theories face the same problem: they cannot easily be extended to human infants and non-human animals who may lack concepts such as FEARSOME or DANGEROUS. Moreover, we know that full-blown emotional episodes can be elicited by low-level nonconceptual cues like oxygen deprivation or a loud fierce growl.

In response to essentially this problem, many philosophers have endorsed so-called perceptual theories of emotion (de Sousa 1987; D'Arms & Jacobson 2000; Döring 2003; Prinz 2004; Tappolet 2012, 2016). On this view we *see* (or in other circumstances, *hear*) the fearsomeness or dangerousness of the grizzly bear; and we see (or rather, mis-see) the dangerousness of the spider. Indeed, Tappolet (2012) suggests that emotions that fail to fit their objects (like fear of an innocent spider) are a form of perceptual illusion, or are at least somewhat like perceptual illusions, for they are apt to persist despite one's knowledge that the emotions in question are inappropriate.

There are three distinct ways in which existing perception-like accounts of the fittingness of emotions can be developed, however, and all confront problems. Note that all three turn out to be domain-specific in nature, suggesting that fear somehow represents fearsomeness, disgust represents disgustingness, and so on. In contrast, the view I will defend shortly is domain-general, holding that it is just the positive or negative valence component of emotions that represent or misrepresent the values of their objects. So both fear and disgust represent the same analog-magnitude property, on this view (badness or maladaptiveness), while differing in their arousal-properties and their motor-urge components (as well as their appraisal-conditions, of course).

One variety of perception-like theory of emotion would claim that emotion-specific evaluative concepts are bound into the content of one's perception of the emotion-eliciting stimulus. This account would build on a general view of perception that allows concepts to be bound into its contents, in such a way that one can hear someone as delivering a greeting (and not just hear the sounds that they make) and see the object on the table as a tomato, not just seeing its color and shape (Carruthers 2015). So when one sees the grizzly bear one might see it *as* dangerous, or fearsome, or threatening. (This may be the way in which Greenspan 1988 and Roberts 2003 intend their views to be taken.) And just as one can see something as a cat, although it is really a raccoon, so one can see the spider as dangerous, although it is actually harmless. Although this account might well be true of many instances of adult human emotion, it founders on the fact that it requires sophisticated conceptual abilities, and so cannot apply quite generally. It is too intellectualized to apply to infants and many non-human animals.

Of course, theorists always have the option of denying that infants and other animals experience genuine fear, or genuine disgust, precisely because they are incapable of seeing something as dangerous or disgusting (deploying the relevant concepts in perception). But this seems like a desperate move to make. Remarkably, however, psychologists from both sides of the debate over socially constructed versus innate-core emotions have claimed just this; or rather, they claim that only mature humans are capable of *conscious* emotion (Barrett et al. 2007; LeDoux 2012). This is because they embrace a higher-order thought theory of consciousness. Yet it is one thing to say that only mature humans can be conscious *of* their fear, and quite another to say that only mature humans can be afraid. And indeed, all of the other components that LeDoux (2012) includes in his model of emotion (arousal, motor activation, proprioceptive feedback, memory, and perception) are available to nonhuman animals. (Admittedly, it is another matter to claim that all of these factors are represented in the animal's working memory, and so become conscious in the first-order global-availability sense. But again, conscious fear is one thing, simply being afraid is another.)[6]

Another form of perception-like theory would keep emotions nonconceptual through-and-through (hence making the theory applicable to infants and even quite simple animals), as most perceptual theorists of emotion actually do. Thus one might claim that, in addition to emotion-specific motor dispositions, arousal, and valence, emotional appraisals of a stimulus also generate a nonconceptual signal representing what is sometimes called the "formal object" of the emotion (fearsomeness for fear, disgustingness for disgust, and so on). This would become a component of the resulting perception of the stimulus alongside representations of color, shape, and other analog magnitudes. So when one sees the grizzly one would see its size, shape, motion, and so on; and one would become aroused and have an urge to run away; but in addition, one's perception would include a nonconceptual, analog-magnitude, representation with the content *dangerous*. This is a possible view. The main problem with it is that we have no evidence of the existence of such signals.

Moreover, it is quite unclear what such an analog-magnitude signal would be supposed to do, or what role it could have. It isn't needed to activate emotion-specific motor plans, since those emerge directly out of the initiating appraisal process. And it would be of no use in adjudicating among competing emotions and desires, for it is the common-currency valence component of emotion that enables that. Nor is it even necessary in order for one to conceptualize oneself as being in danger, or as being in the presence of something disgusting. For activation of the relevant concepts can get built into the routine motor outputs of the relevant emotions once people learn the emotion-terms in question. Or alternatively, one can develop recognitional

---

[6] Notice that Barrett and LeDoux commit essentially the same error that we attributed to Batson et al. (1988) in Section 4.5. All assume that if one is feeling guilty about something one will be thinking about guilt, or at least activating the concept GUILT.

templates for the mixture of contextual cues, patterns of arousal, motor activation, and valence distinctive of each emotion.

A third possibility is the one developed by Prinz (2004). This holds that it is the entire syndrome of emotion-specific effects produced by the emotional appraisal of a stimulus that counts as a representation of the formal object of the resulting emotion. Thus when one confronts the grizzly, the entire suite of fear-specific effects (arousal and negative valence, combined with an urge to run or freeze, depending on the affordances of the situation) qualifies as a representation of dangerousness. This is because it carries information about the presence of danger, and has been designed by evolution to do so, and thus has the function of doing so. But this is "representation" in a quite different, non-mental, sense, for there is no consumer-system of the mind down-stream of the emotional episode that treats it as a representation of danger. There is no process that "computes over" the entire syndrome of effects to generate further mental states or actions—unless it is just recognizing oneself *as* afraid, or *as* in danger, and/or becoming disposed to say so. But these further effects likely played no role in stabilizing the various emotional systems themselves.

Nevertheless, Prinz's account does provide a way of saying how an emotion can be mistaken or unfitting, even if it doesn't really qualify as perceptual or representational. When one undergoes the same syndrome of effects when confronted with the harmless spider, one is in a state that has been designed to respond to danger. But in this case the appraisal system has malfunctioned: because one has mis-appraised the significance of the spider (likely as a result of previous affective learning or conditioning), one's fear-response is no longer tracking real fearsomeness.[7]

The right form of perceptual or perception-like theory of emotion, I think, is the one mentioned briefly earlier. Appraisal of a stimulus produces domain-specific effects on arousal, cognition, and behavior. So fear is generally high-arousal, whereas disgust is less so; fear causes people to be more risk averse, whereas anger causes them to be more risk seeking; fear causes distinctive facial expressions combined with an impulse to escape, whereas disgust produces a different facial expression combined with an urge to retch, and so on. None of these effects are themselves evaluative. The only

---

[7] The *felt bodily stance* theory of emotion (Deonna & Teroni 2015) is somewhat similar to Prinz's. It claims that the only representational components in an emotional episode are the representations of the appraised object or event (e.g. the approaching grizzly) and the representations of one's consequent bodily changes and motor dispositions (e.g. the impulse to run). While this can allow for an account of the fittingness or unfittingness of emotion similar to Prinz's, it is plainly inadequate, because missing the directed-valence component of emotion altogether. So it can't explain how emotions can be traded off against one another in decision-making.

evaluative output of emotional appraisal is valence, with negative valence nonconceptually representing the target as bad (maladaptive) and positive valence nonconceptually representing it as good (adaptive). When one responds to the innocent spider with fear, then, it is the negative valence involved that misrepresents its evaluative character. On this view, one's fear-response doesn't represent the spider as dangerous (whether conceptually or nonconceptually), but just as (nonconceptually) *bad*.

This sort of account is consistent with all the evidence, and comports nicely with what the science of affect tells us about affective states generally (see Chapter 2). It explains how differing emotions can be traded off against one another through the common currency of valence. And it allows that emotions can be incorrect, and can misrepresent the evaluative nature of their targets. Yet at the same time it makes minimal cognitive and conceptual demands on creatures capable of emotion. In fact the same account might even apply to invertebrates like honey-bees, whose overall behavior suggests that they are capable of something resembling fear or anxiety (Bateson et al. 2011; Tye 2017).

It is worth noting that this account of emotional evaluation and mis-evaluation is very different from the sense in which Prinz (2004) thinks emotions can be mistaken or inappropriate. Moreover, the two can come apart. Consider the following pair of cases. In both, someone stops his vehicle at the top of the steep drive leading down to the metal gates in front of his home, puts the car in park, and gets out to open the gate. Before he can do so, the car slips out of park and starts rolling down the hill towards him, picking up speed. Now in one case, his response is anger: he curses the car, and has a disposition to lash out at it. But in the other case, his response is fear: he initially freezes in terror, before trying to leap aside. The arousal components of the emotions in the two cases are similar, while the behavioral dispositions are quite different. Yet in both cases the valence component is the same: it represents (correctly) the event of the approaching car as bad (maladaptive). So the evaluative component of the emotion the person feels is correct in either case. But the overall emotion itself is inappropriate or "ill-fitting" in the case of anger, but appropriate in the case of fear. In the anger case the approaching car has been mis-appraised as a signal of disrespect or attack, which is incorrect; but in the fear case it is appraised (correctly) as a signal of approaching danger.

If we bear in mind the fundamental distinction drawn in Chapter 2 between the input and the output of affective states, then we can see how there is room for both forms of emotional error, in fact. There can either be a mistake at the input stage, when the stimulus gets appraised against standing values embedded in emotion-specific appraisal systems (whether innate or constructed); or there can be an error in the valence component of the output, representing that the stimulus is adaptive when it is really neutral or maladaptive; or both. (And then in addition, of course, there can be further sources of error in the overall distribution of value among the various emotional and other affective systems.)

There is yet another kind of emotional ill-fittingness, however, which is normative in a different sense, not involving either misappraisal or a misrepresentation of adaptive value. Consider shame, which arguably reflects an appraisal that some property of oneself would, if known, lead to one being socially devalued (to some degree) by community members (Sznycer et al. 2016, 2018). And consider a woman from a traditional background who feels ashamed when getting undressed for a routine check-up by a male doctor. In the community that she comes from, shame may well be a fitting emotion—others would, in fact, think badly of her if what she is doing were to become known. But in another sense both she and we might judge that shame is *not* fitting—getting undressed for a doctor's appointment *shouldn't* lead to any negative evaluation; the community are mistaken in valuing modesty of that sort in the way that they do.

Although the resulting picture of emotional fittingness(es) outlined here is not exactly like anything in the existing literature, it doesn't require any major upheaval in familiar ways of thinking. The claim that we need to countenance erroneous pleasures and displeasures more generally, in contrast, may prove harder for many people to accept.

5.6 Erroneous Pleasures and Displeasures

As was remarked at the outset of Section 5.5, one doesn't normally think of pleasures and displeasures as being the kinds of thing that can be correct or incorrect. The idea that some pleasures can be harmful or bad for one is a familiar part of common sense, of course, as is the idea that some displeasures can be beneficial. But the value-representing theory of valence goes further. It claims that in such cases one's hedonic states can be erroneous or incorrect. Since pleasure in smoking tobacco represents it as good (adaptive), whereas really it is harmful, the pleasure smokers feel is erroneous or mistaken. And since the aversion many children have to broccoli and other vegetables represents eating them as bad (maladaptive), whereas really they are healthy, the children's dislike is erroneous, too.

Even in connection with the pleasure that most people take in sugary foods and drinks, as well as in fat-laden and easily digestible calorie-rich foods like beefburgers, nutritionists don't say that these pleasures are themselves incorrect or erroneous. Instead, they might bemoan the fact that the initial default settings of the human appetitive and taste systems, which evolved in conditions when sugar and fat were relatively scarce, are now maladaptive in the modern world (hence the obesity epidemic). Our evolved preferences are said to be disfunctional and harmful given the easy availability, nowadays, of processed sugar and fat, rather than erroneous. The representational account of valence, in contrast, is committed to the latter. Pleasure in sugary drinks represents them as highly adaptive by default and can make the thought of consuming them seem very attractive, when in fact (given their plentiful availability) they are only mildly adaptive. In which case, pleasure here represents such drinks as being much better than they really are.

It is doubtful whether implementation of this change in how we think about pleasure and displeasure has any practical importance, or makes any practical commitments, however, for we can get similar points across already. We can say that it is a pity (it is bad) that some people enjoy smoking, because smoking is harmful. And we can say that it is a pity (again, it is bad) that most children dislike vegetables, because vegetables are good for them. But the representational theory of valence has not been introduced because of its practical benefits, but rather for its theoretical ones. It provides the best scientific account of the nature of the states in question, helping us to explain how, and why, pleasure and displeasure play the roles that they do in affective learning and decision-making, not only in humans but in many other creatures. Or so I am arguing in this book. These theoretical gains can remain in place, untouched, whether or not common sense ever picks up on and makes use of the idea of erroneous pleasure and displeasure.

Moreover, common sense is mostly in the business of predicting and explaining individual behavior. And while it is possible to know something about the adaptiveness of mental valences at a population level, this is almost impossible at the level of the individual. There are, of course, individual differences among people in the initial innate settings of their affective systems. The starting-state effectiveness or strength of primary rewards and punishments will differ among people; and there will be individual differences in affective learning mechanisms, too. (Some people are more susceptible than others to top-down effects on evaluation, for example.) It is possible that some of these differences are adaptations. (Some theorists have speculated that psychopaths might fall into this category, and that psychopathy and pro-sociality are so-called "balanced polymorphisms," each being adaptive in the presence of the other; McGuire et al. 1994; Murphy & Stich 2000.) But most are just instances of normal phenotypic variation, resulting mainly from genetic recombination but also from occasional mutations. These differences are then impacted by wide variations in people's home and cultural environments, together with a myriad of individual-specific experiences.

The resulting individuals, with their specific sets of desires, dislikes, goals, and emotional dispositions then interact with a world full of noisy (often seemingly random) and immensely complex physical and social events. As a result, the question whether any given desire (let alone the specific strength of that desire), correctly represents the adaptiveness (and degree of adaptiveness) of its object, makes little sense. Or rather, given the enormity of the mesh of interlocking causal factors in any individual's life outcomes, attempting to answer that question is deeply intractable. So the correctness or incorrectness of individual people's pleasures and displeasures (qua representations of adaptive value) can play little or no role in explanations pitched at the individual level.

It may be worth stressing that when one claims that enjoyment of smoking misrepresents it as good, one need not be claiming that it isn't really pleasant. One can allow that smoking provides a pleasant experience for those who enjoy it. Notice, however, that there are also normative rather than experiential uses of "pleasant" and "unpleasant" that communities use to inculcate the values they want people to have. Thus parents will tell their teenage children that smoking is a "filthy" or "revolting" habit and they tell their youngsters that broccoli is delicious. But it remains true that many smokers enjoy smoking, with their experience (mis-)representing the activity (nonconceptually) as good. And many children really do dislike the taste of broccoli, with their experience (mis-)representing it (nonconceptually) as bad.

While affective learning is generally reliable and adaptive in real-world contexts (especially among animals), of course it can misfire, issuing in erroneous pleasures or displeasures. And experimental psychologists routinely bring about such outcomes in the course of their experiments, getting a rat to dislike the presence of an innocent light, for example, by pairing it with pain. Among humans, living and learning in richly elaborated cultures as they do, the potential for erroneous pleasures and displeasures is greater. Processes of cultural evolution and adaptation, as well as competition among cultural groups, provide some constraints. For a cultural group that adopts highly maladaptive norms is likely to get out-competed by neighboring ones. Nevertheless, as Boyd & Richerson (1992) demonstrate, punishment

Feelings Versus Representations of Value   **109**

(and especially meta-punishment and meta-reward—that is, disapproval of those who fail to punish infringements of social norms, and approval of those who do), can stabilize just about anything within a culture, no matter how arbitrary or maladaptive. Hence the pleasure someone takes in something (experiencing it as nonconceptually good) will often diverge considerably from the actual adaptive value or disvalue of the thing.

5.7 Merely Sub-Personal or Extended Egoism: A Dilemma

This section confronts an important objection to the value-representing account of valence outlined in the present chapter. It takes the form of a dilemma. It can seem that no matter which of the two horns of the dilemma we opt for, the result is a kind of egoism rather than full-blown pluralism.

On the one hand, a hedonist might agree that feelings of pleasure and displeasure are representations of adaptive value and disvalue. But it might be said that this fact is a sub-personal one, to be found among the underlying mechanisms of human and animal decision-making, not at the level of personal choice. From the perspective of the agent, it might be said, all decisions are taken to secure or avoid the good or bad feelings that get bound into our future-directed imaginings when we simulate potential actions or outcomes. From the perspective of the agent, these feelings are just intrinsic properties of experience. But they might well be realized in physical "tags" of some sort (as suggested in Section 3.4) and these tags might well be representations of adaptive value from a cognitive-science perspective. The first horn of the dilemma is thus that motivational hedonism and the value-representing theory of valence can both be true, but operating at different levels of organization: personal and sub-personal, respectively. And it can then be true, just as hedonism has traditionally claimed, that people's decision-making (at the personal level) is all about maximizing good feelings and minimizing bad ones.

Suppose, on the other hand, that the representational theory of valence is true of the personal level, characterizing what it is that people are trying to achieve or aim at in their decision-making. In that case (and this is the other horn of the dilemma) the result would be, not full-blown motivational pluralism, but rather a kind of extended egoism. For recall that positive valence is said to be an analog-magnitude representation of degrees of adaptive value/inclusive fitness, whereas negative valence is an analog-magnitude representation of degrees of adaptive disvalue, or inclusive *un*fitness. But if

110 Human Motives

all decision-making aims at those values, then the resulting account turns out to be pretty close to being a form of egoism. It appears that everything one does is done to insure the continued survival and flourishing of oneself, one's relatives, and one's descendants. No room seems to be left for true—non-instrumental—altruism towards non-relatives, nor for intrinsic motivations to act justly and to avoid acting wrongly. (Nor, indeed, would there be room left for intrinsic motivations to save the whale, preserve Monarch butterflies, nor any other goal that pluralists think some of us are intrinsically motivated to pursue.) According to the second horn, then, the upshot of the present chapter is that motivational hedonism has been refuted, but only to be replaced by a slightly extended version of motivational egoism.

In order to slip between the horns of this dilemma, we need to draw a distinction between the referential correctness-conditions of a signal (needed for explanatory purposes in cognitive science) and their mode of presentation to the subject.[8] The distinction is one that can be applied to all forms of perception (as we will see in Chapter 7), not only to perceptions of value. From a cognitive-science perspective, color-experiences represent reflectance properties of surfaces, for example, and pain-sensations are often said to represent tissue damage. But people perceiving colors need have no conception of reflectance properties, and people and animals feeling sensations of pain need have no idea of tissue damage. Rather, in both cases the way in which the referential correctness-conditions get presented to the experiencers are as analog-magnitude qualities that bear similarity-and-difference relations to other properties of the same general sort (Rosenthal 2010; Lau et al. 2022).[9]

Likewise, then, people experiencing pleasure (whether consummatory or anticipatory) need have no conception of adaptation and inclusive fitness, and people experiencing displeasure need have no idea of maladaptiveness, either. Instead, people's experience of valence is comprised of a pair of object-directed or event-directed analog-magnitude properties that admit of

---

[8] I am drawing here on the famous Fregean distinction between sense and reference, of course; only without any commitment to the claim that sense *determines* reference—indeed, while denying it. On the contrary, the reference or correctness-conditions of a representation get fixed in the manner outlined in Section 5.4, as whatever subset of the information it carries explains its stabilized role.

[9] Note that the similarity spaces that constitute modes of presentation don't have to map smoothly onto similarities at the level of reference/correctness-conditions, for the former track what is most important/adaptive given the needs, life-ways, and learning history of the organism, rather than the actual physical resemblances among objects. So a judgment that one color or one smell is very similar to another can be correct, even though the physical properties causing the experiences in question are very unlike one another. And one-and-the-same chemical odorant might be presented to members of two different species differently, located in differing similarity-spaces with distinct functional roles. In short, in order to meet the challenge to informational theories of content raised by Pautz (2014) we can appeal to teleo-informational theories of the sort that I am assuming here (Rupert 2018; Shea 2018).

degrees and allow comparative judgments of extent (mapping onto a common scale), while being in some sense opposites.

It is hard to characterize, using concepts, how valence presents itself to people, just as it is hard to say what seeing red is like. Perhaps the closest one can come, is to say that positive valence directed toward a thing or event makes that thing or event seem (nonconceptually) good—one sees or experiences it as good—and negative valence directed towards something makes it seem (nonconceptually) bad. Certainly the valence component of affect is spontaneously and directly expressed in both judgment and speech using the concepts GOOD and BAD, as we noted in Section 5.2. Just as perceiving something red is directly expressible in the judgment, THAT [surface] IS RED, and feeling a pain sensation in one's toe can issue directly in the judgment, PAIN THERE [in the toe], so enjoyment of a conversation with a friend is directly expressible in the judgment, THIS [activity] IS GOOD, and a painful experience can issue directly in the judgment, THAT [pain sensation] IS BAD. Moreover, valence has an impact on decision-making of just the sort one might expect if it represented degrees of goodness and badness: positive valence directed at something makes it seem choice-worthy and negative valence makes it seem rejection-worthy.

Valence thus presents us with perceived values and disvalues (or so the arguments advanced in Sections 5.2 and 5.3 would suggest). It is, from the perspective of the subject, silent about the nature of those values. And it is this perspective that best characterizes what people are aiming at when they take decisions, and that seems most relevant to the task of vindicating our practices of morally evaluating actions and agents. Consider people who help a stranger in need because the act of helping strikes them as an intrinsically good thing to do. This seems sufficient to undergird the judgment that they acted well and altruistically, and to contribute to our evaluation of them as good people. Likewise, consider someone who keeps a promise because they anticipate feeling guilty if they don't, and their anticipatory guilt at the thought of promise-breaking in these circumstances makes their inaction seem intrinsically bad. This appears sufficient to warrant a judgment that the person acted justly (for the sake of justice), and to contribute to our evaluation of them as a just person.

It is only for scientific explanatory purposes that we need to appeal to adaptive value and disvalue to provide the correctness conditions for positive and negative valence. For those are the natural, causally efficacious, properties that valence carries information about, and which serve to explain how affective learning and decision-making systems have become stabilized in the way that they have. If those systems are acting as designed, then

112   Human Motives

people will, in general, be acting in ways that advance their inclusive fitness. But that doesn't mean that people aim, from their own subjective perspective on the world, to improve their inclusive fitness—quite the contrary. What they aim at is securing what is good and avoiding what is bad (or what they take to be so or see as such).[10]

Not all decision-making is conscious, of course. But it is controversial whether people can be judged or held morally responsible for unconscious influences on their actions. Indeed, there is something of a consensus in the philosophical literature on so-called "implicit bias" that people should not be judged on the basis of attitudinal influences of which they are unaware (Holroyd 2012; Saul 2013; Levy 2014; Brownstein 2019)—except that there is a case to be made, given the public attention paid to such attitudes over the last 20 years, that people *should* be aware of the existence and likely influence of implicit biases, and should take steps accordingly. Suppose this is right: people can't be judged on the basis of unconscious attitudes. Then if people are unaware that their choices reflect feelings that have adaptive value and disvalue as their (referential) correctness conditions, it will turn out that the possession of such correctness-conditions does nothing to undermine the claim that their prosocial actions deserve moral credit, for what people are consciously aiming at is to do good for others, and to avoid injustice.

In previous work I have argued that unconscious influences on decision-making *can* be subject to moral evaluation, because of what they can reveal about the character and values of the agent (King & Carruthers 2012, 2022). People's unconscious attitudes are a part of them, and are parts of what make them the kinds of people that they are. But it remains true that conscious, reflective, decision-making is much *more* revealing, since considerations entertained in conscious reflection are "globally broadcast," giving the entire set of one's values a chance to influence the outcome (Dehaene 2014; Levy 2014). More importantly, however, the fact that people make choices that are (in a sense) about maximizing their inclusive fitness shows us nothing about any individual person's character, for the correctness-conditions for the valences that guide decision-making are the same for both the saint and the

---

[10] Notice that there is no parallel distinction to that between reference and mode of presentation that can be used to rescue intrinsic-feeling accounts of valence from entailing motivational hedonism, and hence from undermining the grounds for moral evaluation of actions and agents. Indeed, the claim that people do everything that they do to secure good and avoid bad feelings for themselves is already pitched at a level equivalent to that of mode of presentation. Nor can the distinction be deployed to rescue imperativist accounts of the sort to be discussed in Chapter 6, either. In fact, the main protagonists of such accounts (Barlassina & Hayward 2019a, 2019b) are quite explicit that they intend to be characterizing the phenomenology of conscious decision-making.

axe-murderer. What is revealing about character are the things that strike people as (nonconceptually) good or bad.

My response to the dilemma presented at the outset of this section, then, is to agree with the second horn that when people make decisions they do so on the basis of what pleasure and displeasure represent. But we can then distinguish between the represented properties that we need to appeal to for explanatory purposes in cognitive science (adaptive value and disvalue), on the one hand, and the modes in which those properties are presented to agents themselves in their decision-making (as analog-magnitude quantities of goodness and badness), on the other. What people aim at when taking decisions, then, is to achieve what is good and avoid what is bad. The result is motivational pluralism.

5.8 Conclusion

This chapter has compared and contrasted two theories of the nature of valence. One claims that pleasure and displeasure are intrinsic properties of certain experiences, as elaborated and discussed more fully in Chapter 3. When conscious, the valences have distinctive subjective "feels" or qualia and they influence decision-making directly when combined with estimates of likelihood. Positive feelings (pleasure), when embedded in future-directed representations of actions and events, make those options seem choiceworthy. Negative feelings (displeasure) felt in anticipation make the options in question seem worthy of being rejected. And the upshot is a form of motivational hedonism: all decisions are taken to insure the greatest expected balance of good feelings over bad feelings.

The contrasting theory claims that valence is an analog-magnitude representation of adaptive value and disvalue. Its role in decision-making is to enter into computations of expected value, with representations of outcome values being combined with representations of the costs involved together with the likelihoods of success. The upshot is a pluralistic account of decision-making and a vindication of altruism and morally motivated choice (at least for many people, on many occasions). When one anticipates helping someone in difficulty, the pleasure one feels represents the act of helping as good (if one feels pleasure at all, of course; much depends on group membership, individual personality, and affective-learning history); and that is then at least part of the reason why one chooses that option, if one does. Likewise for fulfillment of an obligation: the intensity of the guilt one feels (or may feel) when one anticipates acting wrongly represents the action in question as being bad to an equivalent degree; and that is then at least part of the reason why one forebears from performing the action (if one does).

Over the course of the chapter, a number of reasons have been presented for preferring the value-representing account to the intrinsic-feeling one. First, there is a puzzle about why evolution should have built a decision-making system that is all about making one feel good and avoiding feeling bad; whereas a decision-making system that computes over adaptive values makes perfect evolutionary sense. Second, the value-representing account fits smoothly into the most promising approach to consciousness, which is some form of reductive representationalism, whereas the intrinsic-feeling account has to postulate a brute (and non-explanatory) identity. And most important, not only does valence check all the boxes for qualifying as a representation, but on most theories of representational content it can be shown to represent adaptive value and disvalue. So the value-representing theory of valence emerges as by far the superior of the two, but that doesn't yet mean that is it the best account overall, for we have yet to consider imperative theories of valence. That will form the topic of Chapter 6.

6
Indicatives Versus Imperatives

This chapter has two main goals, which are partly overlapping. One is to defend the value-representing theory of valence outlined in Chapter 5, comparing it with accounts that construe valence, not as indicative (representing—correctly or incorrectly—properties of the world), but rather as a kind of imperative. While developed initially to provide theories of the painfulness of pain, imperative accounts have now been extended into theories of pleasure and displeasure more generally. It is these generalized accounts that will be considered here. (We will return to the case of pain, in particular, in Chapter 7.) The second main goal of the chapter is to articulate and then critique forms of imperativism about valence that entail motivational hedonism (not all do, as we will see). The upshots of the chapter (when combined with the conclusion reached in Chapter 5, and pending the discussion of pain in Chapter 7) are twofold: the value-representing account provides the best overall theory of valence, and pluralism rather than hedonism provides the best account of human (and animal) motivations.

6.1 Two Forms of Imperativism

This section is largely expository. It explains the different varieties of imperativism and defends them against some initial criticisms. As usual throughout this book, the goal is to deploy the steel-man strategy, constructing the strongest, most plausible, version of such accounts before developing a critique.

There are two basic kinds of imperativism about valence (one of which admits of a pair of closely related sub-varieties, as we will see). Both deny that pleasure and displeasure have indicative (or declarative-like) correctness conditions. They claim, rather, that valence is imperative-like, with fulfillment conditions or satisfaction conditions. While the value-representing account ("evaluativism," for short) views pleasure as having the content, *this is [nonconceptually] good*, and displeasure as having the content, *this is [nonconceptually] bad*, imperativism suggests that the former really has the content, *more of this!*, whereas the latter has the content, *less of this!*. The two

Human Motives: Hedonism, Altruism, and the Science of Affect. Peter Carruthers, Oxford University Press.
© Peter Carruthers 2024. DOI: 10.1093/oso/9780198906131.003.0006

116   Human Motives

kinds of imperativism then differ in what they take to be the referent of "this." More on that in a moment.

Some critics of imperativism take the analogy between valence, on the one hand, and commands or imperatives, on the other, much too literally. Aydede & Fulkerson (2019), for example, think that imperativism requires a consumer system (in fact they talk about "the experiencer," or the person as a whole) that listens to the command and evaluates the authority of the source, deciding whether or not to obey. They draw a comparison with protestors in a town square being commanded to disperse by the police. The protestors can choose whether or not to obey, depending on whether or not they accept the police's authority on the matter. But this is a far cry from what is actually intended by imperativists. Rather, we should think of valence as an abstract, non-behavior-specific, activated motor plan, which pushes for implementation in competition with others, and which will issue in action by default if unopposed and if implementation is possible in the circumstances. In effect, the suggestion is that valence has the content, *do something—anything—to get more/less of this!*

Imperativism is fully consistent with reductive representationalism about phenomenal consciousness. It claims that the phenomenology of valence reduces to an imperative-like urge to do something, provided that the urge in question occurs in whatever way constitutes a representational state as conscious (e.g. by figuring in working memory). But it lays greater stress on the attitude-component of affective feelings than does evaluativism. According to the latter, in addition to the contents of the experience into which valence is bound (providing the referent of "this" in *this is good*), pleasure also embeds an analog-magnitude representation of goodness that can be correct or incorrect to greater or lesser degrees. According to imperativism, in contrast, valence is realized in the *attitude* one takes towards the experiences or contents in question. The attitude is constituted by an urge of greater or lesser strength to bring about or continue (in the case of pleasure) the referent of "this" in *more of this!* and by urges of varying strength to avoid or discontinue (in the case of displeasure) the referent of "this" in *less of this!*. These urges can then be fulfilled or not, either absolutely, or to some greater or lesser degree.

One the two main forms of imperativism is world-directed whereas the other is experience-directed. Consider fear caused by an approaching grizzly bear. On the world-directed view, the "this" in *less of this!* refers to the approaching grizzly (Martínez 2011 tentatively suggests a view of this sort). The negative-valence component of one's fear is an imperative-like urge to do something to stop or get away from the thing or event in question.

But it is maximally unspecific about what one should do (run, freeze, climb a tree, shoot at the animal, or whatever). It can be interpreted as saying something like, "do something—anything—to get less of this!" According to the experience-directed form of imperativism, in contrast, the "this" in *less of this!* refers to the *experience* of the approaching grizzly. Negative valence is a maximally unspecific urge to do something to bring an end to the experience in which it is embedded (Barlassina & Hayward 2019a, 2019b defend a view of this sort). Presumably the same range of actions that might implement a world-directed imperative can be drawn on to satisfy the corresponding experience-directed urge (running, freezing, climbing a tree, and so on).[1]

Barlassina & Hayward (2019b) draw a distinction between two subtly different versions of the experience-directed account of valence. In one form, the imperative refers just to the experience in which it is embedded, such as the visual and auditory representations of the approaching grizzly. But in the other version, which they dub "reflexive imperativism," the "this" in *less of this!* refers, reflexively, to the entire experiential state, including the imperative urge itself—so it refers not just to the sights and sounds of the grizzly, but also the urge to put a stop to them. Barlassina & Hayward argue at some length that the reflexive form of imperativism about valence is the better of the two—indeed, that it is the best of all three, including the world-directed form of imperativism.

One initial worry one might have about the two experience-directed kinds of imperativism concerns their meta-representational nature. For notice that valence, on such accounts, refers to the experience of which it is a part, and experiences are representational states. (Even if one denies that experiences are representational, as some philosophers do, valence must at least be meta-mental. For everyone agrees that experiences are *mental* states.) Why might this be a problem? Well, it is greatly disputed whether any creatures besides humans are capable of meta-representation, or of representing their own or others' mental states (Penn et al. 2008; Smith et al. 2014; Heyes 2015; Carruthers & Williams 2019). But valence is thought to be common to all organisms that are capable of evaluative learning. This includes almost all living creatures, including many insects and other invertebrates, as we noted in Section 3.2. So it might seem that experience-directed forms of imperativism come burdened with a highly controversial commitment.

---

[1] One might wonder why simply closing one's eyes shouldn't be a satisfactory way of bringing an end to the experience of the approaching bear, if ending the experience is what one feels the urge to do. But of course one can foresee that this will just lead to more negatively valenced experiences (e.g. pain) in the future. And notice that in other circumstances, such as watching frightening events in the cinema, people do sometimes respond by closing their eyes or looking away.

118 Human Motives

Although this implication of experience-directed imperativism may be surprising, it need not present a deep difficulty for the approach. For notice that valence, on this view, refers to the experience of which it is a part via a pure indexical. (In philosophers' jargon, it refers to that experience "de re" rather than as such.) So it could do its work in the absence of anything resembling a "theory of mind," and could do so in creatures that lack mental-state concepts of any sort. In contrast, the debates and skepticism about animal capacities for meta-representation concern exactly this: theory-like and/ or concept-like representations of the mental. In fact, the "this" in *less of this!* and *more of this!* might be said to be an instance of what Carruthers & Williams (2022) call "model-free metacognition." They argue that meta-representational signals of a model-free sort are widespread among animals (even in invertebrates like bees), especially in motivating curiosity and information-search. Such behaviors are initiated by appraising the significance of signals with the content, *not known*, Carruthers & Williams argue—which are meta-representational in nature. But this signal can exist and do its work independently of any theory-like model of the mind, and independently of any mental-state concepts. Similar claims could then be made about the meta-representational nature of valence.

What does decision-making look like, from the perspective of imperativism? It will comprise competition among imperatives of differing strengths, modulated by likelihood. Whereas evaluativism sees decisions as resulting from calculations of expected utility—which take outcome values, likelihoods, and costs as inputs—imperativism sees them as resulting from a form of competition among urges to act in which the strongest urge wins. And presumably, on this view, estimates of outcome-likelihood modulate or down-regulate the strength of the related urge. When engaged in prospective reasoning, then, one imagines or otherwise represents the various outcomes. Those representations are received and appraised by one's affective systems, and the valence produced is comprised of urges to get or avoid the relevant events (or the relevant experiences of those events). When one sees an outcome as less likely, this will reduce the urge to get it (or the experience of it). And when the actions involved are predicted to be effortful, a negative urge (inhibiting action) will result, subtracting from the urge to act.

What, then, of evaluative learning and conditioning? How does this appear when seen through the lens of imperativism about valence? It seems that all or most of the key findings can be transposed into this alternative framework. Anticipatory motor-urges, created from innate or previously learned values, can be compared with the actual urge-to-secure-more that occurs at the consumption stage. If the consummatory urge is greater than anticipated, then the stored value for items or events of that sort is ratcheted upwards by some increment, whereas if the current urge is lesser than predicted, the stored value is ratcheted downwards. Moreover, affective learning systems can be set up to create secondary urges to obtain or avoid things that are predictive of or associated with primary urges.

Now recall from Section 5.1 that the intrinsic-feeling account of valence postulates a kind of mis-match between one's stored values, appraisal against which at the input stage produces an affective response, and the intrinsically good or bad feelings that attach to one's experiences as output. And note that imperativism, too, postulates a sort of mis-match between one's stored values that get activated by the input and the nonspecific motor urges (positive and negative valence) that are produced as output. In connection with the intrinsic-feeling account this mis-match resulted in a puzzle: why would evolution care about what people feel? But no such puzzle arises for imperativism, for of course evolution cares about what organisms *do*. Indeed, one might think that all of cognition is ultimately in the service of action, for it is the actions one performs, or doesn't perform, that impact one's inclusive fitness most directly. So there is nothing especially puzzling about the suggestion that the common currency of decision-making should be comprised of non-specific urges to act.

Experience-directed forms of imperativism do leave us with a puzzle, however. For why would evolution have built the core architecture of human and animal decision-making in such a way that the action-urges in which it traffics are urges to secure or to avoid certain experiences? Granted, experiences are generally pretty reliable indicators of the worldly and bodily objects and events they represent. So if an outcome event would increase one's fitness, an unspecific urge to act in such a way as to secure an experience of that event will generally be adaptive too, for normally the only way to produce the experience is to bring about the event itself. But whence the dog-leg through one's experiences? Why doesn't decision-making traffic in urges to secure those adaptive events directly? Indeed, the experience-directed account looks even stranger when we recall that incentive-salience ("wanting" in Berridge's 2009 terminology) is comprised of two parallel components: a specific motor-urge to approach or bring about the positively evaluated thing or event combined with anticipatory positive valence (pleasure) bound into the representation of that thing or event (Miller et al. 2014). The former is world-directed on anyone's account. It appears quite strange, then, that the accompanying non-behavior-specific urge to act (anticipatory pleasure) should be very different in kind, directed at the anticipated *experience* rather than the worldly object or event.[2]

This is, I think, an important consideration favoring world-directed imperativism over the experience-directed forms. However, it isn't yet a reason to favor world-directed imperativism over value-representing accounts of valence, for according to the latter, decision-making is about anticipating the value or disvalue of future events, and then selecting actions to secure or avoid those values. Evaluativism is equally world-directed.

Importantly for our purposes, world-directed and experience-directed forms of imperativism have quite different implications for the debate over motivational hedonism. If valence is comprised of world-directed and body-directed imperatives, then motivational pluralism results, for one will have intrinsic, non-self-directed, urges to achieve many types of worldly event and outcome. And as a result of social conditioning, some of these urges are likely to be altruistic ones, directed at benefiting another person as an ultimate end. Others are likely to be based on moral norms, providing intrinsic urges to forebear from actions that produce anticipatory guilt, for example.[3]

If either kind of experience-directed imperativism is correct, in contrast, then motivational hedonism is entailed, for all decision-making will be about securing or avoiding certain experiences for oneself. When one acts to reduce someone's suffering, for example, because appraisal of the imagined outcome results in positive valence (pleasure) being bound into the imagined result, one will be responding to, and implementing, an imperative-like urge to get more of those imagined experiences for oneself. One is acting to secure an *experience* of helping that will include an urge (pleasure) to have more of that very experience, for recall that on this account, the "this" in

---

[2] Barlassina & Hayward (2019a) seem to think that incentive-salience ("wanting") is entirely comprised of a world-directed imperative or motor-urge. This is a definite mistake. Incentive-salience also includes anticipatory pleasure, which makes the wanted object or event seem attractive, and which figures in down-stream decision-making processes about whether or not to pursue it. Unless they acknowledge the valence component of incentive-salience (a maximally unspecific experience-directed motor urge, on their view) Barlassina & Hayward can provide no account of decision-making. And without the distinction between anticipatory and consummatory valence, they can provide no account of evaluative learning, either. We will return to this point in Section 6.3.

[3] A closely related account of valence is offered by Cochrane (2018) and is similarly world-directed, issuing in pluralism about motivation. It is not directly imperative in nature, however. Rather, positive valence is said to be the detection of the extent to which automatically activated attractant motor-plans are succeeding; and negative valence is the detection of the extent to which avoidance motor-plans are succeeding; in both cases the only direct downstream effect of pleasure or displeasure is to ramp up attentional engagement, thereby boosting the motor activity in question. While this account can avoid many of the problems that confront imperativism, it fails at the first hurdle. It cannot account for the common-currency nature of valence. This is because the impact of valence on decision-making is an indirect one, operating in the same way for both pleasure and displeasure: it increases attention (with the latter then boosting imperative urges that compete with one another for control).

more of this! will refer to the experience of helping, not the actual helping itself.

Although it is experience-directed imperativism that matters most for the topic of this book, much of our discussion will concern imperativism in general, for if any form of imperativism is true, then the value-representing account of valence is false. We will return to some of the arguments that have been used to support experience-directed imperativism in Section 6.5, since many have been intended also as criticisms of value-representing accounts.

6.2 Imperative Versus Indicative Content

This section will continue to explicate imperativist views of valence, focusing especially on how the contents of the imperatives are determined. But it will also begin to compare and contrast imperativism with evaluativism. The upshot is that imperativism isn't adequately supported.

What is imperative content, and how is it determined? Just as indicative representations carry information about things that already exist (or purport to do so), so imperative ones carry information about the future.[4] As we saw in Section 5.4, the content of an indicative representation is comprised of a subset of the things that reliably cause it. That subset is picked out by its role in explaining how the down-stream uses of the representation in question became stabilized, either by evolution, learning, or direct contributions to individual survival (Shea 2018). Likewise, we can say that the content of an imperative representation is a subset of the things that it reliably causes, where the causing of that subset explains why the system comprising the representation works as it does. A motor representation of a right-handed reach, for example, reliably causes activity in the muscles and joints of the right arm and hand; and it reliably causes perturbations in the air through which the arm passes. But it doesn't represent muscular activity, nor does it represent air movements. Rather, it both causes *and* represents the completion of the reach, since that is the sort of outcome that has helped stabilize the organization of this aspect of the motor-control system.

Cognitive theories of action-selection and movement-control are hierarchical in nature (Todorov & Jordan 2002; Jeannerod 2006; Scott 2012; Merel et al. 2019). Intentional action begins with an abstractly specified goal with imperative content, such as, *drink from that mug!* Unless inhibited, this will

---

[4] Our focus here is just on nonconceptual forms of representation. As we noted in Section 5.4, there may be additional constraints on the contents of concepts and of conceptual thought.

122   Human Motives

cause a cascading sequence of increasingly specific motor commands involving limb-selection, trajectory of reach, and the details of the subsequent grasping and lifting movements. These are fine-tuned by interactions between anticipated and experienced sensory feedback (mostly proprioceptive and visual), and the choices at each stage are influenced by the affordances of the environment (such as the orientation of the handle on the mug), as well as by comparative estimates of ease-of-acting (Cos et al. 2014).

Imperative theories of valence can fit smoothly at the very top of the action-control hierarchy. The negative valence produced by fear of a bear reliably causes *some* sequence of actions to avoid the threat. (In this context freezing qualifies as an action.) Hence it can be thought of as a maximally general motor command with the content, *less of this!*, or *stop this!* At the same time, a number of more-specific motor imperatives will have become active, either directly caused by the appraisal mechanisms producing the fear (such as an urge to run), or by the affordances of the environment, or both.[5] The top-level imperative can have a releasing function with respect to lower-level ones that have become activated independently, while at the same time competing for overall control with other valenced attitudes, such as a desire to approach closer if one is a crossbow hunter whose goal is to shoot the bear, or a biologist wanting to study its behavior from close-up.

Imperative theories of valence comport nicely with widely accepted philosophical theories of desire. Many take the view that a desire is a disposition towards action. (Note, however, that many philosophical treatments of desire fail to distinguish between felt desires—which are affective states—and goals and intentions, which are not.) To desire something is to be disposed to act in such a way as to obtain it (Anscombe 1957; Smith 1987). It is equally widely accepted among philosophers that desires have a world-to-mind direction of fit (Searle 1983). That is to say, desires don't describe the way the world is, but are designed to change the state of the world to fit or realize their own contents. It is but a small step from these ideas to claiming that the valence component of desire (the component that represents something other than the desired object or event) is an imperative with the content, *get that!* (or, in the case of a negative desire or aversion, with the content, *avoid that!*).

---

[5] It is worth noting that perception of features of the environment that afford or facilitate well-practiced actions can activate related motor-plans directly. Perception of familiar tools, for example, automatically activates the motor-plans for using them, which need to be inhibited by top-down executive signals if they are not to be carried through to completion (Frith et al. 2000; Negri et al. 2007). As a result, people with certain forms of frontal-lobe damage suffer from what is called "utilization syndrome." They have difficulty inhibiting themselves from grasping and using things in accordance with their familiar affordances (Lhermitte 1983, 1986).

While the value-representing theory of valence doesn't deny that desires often lead to changes in the world, of course—nor that they do so as part of their function—it denies that desires have imperative content. And it also denies that they have world-to-mind direction of fit. Rather, desires are comprised of two indicative components: a representation of the desired object or event, and an analog-magnitude representation of the adaptive value of that object or event. This will seem counter-intuitive to many philosophers, and is the source of one of the main arguments advanced against evaluativism (Aydede & Fulkerson 2014; Barlassina & Hayward 2019a). Moreover, given that one accepts some form of informational approach to representational content, one might think: how can desires *not* have imperative content? For they are apt to bring about the events that they target, and hence carry information about those events.

Evaluativists can (and should) reply that the valence component of desires is too functionally remote from action to carry imperative content. (They should also insist that common-sense intuitions can carry no weight against our best science, which is what evaluativism claims to embody.) This is because on all views, valence only influences action via processes of downstream decision-making. Once decisions get made, the resulting goals and intentions have imperative content, for sure. But those are no longer affective states (they are "cool" rather than "hot," in the sense of Metcalfe & Mischel 1999). Put differently: the valence component of desire doesn't motivate anything directly. Rather, it provides input to planning and decision-making processes in which it is combined with estimates of likelihood and compared with the likelihoods and degrees of valence of other desires and affective states. The output of such processes is generally an imperative representation (such as an intention), but the inputs to those processes—including the valence component of affective states—is not.[6]

It is worth noting, too, that the valence attached to a future-directed representation of an action or event carries no more information about the occurrence of that event than do the estimates of likelihood with which it interacts (which are indicative representations on anyone's view). Even strongly positive valence won't lead to action if the estimate of the likelihood of achieving the event is sufficiently low. And conversely, a very high estimate of the likelihood of achieving an outcome *will* issue in action when combined with even a weakly positively valenced representation (provided that there is

---

[6] While intentions themselves are best thought of as high-level motor representations, they nevertheless interact with affective systems. As we have noted before, appraisals of progress towards achieving a goal issue in experiences of reward (pleasure), and appraising an obstacle to achieving a goal, or the goal's likely frustration, causes an experience of displeasure (Juechems & Summerfield 2019).

124 Human Motives

lesser overall competition from any other future-directed representations, of course—this provides yet another factor that weakens the amount of information about future action carried by valence). It is not the quantity of information carried about future action, then, that could fix the imperative nature of valence, for that is fairly modest.

It should be noted, in addition, that it is no argument against the value-representing theory of valence that valence carries hardly any information about the stimulus, for many states that have indicative content on anyone's view carry almost zero information about sensory input. Think, for example, of perceptions of speaker-meaning. This tells us nothing about the nature of the sound-stream. As is familiar, there are (quite literally) no end of possible sound-streams that might be used to express a given thought; and then once that is extracted, and literal meaning represented, it has to be combined with information about the context together with mentalizing information concerning what the speaker knows, wants, intends, and so on. But this typically happens in real time, and the result is (in my view) genuinely a perception of meaning (Carruthers 2015). Here the information carried by the final state (or rather, the component of the state that represents the speaker meaning) is just something like, *she is saying that P*. Everything else has dropped away. The final representation carries very little information about the stimulus (albeit quite a bit of information about the world, of course; in particular, about what the speaker means).

The appraisals that issue in affective states are like this, too. By the time one gets to the output of the process, there may be little or no information carried about the sensory input. This is because indefinitely many kinds of sensory input can issue in the same or a similar appraisal, outputting the same extent of valence. But it is also because (just as in the speaker-meaning case) the sensory input needs to be recognized and integrated with other sorts of information in the course of appraisal, about the context and about the state of one's own body among other things. So by the time one gets to the output of the appraisal process, the only information carried is information about the current value of the stimulus, not the stimulus itself (nor the context, nor one's bodily state). The fact that valence carries very little information about sensory input is neither here nor there; the same is true of perceptions of speaker meaning.

We noted earlier that anticipatory valence appears to carry comparatively little information about down-stream action, for the latter only occurs on the other side of the processes involved in decision-making. In contrast, valence carries full information about the current value of the target object or event (or at least, about the organism's estimation of that value). This is because it occurs immediately down-stream of the evaluative appraisal process. Indeed, it is one of the primary outputs of that process. Moreover, it is the evaluative information carried by valence that best explains how its role in decision-making has become stabilized. We thus have good reason to prefer the value-representing account.

Now recall from Section 2.3 that the appraisals of value that issue in desires and other affective states are apt to cause motor activations as part of their output, alongside the valence and arousal dimensions.[7] Both evaluativists and imperativists should accept this. The appraisals of danger that result in fear produce motor-urges that will issue in a fear-face by default (unless top-down inhibited), and also generally in a motor-urge to get away. And desires, too, automatically activate motor-urges to approach or retreat. So the overall affective state of desire is partly imperative on anyone's account: all affective states have an automatic motoric component. Imperativists think that the valence component of affective states, too, is an imperative one, but is maximally unspecific (*do something to get/avoid that!*). Evaluativists about valence, in contrast, claim that valence, itself, is not an imperative, but is rather a nonconceptual representation of value. These representations enter into decision-making processes whose upshot is (among other things) to either release or inhibit the motor-urges that are already in train.

In Section 6.1 we raised a problem for experience-directed forms of imperativism: how and why did evolution select for an affective system whose valence outputs are so different in nature from the appraisal processes that give rise to them? The latter match incoming representations of the world or body, together with contextual factors, against stored values; but the former are said to be urges toward action to secure *experiences* of worldly or bodily events. One might wonder whether a similar sort of evolutionary puzzle arises for evaluativism. In particular, how and why did evolution structure the affective systems so that (in addition to arousal) they produce two very different sorts of output: on the one hand, urges towards action that are affective-state-specific while also depending on prior learning; and on the other hand, representations of adaptive value? Imperativism, in contrast, can claim that there is just a single sort of output here: urges towards action of greater and lesser specificity (with valence being maximally unspecific).[8]

---

[7] Thereafter the three types of output are likely to interact, of course. Among the initial motor outputs of an evaluative appraisal will be a tendency for attention to get pulled toward the stimulus; and the bodily arousal processes are often treated as a signal of the importance, or urgency, of what is being appraised, likely strengthening or weakening both motor-preparation and initial attentional tendencies. With the stimulus then being processed more or less deeply, the valenced output, too, is likely to change (being ramped up or down).

[8] At this point we are setting aside expressive actions like the fear-face, the anger-face, and so on. Both imperativists and evaluativists can accept that these likely have distinct (social-communicative) functions rather than instrumental or goal-directed ones.

This challenge to evaluativism is easily met, however, by drawing on the widely accepted distinction between model-free and model-based learning and action-selection (Dickinson & Balleine 1994, 2002; Gläscher et al. 2010; Dayan & Berridge 2014). The latter utilizes causal models of the environment to construct and compare plans, and to issue in decisions. It is flexible but comparatively slow. Model-free processes, in contrast, are fast, and are relied on by default—especially in circumstances where one needs to act immediately, without planning. In the case of fear, for example, there are overlapping but partially distinct brain networks that control behavior depending on the immediacy of the threat (LeDoux 2012; Adolphs & Anderson 2018; Mobbs 2018; Mobbs et al. 2020). When a predator is still distal but approaching, one may have time to plan one's mode of reaction or escape; but when a predator is actively attacking one needs an immediate response. In short: the action-urges produced by affective states are for the immediate future, whereas anticipatory valence is for use in decision-making over longer time-scales. These differing outputs are responses to distinct types of adaptive problem.

Our consideration of the respective merits of imperativism and evaluativism in this section has thus far provided some reason to prefer the latter. Indeed, perhaps imperativists can be forced to admit that valence is at least a form of what Millikan (1995) calls a "pushmi-pullyu" representation, having indicative as well as imperative content. This is because valence (even if it is also an imperative) reliably carries information about the adaptive value of items or events in the environment or body, and because the presence of such information explains how valence's role in decision-making and evaluative learning has become stabilized. Plainly, creatures would not have come to have the primary (unlearned) imperative urges that they do unless those urges generally led them to acquire items of adaptive value, or to avoid ones of adaptive disvalue. And affective learning systems would not have been set up to create the secondary imperatives that they do except that they service the same adaptive values. So valence is at least a representation of adaptive value and disvalue. The burden of proof then falls on imperativists to show that valence also has imperative content.

Imperativists might reply that although valence carries information about adaptive values and disvalues, and wouldn't have had the roles that it does unless it did so, it still doesn't qualify it as a representation of value, for there is no consumer system that treats it as such. Rather, the imperatives that result from appraisals of value just compete with one another to control the behavior of the organism. But this reply fails. Valence does, indeed, feed into at least some consumer systems that unequivocally treat it as a representation of value (at least among humans), for the positive valence generated when one sees something one wants will lead one, by default, to judge, and to say, that it is good. Likewise, the negative valence created by the sight of a moldy slice of bread will lead one (again, by default) to judge and to say that it is bad. So valence does actually have down-stream effects of the sort one might expect of a nonconceptual representation of value, even apart from the role that it plays in decision-making (which is in dispute here, of course).

It seems imperativists should concede that valence is also a representation of adaptive value and disvalue. Can the equivalent case be made against evaluativism? Should evaluativists accept that valence is *also* a maximally unspecific imperative? No, they needn't do so. This is because, as already noted, valence doesn't issue in action directly; nor does it provide any direct impetus towards action. Rather, it feeds into a decision-making system that takes varying degrees of valence as input, combines those together with representations of likelihood, computes the expected value of each option, and issues in decisions to act or forebear from action. It is only the latter states that need to be assigned imperative content.

The upshot of this section is that valence is *at least* a representation of value. It seems that imperativists, just as much as evaluativists, should accept this. But imperativism claims that in addition, valence possesses maximally unspecific imperative content, whereas evaluativism denies it. The two views are accompanied by competing pictures of how decision-making is structured. According to imperativism, decision-making is comprised of direct competition among imperatives (urges to action or inaction) of varying strengths, with those strengths modulated by the likelihood of the outcomes. According to evaluativism, in contrast, decision-making involves computations of the expected value of the options, integrating outcome values, likelihoods, and costs. It is worth noting that the latter interpretation is the one widely accepted by scientists working in the fields of decision-making and neuroeconomics (Glimcher & Rustichini 2004; Loewenstein et al. 2008; Levy & Glimcher 2012). So we need powerful reasons to overturn what is close to being a scientific consensus. As yet, none have been forthcoming.

6.3 Consummatory Pleasure Is about the Present

This section focuses on the two modes in which valence can occur: either in anticipation of the future, prior to action, or during consumption, in the present. Imperativism is committed to the view that even in the latter case valence is future-directed (*get more/less of this [in the future]!*). But both common-sense and affective science suggest that consummatory pleasure and displeasure are present-tensed, directed at what is happening concurrently.

Imperatives, by their very nature, are future directed. An imperative like *do something to get more of this!* is apt to produce future actions of the sort that might secure more of the event or experience designated by "this." As a result, the imperative theory of valence looks most plausible as an account of the kinds of anticipatory pleasure and displeasure that figure in prospection and future-directed decision-making. When one imagines doing one thing or another, or causing one future event or another, and feels some degree of positive or negative valence as a result, what one feels can be construed as an unspecific urge (of greater or lesser strength) to do something to obtain or avoid the imagined outcome. Imperativism looks much *less* plausible, however, as an account of consummatory or present-tensed pleasure and displeasure.

It is true, of course, that when good things happen, one often wants them to continue. While enjoying the taste of a strawberry or the sound of one's favorite piece of music one often feels an urge to eat another strawberry or to continue listening to the piece. Likewise, while bad things are happening one generally wants them to stop. While in pain during a routine prostate exam one likely wants the exam to be over (and the pain to stop) as soon as possible. But on the face of it, one wants pleasures to continue *because they are pleasant*; they aren't pleasant because one wants them to continue, as imperativism suggests. Similarly, when one wants the pain to stop it is *because* it is unpleasant; it isn't unpleasant in virtue of one's urge to get it to stop.

In fact, imperativism inherits all the problems associated with desire-theories of pleasure and displeasure, discussed in Section 3.4. For desires, too, are distally directed towards non-actual events. It is quite unclear what it could mean to desire something one already has. Indeed, Heathwood (2007), when confronting this difficulty as part of his defense of a desire-theory of pleasure, is forced to resort to mere metaphors. He says that a pleasant experience is one that one "gives a thumbs-up to" or that one "is into." It is equally unclear what it could mean to direct an imperative or a motor urge at something one currently has, unless it is an urge to retain it into the future. But one seemingly has the urge to retain it, if one does, *because* it is pleasant. Its pleasantness isn't constituted by one's urge to extend or retain it.

Heathwood (2007) helpfully draws attention to a class of momentary pleasures and displeasures, which can seemingly exist in the absence of any future-directed desire, or any future-directed urge. When strolling through a park, for example, one might pause to sniff a flower, enjoying the scent, without feeling any urge to continue sniffing. One sniffs, enjoys, and moves on. Likewise, when one completes a task of any sort one generally feels pleased, but often without feeling any urge to repeat it or perform another. And when one experiences what one knows in advance to be just a momentary pin-prick, the sensation is unpleasant, but there doesn't appear to be any urge to do anything about it. Of course, there is a signal resulting from the pinprick that in some instances might be characterized as meaning something along the lines of "seek less of this." This would be the learning signal created by matching the current displeasure against one's (less unpleasant) expectation, designed to alter one's stored negative evaluation of events of that sort. But this actually carries, not future-directed imperative content, but rather an analog-magnitude measure of the difference between the expected and experienced painfulness.

Imperativists can choose to dig their heels in and reject these intuitions. They can insist that, despite one's intuition to the contrary, pleasure in the present *is* constituted by a future-directed urge to continue the event or experience; and displeasure *is* a future-directed urge to bring an end to the event or experience. Likewise, they can insist that when one enjoys the momentary scent of the flower, one *is* aware of an urge to do something to continue the experience. For after all, pleasure is an imperative urge, on this view, and one is aware of the pleasure. It may just be that the urge to continue the experience dies away too quickly to influence one's behavior. Similarly for the momentary painful pin-prick: it can be said that one was actually briefly aware of the urge to make it stop (for that is what painfulness is); but it, too, subsided as quickly as the pain sensation did.

It is much harder to accept that when one completes an effortful task one feels an urge to continue it or embark on another one. One feels pleased when one finishes writing a paper, for example; but this surely doesn't implicate any urge to keep writing, or to start writing another. Indeed, whenever one achieves a goal or fulfills an intention one generally feels pleased. On completing the goal of cutting the grass this afternoon one feels satisfied— one "takes pleasure in a job well done," or at least in a job completed. But one feels not the slightest impulse towards more grass-cutting—or so it seems. Nor is this example at all exceptional. There are many, many, everyday tasks that have a discrete end-point. When that end-point is achieved, one is generally pleased. The task in question can be ticked off one's list of things to do, and that in itself is usually rewarding (pleasant). But one seems not to feel the slightest impulse to keep on doing what one had been doing. But imperativism entails that one does, since pleasure is claimed to be an imperative with the content, *more of this!*.

I would agree, of course, that common-sense intuitions are of limited value, and should be set aside whenever they conflict with even moderately well-established science. The trouble, however, is that it is unclear that anything in the science of affect supports imperativism about pleasure and displeasure. On the contrary, the standard interpretation of the nature of affective learning offered in the field is the one adopted by evaluativism. It is that one's stored values get updated when appraisals of the likely future value of an event get confronted with the results of an appraisal of the *current* value of that event when it is experienced in the present. And consummatory pleasure and displeasure are representations of current value.

Indeed, imperative theories of pleasure and displeasure sit uneasily (at least) with one of the core findings of affective science and neuroscience. This is the double dissociation between "liking" (or consummatory pleasure) and "wanting" (incentive-salience, which includes anticipatory pleasure), discussed in Section 2.6. Recall that there are separate subcortical "hotspots" underlying each, stimulation or suppression of which can result in changes in wanting (such as eating much more vigorously, or working harder to obtain food) without altered pleasure-responding, and vice versa (Berridge & Kringelbach 2008, 2015). More specifically, if the incentive-salience system is completely suppressed while leaving the liking system untouched, then animals will seemingly respond with normal pleasure to drops of sugar-solution placed directly into their mouths, but will make no attempt to obtain those drops for themselves. This is quite puzzling if pleasure is constituted by an imperative or motor-urge with the content, *more of this!*. For one would think that a motor-urge would provide some impetus towards obtaining more.

As we also saw in Section 2.6, the same dissociations seem to occur among humans. In particular, consider individuals with depression or certain forms of schizophrenia who have been diagnosed with "anhedonia" (lack of enjoyment), but on the basis of retrospective and/or anticipatory questionnaires. It turns out they can show just as much enjoyment of a current stimulus as controls do when using measures of contemporary pleasure, while at the same time showing greatly reduced anticipation of pleasure, and while being much less willing to work for pleasure (Gard et al. 2007; Dichter et al. 2010; Sherdell et al. 2012). Again, this is quite puzzling if pleasure is comprised of an imperative of any sort, or of an urge to get more.

Recall from Section 6.1, however, that Barlassina & Hayward (2019a) seem to think that "wanting" is entirely comprised of a world-directed motor-urge, and that the experience-directed motor-urge that constitutes liking can only impact the world via the functioning of the wanting system. In that case it would make sense that with the latter system suppressed, there would be no action. But as we noted previously, this is a mistaken account of incentive-salience ("wanting"), which comprises both motor-activation *and* anticipatory pleasure. Moreover, unless one allows that incentive-salience comprises future-directed anticipatory pleasure one can give no account of evaluative learning, for the latter requires current pleasure to be matched against anticipatory pleasure to issue in the error-signals that drive learning.

To accommodate the data, imperativists of all sorts need to say the following. Consummatory pleasure is a maximally unspecific motor-urge created in response to, and directed at, some current experience or current event. That urge is received as input by the incentive-salience system, where it is one of the factors whose appraisal issues in both specific world-directed motor-urges together with anticipatory pleasure (an anticipatory non-specific motor-urge, for an imperativist) directed at the results of the anticipated future action. This anticipatory pleasure/motor-urge then interacts with other competing anticipatory pleasures/urges and estimates of likelihood in decision-making processes, the result of which is to either release, activate, or suppress some specific set of world-directed motor instructions.

Now, notice that on this account the pleasure one takes in a current experience or current event (the motor-urge caused by that event, for an imperativist of any stripe) fails to have any direct impact on action. Indeed, its relevance to action is really quite indirect. Its only roles are (1) to provide input to the appraisal processes that issue in preparatory motor-activation and anticipatory pleasure, where the latter then enter into subsequent decision-making processes to select an action; and (2) to provide feedback to be compared with any previously generated anticipatory pleasure relating to the current event for purposes of evaluative learning. As a result, it is quite hard to see any justification for the claim that consummatory pleasure has imperative content. It is much more plausible to claim that it has evaluative content, resulting directly from an appraisal of the value of the current stimulus. And if consummatory pleasure has evaluative content, then so must anticipatory pleasure, or one can no longer endorse a common-currency theory of valence. The conclusions reached in Section 6.2 are thus further reinforced.

Before concluding this section, we should consider whether evaluativism about valence has the resources to explain what Barlassina & Hayward (2019a) call valence's "loopy regulative profile," since they present this as an objection to evaluativism. When one takes a bite out of a ripe strawberry, pleasure at the taste motivates one to take another bite, which in turn produces more pleasure, which in turn motivates yet another bite, continuing

132 Human Motives

until sensory-specific satiety is reached (or one runs out of strawberries, or one decides one has something better to do). This is claimed to support imperativism: pleasure at the first bite has the content, *more of this!*, which motivates taking another bite, which results in a second state with the content, *more of this!*, and so on. In contrast, the loopy regulatory profile of pleasure is said to be difficult for evaluativism to account for. But it is not.

In fact, this sort of case is better explained in a way that utilizes the fundamental distinction between "liking" (current pleasure) and "wanting" (incentive-salience, including anticipatory pleasure), which is fully consistent with evaluativism about pleasure, as we have seen. One takes one's initial bite of the strawberry because, as a result of previous affective learning, the thought of eating it is appraised positively, resulting in anticipatory pleasure. The positive valuation of the resulting taste when one takes that bite (current pleasure, having the content, *this is [nonconceptually] good*, for an evaluativist) is then one of the inputs received by the future-directed appraisal system. Assuming that the latter has not been suppressed by depression or an interfering experimenter, that system is led to anticipate that the next bite will be good, too, as well as issuing in a preparatory motor-urge. The anticipatory pleasure accompanying one's representation of the second bite leads to a decision to take it, which in turn results in more current pleasure, and so on. The "loopy regulatory profile" of pleasure is thus explained.

6.4 Valence and Imperatives in the Brain

There are a number of respects in which imperativism about valence is deeply problematic, as we have seen. But there is an additional argument against imperative theories, this time grounded in quite general facts about the brain networks involved in affect, intention, and action, respectively. For the imperative theory seems to make clear predictions about where, in the brain, signals of pleasure and displeasure should be found. But those predictions turn out to be wrong. I will try to make the discussion as untechnical as possible, giving limited references. But the underlying science is now quite well established.

One would expect that imperative content would be realized in networks closely related to those that initiate and control motor actions, for as we noted earlier, the imperative contents *more of this!* and *less of this!* amount to maximally unspecific motor instructions (*do something to get more of this!* and *do something to get less of this!*). One might therefore expect pleasure and displeasure to be realized in some of the more abstract (less movement-specific) regions of premotor cortex. This is located in a band across the outside upper surface of prefrontal cortex, immediately anterior to motor cortex (which in turn lies just forward of the central sulcus that separates frontal from parietal cortices). Alternatively, one might think of imperative content as being tantamount to an active goal to sustain or get more of (or eliminate or have less of) the event or experience in question. This leads to a similar prediction, since the networks for prospective memory ("what am I going to do?") and for active goal maintenance are centered on the anterior and dorsolateral prefrontal cortex, which partly overlaps the regions just mentioned (Poppenk et al. 2010; Momennejad & Haynes 2013; Cona et al. 2015).

Where, then, are pleasure and displeasure found in the brain? Not in the regions just described. Simplifying hugely, positive valence is realized in networks linking especially subcortical regions of the ventral striatum with regions of orbito-frontal cortex, which is located just behind the eyes, beneath the *lower* surface of prefrontal cortex (not on the upper surface, as are goals and high-level motor plans). Negative valence, in contrast, is mostly realized in networks linking a distinct set of subcortical regions in the ventral striatum with the anterior insula (hidden in the fold between temporal cortex and the lower outside surface of prefrontal cortex), and a separate set of regions of orbito-frontal cortex (Grabenhorst & Rolls 2011; Yarkoni et al. 2011; Chikazoe et al. 2014). Again, these are quite distinct from regions of the brain closely involved in goal-maintenance and motor-urges.

Orbito-frontal cortex is thought to code for outcome values alone, binding valence representations computed in interaction with subcortical structures with incoming sensory or imagistic representations. Nearby regions of ventromedial and medial prefrontal cortex (on the lower *inside* surface of prefrontal cortex, located in the gap between the two hemispheres) are thought to integrate valence with likelihood and energetic costs to provide representations of overall expected value. And then competition among options and with existing goals is resolved through interactions between anterior cingulate cortex (just above medial prefrontal cortex on the inside surface of the brain, immediately above the corpus callosum) and dorsolateral prefrontal cortex (where current goals and intentions are realized), issuing in decisions to act (Wallis 2007; Shenhav et al. 2014, 2018).

The evidence from affective neuroscience, then (albeit highly simplified here) suggests that valence, on the one hand, and intentions/motor-urges, on the other, are realized in very different non-overlapping networks in the brain. It is conceivable that cognitive neuroscientists have gotten it badly wrong, and that orbito-frontal cortex, for example, is really a high-level motor area, coding for high-level motor instructions of the form,

134 Human Motives

do something to get more/less of this!. But it would require very strong philosophical arguments to warrant such a wholesale reworking of current scientific understanding. Indeed, it is not clear that anything a philosopher could say, at this point, would (or should) be sufficient to overturn an established scientific consensus.[9]

6.5 Alleged Counter-Examples to Evaluativism

We have developed a number of powerful arguments against imperativism in general (for the most part ignoring the distinction between world-directed and experience-directed varieties). But we have yet to confront all of the criticisms that imperativists have directed at evaluativism, in turn (although some have been considered in passing earlier). Nor have we considered the arguments that are intended to support experience-directed forms of imperativism over the world-directed variety (and hence to support hedonism). We can begin with these.

Barlassina & Hayward (2019a) claim that pure mood states provide counter-examples to both evaluativism and world-directed imperativism. This is because in such cases there is (allegedly) no worldly object or event to be evaluated, so there is nothing there to be represented as nonconceptually good or bad; and nor is there anything to be the target of a world-directed imperative. In contrast, they say, a bad mood can consist of an experience-directed imperative, *less of this!*, referring just to the person's own state of mind. But although moods can lack an identifiable represented cause (their cause can rather be chemical in nature), they arguably focus on the world, nevertheless. For they generally comprise dispositions to regard the world (and one's own bodily state) in a good or bad light.

For instance, the world in general is apt to seem flat and colorless to someone who is depressed (Lambie & Marcel 2002). One thinks about a hike (normally one's favorite weekend activity) and responds, "Meh!" One anticipates listening to one's favorite piece of music and thinks, "Meh!" And so on, as one considers things one normally enjoys. Now, granted, failing to experience positive anticipatory affect is not the same as experiencing affect that is negative; and yet depression is surely a negative affective state. But Barlassina & Hayward display insufficient awareness of the flexible nature of appraisal

---

[9] Note that only a sample of recent papers has been cited here for what I claim to be the scientific consensus. These could easily have been supported by many, many, more. For book-length discussions, see Rolls (2014) and Adolphs & Anderson (2018).

mechanisms, which can operate on higher-order as well as first-order contents, and can shift with the shifting direction of attention.

To illustrate: thinking about going for a hike, and knowing how much one normally enjoys it (for an evaluativist, how it would normally seem nonconceptually good), but failing to have any positive response, that fact itself can become an object of appraisal. It then seems nonconceptually bad that one fails to experience the usual joy at the thought of a favorite hike. In effect, depression can be characterized as a state in which nothing seems attractive, and the fact that nothing seems attractive seems bad. Likewise, when one shifts attention to one's low-energy, listless, bodily state (characteristic of many forms of depression), that state, too, seems nonconceptually bad, especially in comparison with how one's body normally feels. Parallel things can then be said about positive moods, like cheerfulness. Everything is apt to seem good (or better than normal) to a person in a cheerful mood, and the fact that everything seems good (and that one feels full of energy) itself seems good.

Barlassina & Hayward (2019b) go on to discuss a case of neurological damage that they claim provides an instance of pure valence, lacking any sort of intentional object. This is said to demonstrate the correctness of their own form of reflexive imperativism, and to refute both evaluativism and all other varieties of imperativism. For they think the displeasure the person experiences in this case is comprised of a negative imperative with the content, *less of this!*, where the referent of "this" is just that imperative content itself—there is no other content to be rejected or evaluated. The case in question is that of a man who had suffered stroke-damage to the primary and secondary somatosensory cortices in his right hemisphere. (These are the regions of the brain that normally map bodily feelings like touch and pain to specific locations in the body.) The result was that he was unable to feel any sensations of touch, warmth, cold, or pain in his left hand or arm, but the negative affective component of pain (the painfulness aspect of pain) resulting from laser-stimulation of the left hand was preserved (Ploner et al. 1999).

Barlassina & Hayward (2019b) misdescribe the case, however. It does seem that this person was incapable of feeling sensations of any sort in his left arm or hand. When presented with the following potential descriptors for what he might be feeling under various conditions, he rejected them all: "warm," "hot," "cold," "touch," "burning," "pinprick-like," "slight pain," "moderate pain," and "intense pain." Nevertheless, when his hand was subjected to the kind of laser-stimulation that would normally be experienced as painful pain, he spontaneously described an unpleasant feeling, and the intensity of his expressions of displeasure in fact co-varied with the intensity of the stimulation. Although he was unable to localize the feeling precisely (this is one of the normal functions of primary somatosensory cortex), he was aware that it emanated from somewhere within a broad region extending from his left shoulder to the fingertips of his left hand. So there was, in fact, an intentional object for the negative valence (the painfulness) that he experienced. From an evaluativist perspective, he experienced a nonconceptual representation of badness targeted vaguely at his left fore-limb. Expressed in words, the content of his experience might have been rendered somewhat like this: "Something bad is going on in my left arm or hand." There is no difficulty for evaluativism about valence here (nor for world-directed imperativism).

Barlassina & Hayward (2019a) describe one other case intended to support experience-directed imperativism that is worth discussing here, because of the general point it illustrates about incentive-salience and motivation. This is an example of someone eating junk food without enjoyment—indeed, with some degree of disgust, perhaps—who is nevertheless strongly motivated to keep eating, and who does keep eating. (Many of us have found ourselves in just this sort of situation, unfortunately.) The authors claim that the best explanation here favors experience-directed imperativism: the person in question has an experience-directed imperative with the content, *less of this!* (in virtue of which it is unpleasant), while at the same time having an eating-directed or food-directed imperative, *more of this!*. But in fact evaluativists can make essentially the same move, drawing on the distinction between consummatory pleasure (or in this case, displeasure) and future-directed incentive-salience (in this case, the next bite nevertheless seems attractive, and one has an urge to take it).

One might think that a problem remains with the latter explanation, however. For why would appraisal of the taste of the food (which results in current displeasure) lead to anticipatory pleasure and an urge to eat more? (Actually the same problem surely arises for imperativism, too: why do experience-directed imperatives come apart from food-directed ones?) The answer may be specific to the appetite system, in particular, rather than drawing on properties common to all affective-appraisal systems. In fact, recent evidence shows that food preferences and food motivation (as measured by how much of a substance one ingests in comparison with another) are poorly correlated with reported pleasure, in both humans and animals (Small & DiFeliceantonio 2019; de Araujo et al. 2020). Indeed, one of the main reward-signals driving the acquisition of food preferences and consumption motivations comes from neurons that are sensitive to fat and sugar metabolism in the gut (recall from Section 2.5 that it could be appropriate to describe these signals as forms of unconscious pleasure). This gut-brain reward system seems to operate entirely unconsciously, although its output interacts with conscious forms of flavor conditioning in determining behavior. Moreover, only the conscious flavor-appraisal system is influenced by top-down factors of the sort noted in Section 2.7, such as beliefs about value and about healthiness. The result can be strong incentive-salience (motivation to eat more) in the absence of conscious pleasure. Thus eating the next cold and greasy French fry can seem attractive, and one can have an urge to do it, even though the taste of the present one is unpleasant.[10]

Barlassina & Hayward (2019a) and Barlassina (2020) present a number of other alleged counter-examples, specifically directed against evaluativism about valence (some of these relate to pain, in particular, and will be discussed in Chapter 7 where relevant). But all of them either display a lack of appreciation for how multiple distinct appraisals and re-appraisals can be involved in a single affective state, or failure to take seriously the nonconceptual nature of valence, or both. For example, Barlassina (2020) describes the case of someone looking longingly at a cake in a shop window, wanting to obtain and eat it, only to realize that she has left her wallet at home. Barlassina says that since the cake is evaluated as good, evaluativism should say that she is in a positive affective state; but she is not: she is feeling bad. The response here is obvious: the thought of eating the cake is appraised positively, and issues in anticipatory pleasure; but the subsequent realization that it can't be obtained is appraised negatively and results in displeasure. In general, failure to obtain what one wants (from which one anticipates pleasure) results in frustration and current displeasure.

A similar response can be made to Barlassina's (2020) example of a general and a saint, each of whom is being applauded by the populace for their achievements, and each of whom feels pride. But the general revels in (enjoys) his pride, whereas the saint is mortified—a servant of God should be humble. Here is the obvious explanation: both appraise what they did as worthy achievements, and the applause of the people as expressing admiration, and both undergo nonconceptual representations of the goodness of their situation as a result. But the saint, alone, aware that he feels pride, appraises that fact as a betrayal of everything he stands for, and hence experiences a large-magnitude nonconceptual representation of badness directed at himself as a result. In effect, recognizing his own pride causes him to feel guilty.

---

[10] Notice the resemblance between this sort of case and that of drug-addiction (discussed in Section 2.6), where the drug can be strongly incentive-salient (there is a powerful urge to take it, and doing so seems very good and attractive) although the drug is known not to give pleasure. Notice, too, that like the Garcia effect (disgust at a food that had previously caused illness) conditioning of foods via the gut-brain pathway must rely on a fairly sophisticated computational process to identify which previously eaten food has now resulted in high sugar and/or fat contents in the digestive system.

138 Human Motives

In addition, Barlassina & Hayward (2019a) present an example of a medical trainee and an experienced doctor, both examining a patient's serious injury. But only the trainee finds the experience unpleasant, whereas both see the injury as bad. But of course perceptually representing the badness of an injury can be quite different from affectively appraising it as disgusting, issuing in negative valence directed at what one sees. The same general point applies to Barlassina's (2020) example of the person so drugged-up on affect-suppressing painkillers that he doesn't find looking in the mirror at the mess the dentist has made of his mouth unpleasant, although he can see that his mouth is badly damaged. Again, seeing something as damaged is one thing, appraising it as bad with a normally functioning affective system—and hence experiencing displeasure—is quite another.

6.6 Conclusion

This chapter has compared the relative merits of evaluativism and imperativism. The former construes pleasure and displeasure as analog-magnitude representations of adaptive value and disvalue, respectively. The latter claims that they are maximally unspecific motor urges with the contents, *more of this!* and *less of this!* (different varieties of imperativism then interpret the referent of "this" differently). We have seen that there is nothing in the science of affect that favors imperativism, and that the common-sense intuitions that have been thought to support it fail to do so. Moreover, imperativism makes mistaken predictions about where in the brain pleasure and displeasure should be realized, and it offers an account of the nature of decision-making that is at odds with widely accepted scientific models. It also has difficulty making sense of the well-known distinction between "liking" (consummatory pleasure) and "wanting" (incentive-salience, including anticipatory pleasure)—especially given that imperatives are by their nature future-directed, whereas the role of consummatory pleasure seems to require it to be present-tensed. In addition, we have also seen that there are good explanatory reasons for maintaining that valence has indicative content, representing adaptive value and disvalue, but no good reasons for thinking that it has imperative content.

When the arguments and conclusions of this chapter are put together with those of Chapter 5, we can conclude that evaluativism is the best overall theory of pleasure and displeasure (pending further discussion of the case of pain in Chapter 7, and assuming that the theories of valence we have discussed exhaust the options). It beats out both intrinsic-feeling accounts of the sort discussed in Chapter 5 as well as all varieties of imperative theory discussed here. Moreover, since both intrinsic-feeling and experience-directed-imperative views entail motivational hedonism (and since these seem to be the only scientifically informed views that do so), we can now conclude, at least tentatively, that hedonism has been refuted. Not only do people attach value to many different worldly and social properties, appraising the affective significance of events against those properties (including, generally, the welfare of some other people as well as some moral norms), but their valence-based decision-making, too, is often aimed at securing those valued outcomes for their own sakes, and not for the sake of one's own pleasure or avoidance of one's own displeasure.

It is important to note, however, that in rejecting motivational hedonism and embracing pluralism one need not be denying that pleasure and displeasure have ubiquitous roles in decision-making. On the contrary, one should accept (as was argued in Section 2.5 and again in Chapter 3) that pleasure and displeasure are (along with estimates of likelihood) the main determiners of all or almost all choice. But evaluativism about valence claims that mental states of pleasure and displeasure are the representational *vehicles* of the values involved in choice, not the *objects* of choice. What one chooses among are estimated values, not one's own feelings. And what one subsequently aims for are the valued objects or events chosen, not the feelings or experiences involved in their evaluation.

7
Pain

A Test Case

The debates among the intrinsic-feeling, value-representing, and imperative accounts of valence considered in Chapters 5 and 6 also play out (albeit somewhat differently) in theories of the nature of sensory pain. Indeed, pain—and to a lesser extent other sensory pleasures and displeasures—has been thought to provide a decisive counter-example to representational theories of consciousness, thus purporting to under-cut one of the arguments favoring representational accounts of valence. Moreover, one major objection to value-representing theories of pain is that pain and painfulness seem to lack correctness conditions. To feel pain is to be in pain. There seems to be no possibility of error. Even phantom-limb pain is real pain. This chapter will confront these objections, while at the same time defending a value-representing account of painfulness.

7.1 The Science of Pain: A Primer

This section will outline some of the main scientific findings about the nature of pain, its causes, and its realization in the brain. As usual, I will try to keep the discussion non-technical. We begin at the beginning, with the input.

There are multiple different types of nociception receptor (probably at least ten; Tracey 2017). These are distributed throughout the skin and muscle as "free nerve endings," and also to a lesser extent within internal organs (heart, stomach, and so on). They respond to thermal, mechanical, and a variety of chemical stimuli that are potentially damaging or costly. But they also respond to damage to the receptor nerve itself. Some of these pain receptors are specialized for specific types of stimulus, whereas others are multimodal. For instance, one of the receptor channels sensitive to noxious heat also responds to the active ingredient in chili peppers (so to call foods laced with the latter "hot" is more than a mere metaphor). Moreover, differing types of receptor within the same modality can have different activation thresholds. Thus one type of noxious-heat receptor becomes active above

Human Motives: Hedonism, Altruism, and the Science of Affect. Peter Carruthers, Oxford University Press.
© Peter Carruthers 2024. DOI: 10.1093/oso/9780198906131.003.0007

104°F (40°C), whereas another kicks in at 126°F (52°C). Many of these receptor mechanisms are highly conserved, and have been studied in fruit-fly larvae as well as in mammals (Basbaum et al. 2009; Tracey 2017).

Pain-receptor neurons have an unusual property, in that activation of one dendrite will spread to all the others in the same neuron through a form of back-propagation, resulting in the release of inflammatory chemicals into the surrounding area (this is why the redness and swelling caused by a small lesion typically covers a larger area in the skin around it). And inflammation, in turn—besides facilitating repair and recovery—can sensitize the receptors in that area. Hence sun-burned skin, for example, becomes painful to even gentle forms of touch. Since nociceptive sensitization occurs in invertebrates as well as vertebrates, it is presumably adaptive (Tracey 2017), perhaps because surfaces that are already damaged are especially vulnerable to further damage.

There are two main types of nerve-fiber that transmit nociceptive information onwards to the spinal cord, where they synapse with other neurons. A-delta fibers are myelinated for speed, and are of intermediate width. They are responsible for the initial—acute—onset of pain and its precise location. C-fibers are thin and largely unmyelinated, and are comparably slow. They produce a more diffuse follow-up dull form of pain. Other fibers also synapse nearby in the spinal cord, especially A-alpha fibers, which carry proprioceptive information from the muscles and tendons, and A-beta fibers, which carry touch information (some types of C-fiber, too, carry touch, and are responsible for making gentle stroking feel pleasant). A-alpha and A-beta fibers are larger and significantly faster than nociceptive A-delta and C-fiber pain neurons. And because transmission onwards from the spinal cord is influenced by competition among incoming signals, this means that pain can be partially "gated" by movement and touch (Melzack 1996). This is why manipulating and rubbing a just-bruised limb can result in a reduction in the amount of pain one feels (Mancini et al. 2014).[1]

There are a number of different types of congenital insensitivity to pain, resulting from partial development or absence of peripheral nerve pathways. (There are rarer cases of congenital *indifference* to pain, in which pain is experienced but not felt to be bothersome. These will be discussed shortly.) In some forms, the inability to feel pain is combined with loss of peripheral touch and proprioception, whereas in others it is restricted just to pain and

---

[1] In addition, pain can be modulated by back-projections from primary motor cortex during movement. There are two distinct networks emanating from different layers of cortex, one of which can down-regulate the sensory component of pain, the other its affective (painful) aspect (Gan et al. 2022).

142   Human Motives

temperature sensations (Nagasako et al. 2003). Most such people die in childhood, testifying to pain's adaptive value.

After synapsing in the spinal cord, nociceptive signals are transmitted onwards to the brain via two distinct routes (Treede et al. 1999). The so-called "lateral system" passes information via the sub-cortical thalamus to primary and secondary somatosensory cortices.[2] As we will see shortly, this pathway is responsible for the felt sensory aspect of pain, including its intensity, quality (e.g. burning versus aching), and location. The medial system, in contrast, passes via a distinct set of regions of the thalamus to the amygdala, as well as to the insula and to anterior cingulate cortex.[3] This pathway is responsible for the affective component of pain—its badness or painfulness—as we will see shortly. In addition, both routes output to the supplementary motor area of cortex. There is evidence that the motor and arousal components of pain can be activated prior to both the conscious experience of pain and executively controlled action (Tiemann et al. 2018), just as is the case with other affective states (as we noted in Sections 2.3 and 2.4).

There are multiple lines of evidence that the sensory aspect of pain is distinct from its affective component (negative valence/painfulness). This is now widely accepted, even among philosophers (Dennett 1978; Hardcastle 1999; Corns 2014). For one thing, morphine suppresses the painfulness of pain while having little impact on its sensory qualities or intensity (Kupers et al. 1991). Patients say that their pain is still there, and feels the same, but that they no longer care about it. Additionally, placebo reduction of pain (to be discussed shortly) has its primary impact on the affective dimension of pain, with lesser effects on the sensory component. Moreover, the two components can be or become dissociated, as we now discuss.

With regard to congenital syndromes there is only a one-way dissociation. Perhaps because the affective component relies on an appraisal of the significance of sensory signals, there is no known congenital syndrome that destroys the capacity for pain sensation while leaving pain affect intact. But

---

[2] The thalamus is the main sub-cortical way-station to the cortex for almost all forms of sensory information entering the brain. Primary somatosensory cortex is laid out in the form of a somatotopic map across the top of the brain, just behind the central sulcus that separates frontal from parietal cortices. Secondary somatosensory cortex is hidden in the fold between parietal and temporal cortices, located horizontally just above the insular cortex (which is described in footnote 3).

[3] The amygdala is a complex subcortical structure. It has multiple functions, but is centrally involved in the arousal component of many affective states, and also in fear and fear conditioning. The insular cortex is a vertical surface of cortex hidden behind the fold that separates temporal from frontal and parietal cortices. It receives input from all sensory systems (both external and internal), and is centrally involved in the networks that ascribe value to events in a context-sensitive manner. Anterior cingulate cortex is the frontal part of the cingulate cortex, which lies on the inner (medial) surface of the two hemispheres, wrapping around just above the corpus collosum (which is the thick band of neural fibers linking the two hemispheres together). It, too, is a multi-functional brain hub.

there are rare congenital conditions in which capacities for pain sensation remain intact while those sensations are not experienced as painful (Nagasako et al. 2003). For example, Landrieu et al. (1990) document the case of a girl who could detect pinpricks, heat, cold, touch, joint position, vibration, and pressure in a normal manner, and who also had normal reflexive responses and grimacing to a nociceptive stimulus, while at the same time being indifferent to the continuation of that stimulus. In addition to demonstrating that the negative-valence component of pain is distinct from its sensory aspect, this case also seems to suggest that some forms of spontaneous motor responding to pain are independent of its evaluation.

Acquired syndromes, in contrast, demonstrate a double dissociation. We have already noted in Section 6.5 that damage to primary somatosensory cortex can result in complete loss of pain sensation in the corresponding body part, while the affective/unpleasant aspect of pain is retained (Ploner et al. 1999). Recall that the person in question was aware that something unpleasant was happening somewhere in the region of his left arm (when it was laser-stimulated out of his sight), but that he could neither detect nor localize any touch, temperature, or pain sensations in that arm.

The converse dissociation also exists. Damage to the insula can result in so-called "pain asymbolia," which involves loss of the affective, but not sensory, component of pain (Berthier et al. 1988). (In some patients, pain asymbolia also results in lack of responsiveness to threatening gestures or insults.) Symptoms vary from patient to patient, of course, depending on the precise location and extent of the brain damage involved. But in all cases there is normal sensory discrimination of pain stimuli and their location on the body, sometimes combined with grimacing and withdrawal from an unexpected pain stimulus. But even immersing a limb in ice water is described merely as "cold" (not painful), and the patient shows no inclination to withdraw the limb (Schilder & Stengel 1932). And in one case, for example, the patient would hold a lighted match until her fingers were burned, rather than dropping it or blowing out the flame (Rubins & Friedman 1948). These findings appear to show that the insular cortex is a component of the pain-appraisal network whose integrity is necessary for pain sensations to be experienced as painful.

In addition, surgical removal of the anterior cingulate cortex has been used (seemingly successfully) in the treatment of chronic pain (Sharim & Pouratian 2016). These operations are said to leave the capacity to experience pain sensations intact, while rendering them no longer painful (or in some cases, just much less so). Such claims need to be handled with a good deal of caution, however, for I am aware of no studies that have used a

144 Human Motives

sham-surgery control-condition to test for placebo effects. And yet a recent review of sham-surgery controls for other forms of surgery to treat chronic pain (back pain, abdominal pain, and so on) found no evidence of any benefit of real surgery over sham surgery (Jonas et al. 2016)—both were moderately successful. So it is possible that the effects of cingulotomy on chronic pain are entirely placebo-based.

In fact, there are powerful top-down influences on the experience of pain, both placebo (causing reductions in experienced pain) and nocebo (causing increased pain). Placebo effects on medical outcomes have been known about for centuries, of course, which is why use of placebo-involving control conditions is now an essential tool of scientific medicine. Such effects tend to be largest for broadly affective forms of illness, including chronic pain, depression, anxiety disorders, and irritable-bowel syndrome (as well as Parkinson's disease), as we noted in Section 2.7.

But it is placebo effects on pain, in particular, that are especially relevant for our purposes. These have been heavily investigated (Ashar et al. 2017; Petrie & Rief 2019). It appears that placebos can impact pain via two distinct (albeit interacting) routes (Schafer et al. 2018). One is the patient's beliefs and expectations about treatment. These can be influenced in multiple ways, including verbal instruction, confidence in one's health practitioner and the health system generally, as well as the degree of empathy and understanding displayed by the person administering treatment (Petrie & Rief 2019). The other mechanism is conditioning, which has been explored in animals as well as humans. For example, if treatment is started using a regular analgesic drug, but after a while the drug is replaced by a similar-looking placebo, then reductions in felt pain are generally sustained. The patient has come to associate the stimulus with reduced pain to the point where the stimulus alone serves as an analgesic. As one might expect, the strongest placebo effects can be found when the two mechanisms work together in concert (Ashar et al. 2017). If one's initial expectations of treatment lead to a reduction in pain, then that can in turn give rise to conditioned learning of the analgesic properties of the stimulus used as a placebo. In effect, one's expectations can become self-fulfilling.

There is yet a third mechanism of placebo pain reduction that should be mentioned here, which can serve either to reinforce the effects of the others or operate alone. This is distraction (Buhle et al. 2012). As every parent knows, distracting a child undergoing a painful procedure can reduce or eliminate the amount of pain the child experiences. This is just what one would expect, given that pain is (normally) a conscious experience, and given that consciousness is attention-dependent (Dehaene 2014). Thus, if a placebo treatment is initially partially successful, then one's pain will seem to demand (and will receive) less attention, which will further reduce how much pain one experiences.

Expectancy-based placebo effects rely especially on the brain networks that are used in affective appraisal and evaluative processing generally.[4] Indeed, it may be that placebo-induced reductions in pain result from opponent-processing, or mutually inhibitory competition between pleasure networks and pain networks (Leknes & Tracey 2008). Since anticipating pleasure is itself pleasant (as we saw at length in Chapter 3), and since reduced pain is experienced as rewarding, it may be the pleasure generated by one's placebo-induced expectations that serves to suppress the pain one subsequently feels.

Placebo effects aren't just restricted to affective networks in the brain, however; they can also reach deep down into the spinal cord, releasing chemicals that reduce nociceptive signaling (Eippert et al. 2009). They can also be seen in reduced activity in primary somatosensory cortex. But it is unclear whether (and to what extent) these latter effects result from placebo-reduced transmission upwards through the sensory pain-signaling network, or whether they result rather from reduced attention, for we know that focused attention has a direct effect on the amount and nature of neural activity in sensory cortices generally (Voisin et al. 2006; Runeson et al. 2013; Cutrone et al. 2014).

With this sketch of the scientific findings on pain behind us, we can now embark on our discussion of the nature of pain itself, especially the question of which theory of that nature makes best sense of the science. We will begin with the sensory component of pain, before moving on to discuss its painfulness.

7.2 The Sensation of Pain

In Chapter 5 we discussed—and critiqued—intrinsic-feeling accounts of valence. Such accounts have been offered for the painfulness (negative-valence component) of pain, too, as we will see in Section 7.3. But some have also claimed that the sensory component of pain is just an experiential feeling—a sensation—lacking any sort of representational content (Aydede

---

[4] These include the ventromedial prefrontal cortex, orbitofrontal cortex, and the subcortical ventral striatum (Schafer et al. 2018), as we noted in Section 2.7 when discussing top-down effects on all forms of affective feeling.

146 Human Motives

2019; Aydede & Fulkerson 2019). On this view, the sensation of pain is merely a distinctive sort of phenomenal feeling, or qualia.

An initial puzzle for the intrinsic-feeling account is to explain how pain sensations can nevertheless be physically located in specific regions of the body. One feels pain in one's toe (from gout), or in one's calf (from cramp), or in one's back (from a pulled muscle), and so on. But qualia are supposed to be intrinsic properties of experience. Yet surely there are no experiences in one's toe, or calf, or back. Experiences belong to the mind, not the body. Or so most of us believe. But since the phenomenal-feeling account of pain denies that feelings of pain *represent* properties of locations in one's body, it might be thought that it therefore requires us to conceive of the mind itself as being distributed throughout the body, with some mental states themselves being located in one's limbs or in one's torso. That would be a hard pill to swallow.

The best response for an intrinsic-feeling theorist is to claim that these intrinsic pain-sensation qualia attach, not to specific body locations, but rather to *representations* of those locations within the subject's body schema. The latter is a multisensory representation of the body, which is continually updated as one moves (Berlucchi & Aglioti 1997; Maravita et al. 2003; de Vignemont 2010). Much of the time it operates beneath awareness, but it can also be a component in conscious experience. Either way, pain-sensation qualia can be said to attach to it, rather than to the body itself. So a pain in the toe can be an intrinsic felt property of a *representation* of the toe, rather than of the toe itself. Hence, just as valence is supposed to be an intrinsic property attaching to one's experiences of the world (according to the intrinsic-feeling account of valence discussed in Chapter 5), then so too are bodily sensations intrinsic properties of one's experience: in this case, one's experience of the spatial distribution and movements of one's own body.

The real problem for the intrinsic-feeling account is that pain sensations carry information about the body, and the fact that they carry that information explains how the roles of those mental states have become stabilized in one's cognitive economy—in particular, becoming targets of pain-related motivation and giving rise to negative valence by default. (Quite *what* information plays this explanatory role is something we will return to shortly.) So pain sensations seem to satisfy the requirements for qualifying as representational. Now, this is by no means a knock-down argument, for if pain sensations are representational, then they must also be capable of representing wrongly; indeed, it must be possible for them to be completely illusory. But although phantom-limb pain sensations, for example, are felt in a non-existent limb (hence the limb is an illusory component of the person's body schema), we don't count the pain sensation itself as illusory. This is said to be a problem for representational theories of pain (Aydede & Fulkerson 2019). We will return to it in Section 7.4.

Imperativists about valence have generally accepted that the sensory component of pain is a representation of bodily damage of some sort (Martínez 2011; Barlassina & Hayward 2019a), as do most value-representing theorists (Cutter & Tye 2011; Bain & Brady 2014). But not all agree. In particular, Klein (2015) thinks that the sensory component of pain itself has imperative content. We have already seen enough in Section 7.1 to conclude that he is right, at least to a limited degree. For it seems that the sensory component of pain can initiate motor responding directly, independently of evaluative appraisal.

Some care needs to be taken here, however, because sudden-onset pain stimuli can initiate reflexive withdrawal controlled by synapses in the spinal cord, without any cortical contribution. So if actions are movements that are cortically controlled by motor plans, as we suggested in Section 2.2, then reflexively jerking one's hand away from contact with a red-hot saucepan is not an action. Rather, it belongs in the same category as the reflexive knee-jerk caused by one's doctor tapping one's leg beneath the kneecap. It is likely that the motor signals that initiate such movements are too low-level to qualify as representations of any sort, imperative or otherwise.

However, we have also seen that in people with pain asymbolia, who say they aren't bothered by their pain sensations and make no attempt to withdraw their hand from a bucket of iced water in consequence, will nevertheless grimace at the onset of pain, and may make simple initial withdrawal movements (Schilder & Stengel 1932; Berthier et al. 1988). The latter may be reflexive, but the former surely is not. A grimace requires coordinated activation of a number of different muscles, and is cortically controlled rather than emanating directly from the spinal cord. And in any case it seems likely that the sensory pain pathway, because connected directly to motor areas of cortex (as we noted earlier), may initiate simple expressive and avoidance actions independently of any contribution from the affective pathway. In which case one might say that pain sensations (at least those with a sudden onset) can carry imperative contents such as, *make a grimace, say "ouch,"* or, *lift that hand*.

Even if this is accepted, however, similar reasoning to that employed in our critique of the intrinsic-feeling view of valence can be used to show that pain sensations are at least "pushmi-pullyu" representations (Millikan 1995). For in addition to their limited imperative content, they also carry information about the impact of events on the body; and that information surely plays a role in explaining why the sensory component of pain has the functional and computational roles that it does. Which brings us back to the question of what a representationalist about sensations of pain should say about their representational content. What is it, exactly, that pain sensations represent?

Philosophers who have addressed this question (and who think that pain sensations represent anything at all), have been nearly unanimous. Pain sensations represent bodily harm or tissue damage (Cutter & Tye 2011; Martínez 2011; Barlassina & Hayward 2019a), or perhaps risk of tissue damage (Bain 2017). This has the advantage of explaining why pain sensations should be negatively appraised by default, hence reliably acquiring negative valence (being felt as painful). And it seems intuitively correct if one thinks of examples like cutting one's finger while chopping onions, or burning one's hand when picking up a hot saucepan. But it is much less plausible for other forms of pain.

Consider immersing your arm in a bucket of iced water. This will quickly become quite painful. But it is doubtful that the pain represents actual tissue damage, or even risk of damage, since iced water won't cause the skin itself to freeze (resulting in frostbite). Moreover, immersion in water with temperatures significantly higher than freezing is still experienced as painful. It seems more plausible that the cold-temperature pain receptors are responding in a manner designed to maintain thermostasis. The risk signaled is one of hypothermia rather than tissue damage as such.

Now consider heat nociception. Imagine stepping outside in Arizona in August when the temperature is 122°F (50°C) in the shade. It is so hot it hurts. One might describe what it feels like by saying, "My skin is burning." But the skin itself isn't at risk of being damaged in ambient temperatures that high. The risk, rather, is that one will soon be unable to maintain one's core body temperature—the risk is one of hyperthermia. The pain one feels is, plausibly, designed to provide an incentive to do something to cool down— splashing water on oneself, for example, or drinking more; and by staying as immobile as possible. Thus it is beginning to seem as if pain sensations might represent a variety of types of risk to one's bodily integrity, in addition to actual tissue damage.

Muscle pain caused by ongoing exercise is different again. Some free nerve-ending receptors in muscles are sensitive to relatively low levels of the chemicals released during exercise, whereas others only become active at higher levels (Jankowski et al. 2013). The outputs of the former type are negatively valenced, but would not normally be described as painful; rather, they give rise to feelings of fatigue or tiredness. They provide a rough index of one's effort and energy expenditure during various kinds of daily activity, and learning from their feedback is what enables one to estimate whether it would be better to walk to a destination across a small hill or take a longer route around, for example. In fact, choice among actions is always sensitive to the estimated effort required to undertake each of the alternatives, as we noted in Sections 3.4 and 3.5.

Normal muscle pain during more-intense forms of ongoing exercise is produced by the activity of a second group of nociceptor muscle neurons. Their increasingly urgent signaling is what makes it *hurt* to engage in intense exercise. Pain-generating neurons in the muscles respond to a variety of stimuli, including mechanical compression of the muscles themselves, as well as a number of exercise-induced chemical substances released within them. In some instances what might be signaled is risk of tissue damage, since some forms of exercise can result in micro-tears within the muscle fibers. But this can't be the whole story, since micro-tearing (and its associated delayed-onset muscle soreness a day or two later) results only from what is called "eccentric" exercise, in which there is controlled *lengthening* of muscles under tension (such as occurs in one's biceps when lowering one's body from a chin-up, or when raising one's body during a push-up). Forms of painful exercise such as holding one's arms horizontally for as long as one can, or climbing on a steeply-inclined stair-master, don't result in muscle micro-tearing (Contrò et al. 2016; Mizumura & Taguchi 2016).

What is it that non-damaging forms of exercise-induced pain sensations represent, then? Not tissue damage, for these forms of exercise do no damage. Nor do they even represent *risk* of tissue damage, since the muscles in question will simply become inoperable before damage occurs. Moreover, even when employed with maximal effort, there is always a "reserve" still remaining in the muscles themselves, which can be evoked artificially (Gandevia 2001). And in fact, as exercise-induced pain increases, so there is a reduction in central signaling from the motor cortex to activate the muscles in question, even when one continues to try as hard as one can (Kennedy et al. 2014). Signaling between the brain and the muscles appears to be regulated by a complex set of predictive feedback loops designed to ensure that one never exceeds the limits of bodily homeostasis (Noakes 2011).

It seems likely that the pain sensations created by muscle activity during exercise correlate with (and represent) calorific resource depletion (at least in part). All forms of movement take energy, of course, so the negative valence created by normal daily activities can figure into a cost–benefit analysis of the various actions open to one, as we noted earlier. More extreme forms of exercise are much more demanding of energetic resources, not just through the activity of the peripheral muscles themselves, but also via

150   Human Motives

increases in the activity of a range of physiological systems that ramp up oxygen availability (heart rate, breathing rate) and maintain temperature control (sweating, re-directing blood flow to the surface). Moreover, we know that feelings of effort induced by exercise (as measured by one's motivation to stop) are at least partly mediated by feelings of muscle pain (O'Connor & Cook 1999; Norbury et al. 2022).

In addition to calorific costs, however, it may be that pain sensations caused by effortful exercise also signal an opportunity cost. It will help at this point to compare physical effort with contemporary theories of *cognitive* effort. This, too, arguably depends on affective appraisal of an analog-magnitude signal, in this case representing the extent of executive-system engagement (Carruthers 2021); and this signal, too, is experienced as aversive by default. Focused concentration is generally hard (unpleasant), as is continuing to maintain concentration across a series of cognitively demanding tasks. This seems to be an initial—innate—default setting, and can be demonstrated across a range of different species (Winstanley & Floresco 2016; Inzlicht et al. 2018). But processes of normal evaluative conditioning can lead rats as well as humans to shift their default appraisals, to the point where some cognitively demanding activities are experienced as rewarding (Eisenberger 1992; Hosking et al. 2016). Hence people can come to enjoy doing crossword puzzles or tackling difficult chess problems. Degrees of engagement of cognitive effort in a given task are thought to be underlain by computations of the *expected value of control* (Shenhav et al. 2017; Inzlicht et al. 2018). People decide how much effort to invest in a cognitive task by calculating over the estimated value of the outcome, the likelihood of achieving that outcome, and the estimated aversiveness (or otherwise) of exercising the necessary executive control.

Currently the best theory of what it is that signals of cognitive effort represent isn't calorie-depletion in one's prefrontal "brain muscle," as was once believed (Masicampo & Baumeister 2008), for the so-called "ego depletion" model of effort has now been pretty thoroughly undermined (Kurzban 2010; Hagger et al. 2016; Vadillo et al. 2016). Rather, it is thought to be the opportunity cost of not utilizing one's attentional resources elsewhere, for other purposes—such as monitoring the environment for risks and threats, or engaging in mind-wandering or offline planning (Kurzban et al. 2013; Inzlicht et al. 2018). The default aversiveness of cognitive effort can be seen as evolution's best guess at what those opportunity costs are, on average. Now, notice that in the case of vigorous exercise, too, there are opportunity costs in addition to the obvious direct cost of energy expenditure. One could be using one's energetic resources for other purposes. Moreover, intense exercise may leave one physically depleted, making one vulnerable to attack thereafter, for example.[5]

It seems that the message carried by pain sensations resulting from vigorous exercise might be something along the lines of, "Be sure that this is worth it!" In addition to signaling a risk of muscle tearing, the default content carried by exercise-induced sensations of pain (prior to evaluative learning and top-down modulation from cognitive appraisals) can be construed as an evolutionarily selected combination of both energetic costs and opportunity costs. These signals are mapped to somatosensory cortex where the sources of the pain can be localized in the body, but they are also (via a separate route) received as input by cortical and subcortical evaluative networks where they issue (by default) in proportional degrees of displeasure, or painfulness.

The upshot of our discussion is that the best account of the representational content of sensory pain is a pluralist one. Some types of pain represent a combination of energetic and opportunity costs, as we have just seen. Some represent potentially dangerous deviations from bodily thermostasis (either too hot or too cold). Others represent actual or potential tissue damage, whether mechanical, chemical, or resulting from extreme forms of localized heat (e.g. contact with a burning match). In each case the information carried by the pain signals in question, which serves to explain why signals of that sort should be negatively appraised by default (and felt as painful), is markedly different. All of the likely outcomes can be characterized similarly, of course—for all are maladaptive. But that is arguably the content of the negative valence (the painfulness) that is subsequently attached to pain sensations, as we will see in Section 7.3. As for the pain sensations themselves, it seems that the four main types represent different sorts of generally maladaptive properties (energy depletion combined with opportunity costs, hypothermia, hyperthermia, and tissue damage or risk thereof). Consistent with this suggestion, note that the different kinds of pain automatically initiate differing types of ameliorative behavior (ceasing contact with a stimulus in the case of tissue-damage pain and localized hypothermic pain; seeking sources of warming or cooling in connection with body-wide hypothermic and hyperthermic pain, as well as increases in shivering or sweating; and

---

[5] This fact is exploited by persistence hunters, who will chase an animal (normally during the heat of the day), keeping it continually on the move, until it is too exhausted to resist and can be killed at close quarters (Liebenberg 1990). Even cheetahs can be successfully hunted in this way, resulting from a combination of the advantage that human sweat-glands give us in the heat, swift tracking abilities when the animal initially disappears from sight, together with the foresight to fill up with water before beginning the chase.

152   Human Motives

ceasing local and/or global activity in connection with muscle pain). This suggests the existence of specialized pain-sensation sub-systems.[6]

7.3 The Painfulness of Pain

The same three basic kinds of account of pain's painfulness mirror the three types of theory of valence in general, discussed in Chapters 5 and 6. Imperativists say that painfulness is comprised of an imperative with the content, *less of this!*, where "this" can either be held to refer to the bodily state represented by the pain sensation (Martínez 2011) or to the phenomenal experience caused by that state (Barlassina & Hayward 2019b). Intrinsic-feeling theorists say (or should say—see below) that painfulness is an intrinsic property possessed by most pain sensations, where the feeling in question provides feedback in the present for evaluative learning, as well as influencing avoidance-related decision-making when anticipated (Aydede & Fulkerson 2019). And value-representing theorists say that painfulness represents some natural evaluative property, whether bodily harm (Cutter & Tye 2011), the sensation being "bad for one in a bodily sense" (Bain 2013), or maladaptiveness more generally (which is the view I am defending here).

Imperativist accounts of painfulness have nothing new to add to imperativist accounts of valence generally, and are subject to all of the problems discussed in Chapter 6. Specifically, they make mistaken predictions about the brain networks that should underlie painfulness, they seem forced to accept that painfulness is at least a "pushmi-pullyu" representation with indicative as well as imperative content, and they mistakenly make the content of painfulness future-directed rather than present-tensed. Admittedly, the latter error is a bit less obvious in the case of pain than it is for pleasure, and there is no familiar scientific language of "disliking" versus "disincentive-salience" to mirror the well-established distinction between "liking" (pleasure) and "incentive-salience." But the same distinction holds. Painfulness itself is a present-tensed, "consummatory," or feedback signal used in evaluative learning (it is a primitive punisher). In many cases, admittedly, present painfulness gives rise to an anticipation of immediately future painfulness, which will activate avoidance motor-plans by default and make whatever seems to be causing the pain seem bad and to be avoided (disincentive-salient). But the only imperative representations to figure here are the motor urges

---

[6] The representational-pluralist account of the sensory component of pain developed in this section owes a debt to Coninx (2021), as well as to discussions of that paper with Chris Masciari, in addition to the latter's own draft paper on the same topic.

that accompany anticipated continuing pain; and these are distinct from both present-tensed and anticipatory painfulness.

Intrinsic-feeling accounts of painfulness, too, are subject to the same set of criticisms of intrinsic-feeling theories of valence generally, discussed in Chapter 5. Specifically, they give rise to an evolutionary puzzle ("Why should evolution care about feelings, rather than about what those feelings carry information about?"), and they, too, seem forced to accept that the intrinsic-feeling in question is *also* a representation of value, since it checks all the explanatory boxes for being one. Moreover, intrinsic-feeling accounts are inconsistent with representational theories of consciousness. But since the main espousers of the view fully embrace this conclusion, it will be worth considering their own positive theory here, before we transition to their negative arguments against value-representing theories of painfulness in the remaining sections of the chapter.

Aydede & Fulkerson (2019) present and defend what they describe as a psycho-functionalist theory of pain's sensory and affective components. They say that pain experience/pain phenomenology is realized in (and is thus reductively explicable in terms of) a complex set of underlying functional processes. Signals normally caused by tissue damage undergo what they call "m-processing." This includes an appraisal of the signal for its personal significance, priming of motor systems, avoidance motivation, and negative reinforcement of preceding actions. Pain phenomenology itself is thought to split into a nonconceptual experience component (which is not representational) and a nonconceptual desire-like component (which they call "experiential desiring" or "phen-desiring").

This is all quite unfortunate, and surely not the best way to develop an intrinsic-feeling account of pain and pain's painfulness. By lumping everything together under "sensory affect" they fail to distinguish between the motor-urges that one can consciously experience when in pain (e.g. urges to grimace, cry out, cringe away, and so on) and the unpleasantness of the pain itself. Moreover, the learning signal that serves to update one's expected values and negatively reinforces previous actions is *caused by* pain's painfulness (following comparison with the degree of painfulness expected), not constitutive of it. And by describing the overall painfulness feeling as a sort of experiential desiring they confront the same difficulty we noted for imperativism: painfulness is present-tensed, whereas desires are, by their nature, aimed at distal events (e.g. in the future).

A better way to develop an intrinsic-feeling account would be to distinguish clearly between the present-tensed valence component of pain (its painfulness), anticipations of continued painfulness (disincentive-salience), and the motor-urges to which pain gives rise. On this view, the feeling that is the painfulness of pain is among the causal effects of an appraisal of the incoming sensory signals of pain for personal significance in the light of previous learning, context, and expectations. (The sensory signal can itself be construed as a distinct sort of intrinsic bodily feeling, for these purposes.) Moreover, the painfulness-feeling is a primitive punisher, negatively conditioning events and actions that are predictive of it. And when matched against stored expectations of painfulness, it generates an error signal that changes the negative weight attached to events of the sort in question in future appraisals. And then in addition, when expectations are actively formed, they make the anticipated feeling seem intrinsically bad and avoidance-worthy in one's decision-making. This sort of intrinsic-feeling view will be assumed as the best candidate of this type going forward. (Note, however, that it is still vulnerable to all the main arguments against intrinsic-feeling accounts of valence generally, discussed in Chapter 5.)

Turning now to value-representing theories of pain's painfulness, existing accounts characterize the content represented too narrowly. If painfulness is a representation of bodily harm (Cutter & Tye 2011) or of "badness in a bodily sense" (Bain 2013), then it cannot form part of a common-currency of negative valence generally. These theories would leave unexplained how one can affectively weigh up a certain degree of physical painfulness against a certain amount of social disapproval or a certain degree of disgust. Indeed, all of the reasons that favor a common-currency view of valence, outlined in Section 2.5, by the same token speak against these representational theories of painfulness. In fact, the only account that has the required generality is the one outlined in Section 5.2. This holds that painfulness (and negative valence/displeasure generally) is a representation of some degree of maladaptiveness. In short, painful events are represented (nonconceptually— certainly not conceptually and as such, of course) as maladaptive. This is the property we need to appeal to in explaining how the pain system, its default appraisal of sensory pain signals, and the structure of the surrounding learning and modulating systems have been designed and stabilized.

It is a consequence of this account (as it is of any value-representing theory of painfulness) that many painful pains *mis*represent the sensational component as bad and/or maladaptive. Thus the pain involved in a prostate exam represents what is happening as (nonconceptually) bad, when it is in fact (in the context of modern medicine) highly adaptive. Section 5.6 argued, when discussing valence generally, that this sort of consequence of value-representing theories doesn't amount to a serious objection to such accounts.

Sections 7.4 and 7.5 will discuss whether it causes any problem for the value-representing theory of the painfulness of pain, in particular.

In many cases, of course, it will be quite hard to know whether a given pain is representing what is happening correctly or incorrectly, let alone to what precise extent it is doing so. While the default painfulness of pain is plainly adaptive, and while the learning and top-down pain-modulating systems have likewise been structured by natural selection (and so are presumably adaptive on the whole), in any given case it may be impossible to know whether the results of that learning, or of that top-down modulation, are themselves adaptive or not. And it will be even harder to know whether the extent of painfulness felt in any given case matches or diverges from its degree of maladaptiveness, and if so by how much. But this is just an epistemic limitation (albeit a deep one); it cannot form the basis for a challenge to our account of the *nature* of pain and painfulness.

7.4 Erroneous Pains

One problem confronting an indicative-representation theory of pain and painfulness (as opposed to an imperative-representation one) is that we ordinarily think that to *feel* pain—to *experience* pain—*is* to be in pain; and the extent of one's pain is just the extent to which one feels it (Aydede & Fulkerson 2019). In fact, there appears to be no room for an is/seems distinction in the case of pain: to feel pain is to be in pain. Indicative-representation theories, in contrast, imply that some pains are illusory or incorrect. Moreover, it isn't just ordinary folk who would reject the latter view. No pain scientist would tell a patient that the pain they feel in their phantom limb doesn't really exist, or isn't really pain. (Indeed, the International Association for the Study of Pain defines pain—in part—as "an unpleasant sensory and emotional *experience*" [emphasis added].) But on a representational theory, this appears to be what one has to say: the experience of pain in a phantom limb represents the presence of tissue damage in the limb and represents it as maladaptive. But it is neither of those things (or it isn't *directly* maladaptive, at any rate; for as Martínez 2015 points out, feelings of pain can be like email spam—they interrupt and distract).

On one level, this is not a deep problem. It is as if we had opted to use the word "see," not as a success-verb, but rather just to refer to visual experience as such, whether veridical or not. This wouldn't prevent visual experiences from having correctness-conditions, of course. In that case, instead of saying

156 Human Motives

that someone hallucinating a pink elephant isn't really *seeing* a pink elephant, we would say, "Yes, you see it; but there is no elephant there." And note that we do sometimes use the word "hear" to refer just to the experience of hearing, as when we describe a schizophrenic patient as "hearing voices." But no one thinks this conflicts with the representational nature of audition.

In the same way a pain-scientist might say to someone with phantom-limb pain, "Yes, you have pain in your arm; but there is no arm and no damage there." But then the question becomes: why? Why, if a representational theory of pain is true, do we systematically use the word "pain" to refer to the representing-event, rather than to the event represented? Why do we always use it to refer to the experience of pain, rather than to what is experienced (represented)?

An initial point to make in reply is that the representational theory of pain is not intended as an account of our folk-psychological conception of pain. It is meant rather as a theory of the real *nature* of pain. Moreover, it is easy to see how the folk conception has ended up as it has. This is because pains are not inter-subjectively available in the way that colors, for example, are. The same colored surface can be perceived by more than one person, and if the color is described differently by different people, there can be debate about who is right. In addition, we have a nascent folk theory of the factors that can influence color perception. We know, for example, that a white object seen under a green light will appear greenish, that the same object seen through rose-tinted glasses will appear pink, that the object won't be seen at all in the dark, and so on. As a result, we have use for an is/seems distinction in the case of color. We allow that although something is really white, it seems green to everyone present (when in green light), or pink to one person in particular (when wearing the glasses), or no way at all (in the dark). But the same pain cannot be felt by more than one person. Pains are inherently subjective, in a way that colors are not. Nor do we have much in the way of a folk theory of the processes that cause and modulate pain experience.

It is no surprise, then, that a theory saying that pain experience is, in fact, much like color experience (it is representational) should conflict with our common-sense theories. Nor is it hard to see why the scientists who study pain should adopt the language of common sense, for they can say everything that they want to say within its framework. They can say, "The pain you feel in your shoulder is actually caused by trouble with your heart" (in a case of referred pain); and, "The pain in your arm is caused by persistent firing of the damaged pain-nerves in your shoulder" (in a case of phantom-limb pain), and so on. Moreover, pain scientists are mostly focused on understanding pain and painfulness as part of a search for ways to ameliorate pain.

They are not in the business of explaining how painfulness can be traded off in coherent ways against other forms of pleasure and displeasure, which is where common-currency accounts of valence get to earn their keep. It is, then, but a small step from here, once one accepts the correctness of some form of informational theory of representational content, to saying that the pain felt in the shoulder misrepresents the pain's location, and that the pain felt in a phantom limb misrepresents both the location of tissue damage and its maladaptiveness.

7.5 Pain's Transparency

Aydede (2019) develops a different argument against representational theories of pain and painfulness. It turns especially on a claim generally made by defenders of representational theories of consciousness, that conscious experience is *transparent* to introspection. The claim is that when we introspect our conscious experience we are aware of no properties of the experience beyond those that the experience represents. When we introspect our experiences we "see" right through them, as it were, to the world (or states of the body) represented; thus, there are no qualia, no intrinsic properties, attaching to those experiences themselves. Aydede argues, in contrast, that sensations of pain (on a representationalist construal of them) are *not* transparent to introspection. So representationalism about pain must be false.

Aydede (2019) begins by developing an account of what transparency amounts to in the case of color experience. He argues first, that the content of one's visual experience when viewing a red tomato is, *that is red and round*. Then second, when one introspects that experience, the content of one's introspective awareness is, *I am experiencing that as red and round*. This presupposes, he claims, that one possesses what he calls the "*de re* labeling concepts" RED and ROUND. So the transparency of experience presupposes *de re* (non-descriptive, directly applicable) labeling concepts for the properties represented in experience. Yet, in contrast to the case of visual experience, we lack any such concepts for the properties said to be represented by pain, such as DAMAGE. We can only tell that a body-part is damaged inferentially, not by direct recognition.

The two key premises of this argument are each false, however; and the way in which they are false shows us something important about the content of *both* color experience *and* pain experience. First, color (and other kinds of) experience need not contain concepts at all. A child lacking concepts of redness and roundness can still experience the red tomato, of course. The nonconceptual content of the percept involved will be something along the lines of, *that [shape quality] has that [color quality]*. Likewise, introspecting one's experience requires no concepts beyond the concept EXPERIENCE. The content of one's introspection can just be something like this: *I am experiencing that [roundness quality] having that [redness quality]*. Similarly, someone introspecting an experience of pain in their toe can merely be entertaining the content, *I am experiencing that [pain quality] there*. No further concepts are needed.

It is important to see, in fact, that in neither color perception nor pain perception are the properties that representationalists use to characterize the correctness conditions of the states represented *as such*. Representationalists about color generally say that what is represented by color experiences are reflectance properties of surfaces. For these are the properties that color vision carries information about, and that explain the genesis and stabilization of the perceptual states in question. But of course color vision doesn't require, nor actively involve, the concept REFLECTANCE, nor anything of the sort. Rather, it comprises a set of multi-dimensional analog-magnitude representations that bear various similarity-and-difference relations to one another, as can be depicted in the well-known hue-and-brightness cone (Rosenthal 2010; Lau et al. 2022).

Here we need to recall the distinction introduced in Section 5.7, between the *reference* or *correctness-conditions* of color perception and pain perception, on the one hand, and their *modes of presentation* to the perceiver, on the other. In specifying the correctness-conditions of color perception for explanatory purposes in cognitive science, we need to do it in terms of reflectance properties of surfaces. These are the natural (real) properties that the visual signals carry information about, and that explain the genesis and cognitive role of the resulting visual states. But the mode of presentation of those properties to a perceiver is merely that of a set of analog-magnitude properties of surfaces, which are more-or-less similar or different from other such properties along a number of different dimensions (as already noted, vision scientists capture these relations in the color-cone).[7,8]

---

[7] Recall from Section 5.7, moreover, that these similarity spaces in modes of presentation need not map smoothly onto equivalent physical similarities in the objects represented. Rather, the relevant physical similarities are the ones that matter from the perspective of the organism, impacting fitness.

[8] How are modes of presentation in color experience related to the phenomenon of color constancy, where two surfaces that appear different in color (because of differences in lighting) are nevertheless seen as having the *same* color? Not by identifying modes of presentation with the seeming-differences (as does Thompson 2009). Rather, two distinct analog-magnitudes can be simultaneously components of one's visual experience, one of which represents each surface considered in isolation, whereas the other represents them in a way that is influenced and modulated by the other (and by any other visual cues that might be available). The result is a *layered* representation of color, similar to the way in which shape

Likewise, I suggest, in the case of pain perception. The correctness conditions of sensations of pain (the natural properties that the perceptual states in question pick out or refer to) need to be specified in terms of various forms of bodily risk, damage, or costliness (as we saw in Section 7.2). But from the subject's perspective, there is just an analog-magnitude property instantiated in some specific location or region of the body, which can be distinguished from and compared with other such properties, and which can be more or less intense. Admittedly, in the case of pain, the psychophysical work has not yet been done to specify the nature of its modes of presentation, in the sort of way that vision science has done for color. But common sense already distinguishes among a number of different types of pain sensations, some described in terms of their paradigmatic bodily causes. Thus there are stinging pains, burning ones, icy ones, stabbing ones, throbbing ones, and so on.

Properly understood, the transparency-thesis with respect to color vision amounts to this: when one introspects one's experience of color one is aware of nothing beyond a set of analog-magnitude properties of surfaces that bear similarity-and-difference relations to one another, where these properties are, in fact, nothing over-and-above physical analog-magnitude properties of the surfaces in question.[9] And likewise, then, in the case of sensations of pain. We can say that when one introspects one's pains one is aware of nothing beyond a (different) set of analog-magnitude properties of some-or-other region of one's body, that bear similarity-and-difference relations to other such properties. We can insist that pain sensations are transparent in just the same sense that other perceptual experiences are, in fact.

7.6 Pains as Reasons

Aydede & Fulkerson (2019) and Barlassina & Hayward (2019a) each raise essentially the same objection to indicative-representation theories of pain. The problem is to explain how a pairing of representations of how things are (an analog-magnitude representation of bodily risks, damage, or costs, together

---

perception is layered into context-free perspectival representations of shape (e.g. oval, for a penny seen obliquely) together with an all-cues-considered representation of allocentric shape—in this case, round (Green 2022a, 2022b). Such layering of perceptual content most likely results from the fact that attentional signals directed at midlevel sensory areas of the brain are what select representations for entry into working memory and conscious status, with higher-level contents being added and broadcast as processing continues (Prinz 2012; Carruthers 2015).

[9] Note that the analog-magnitude properties that constitute the mode-of-presentation of color to the perceiver are *identical with* the reflectance properties of surfaces that constitute the correctness-conditions of color perception. So there are no additional properties involved in experience beyond representations of reflectance properties; and color experience can still be transparent to introspection.

with an analog-magnitude representation of badness or maladaptiveness) can explain the motivational and reason-giving role of pain. Underlying the objection is that both pairs of authors assume a version of Humean theory of motivation according to which belief-like states and perceptual states (states with truth-conditions or correctness-conditions) cannot motivate action. As a result, and in contrast, Aydede & Fulkerson argue that the affective component of pain is a nonconceptual desire-like state, whereas Barlassina & Hayward maintain that it is an experience-directed imperative.

We have already responded to one version of this argument (framed in terms of valence more generally) in Section 5.2. But it may be worth revisiting and elaborating on that reply here. There are a number of points to be made. One is that our topic is the real nature of motivation, not our common-sense beliefs about motivation. If the science of affect is best interpreted as demonstrating that indicative representations of value are capable of motivating, whereas common sense denies it, then so much the worse for common sense. Philosophers who approach questions about the structure and operations of the mind by consulting their intuitions on the matter are proceeding in a way that is methodologically unsound (Carruthers 2025). Common-sense beliefs are a poor guide to the real structure of the world (and of the mind).

A second point is that appraisal of the personal significance of incoming sensory pain signals produces two distinct outputs in parallel, one of which *is* genuinely imperative-like. Pains directly activate expressive motor-plans (e.g. for grimacing) as well as avoidance ones (such as an urge to withdraw one's arm from a bucket of ice water). But these are separate and distinct from the experienced painfulness of the sensation (its negative valence). The latter plays two roles: it is a primitive punisher, causing one to negatively evaluate future actions and events of the sort that preceded the pain; and when the degree of painfulness differs from one's previous expectations for events of the kind that produced it, one's stored evaluation of events of that kind is updated to some extent.

Third, neither present-tensed pleasure nor present-tensed painfulness motivate directly, in any case (rather, they play the rewarding/punishing and value-updating roles). It is *anticipations* of pleasure and painfulness that motivate, giving rise, respectively, to incentive-salience and disincentive-salience. This, too, splits into two components: on the one hand, motor-activation of actions that have previously resulted in pleasure or the avoidance of pain, together with motor-activations of the sort that underlie attention to the anticipated event or its precursors; and on the other hand, representations of value or disvalue that play a critical role in decision-making (including decisions about whether to allow the accompanying motoric component to be executed or suppressed).

As we have repeatedly stressed (for instance in Section 6.2), the motivating role of anticipatory valence (representations of future value) is not a direct one; rather, it is among the main inputs to decision-making processes. Anticipatory painfulness (whether a continuation of a current pain or the initiation of a new one) competes with other representations of value and disvalue, modulated by estimates of likelihood, to issue in decisions. The resulting goal-states or intentions have an imperative-like quality. But all of the inputs to the decision-making process itself are indicative ones: representations of the anticipated event, analog-magnitude representations of likelihood, and analog-magnitude representations of goodness and badness (adaptive value and disvalue). If this conflicts with common-sense intuitions, then so be it. No one should think that common sense is a reliable guide to the real structure of the world or mind.

Aydede & Fulkerson (2019), Barlassina & Hayward (2019a), and others develop an additional argument against indicative-representation theories of pain. They claim that the latter cannot explain the rationalizing and justifying roles of pain in cases where the pain itself is a complete *mis*representation. Consider someone whose forearm has become hypersensitive to touch as a result of an earlier injury, so that even light stroking is intensely painful. The stroking does no damage, and the person might know full-well that it doesn't. But we still think she is justified in insisting that her arm not be touched. Likewise, consider someone with phantom-limb pain who requests a pain-killer, although he knows full-well (of course) that there is no ongoing damage to the limb (the damage has already been done: he *has* no limb). But still we think it reasonable when he says, "Doc, please give me something to get rid of the pain in my arm." This objection to indicative-representation theories is sometimes referred to as "the problem of killing the messenger" (Cutter & Tye 2014)—since pain *represents* the presence of something bad, why is it rational to try to get rid of the representation (the messenger, the experience of pain) in cases where nothing bad is really happening, and one knows that nothing bad is really happening?

In reply, one can point out that pain—the experience of painful pain—is a primitive punisher. It teaches one to be reluctant to do anything to bring it about—like touching one's hypersensitive arm, or allowing it to be touched. This has nothing to do with, and is much more basic than, one's beliefs about harm. And by the same token, relief from pain is both envisaged as, and felt as, rewarding and pleasurable (Leknes et al. 2013). So the prospect of

162 Human Motives

reducing or eliminating one's phantom-limb pain is seen as strongly attractive: it has incentive-salience. There is no mystery about why the phantom-limb person requests a pain killer, for he is not trying to "kill" or prevent tissue damage (he knows that none is being done). He is trying to kill *that bad quality there*, the mode in which pain is nonconceptually presented to him (and presented to him in a way that can be indistinguishable from normal cases involving real damage).

There is no difficulty, then, in understanding why the experience of pain can rationalize preventative action in such cases. For rationalization is inherently perspectival. Considering the situation from the perspective of the person involved one sees, of course, that one would be similarly motivated to act. Imagining that one feels intense pain (even one that reflects no real damage), one sees that one would be strongly motivated to get rid of it, and would be greatly relieved—and pleased—when one does. Such people are acting rationally, not only by their own lights, but by ours too.

It might seem harder to show that action in such cases is *justified*, however, for one might think that justified action can require the truth or correctness of the representations on whose basis one acts. (This might be so in one sense of "justified," at any rate; in other uses, justification just tracks reasonableness.) On this view, one is justified in turning right at the lights only if one's belief that this will lead to one's destination is correct. If that belief is false, then the action might have been *reasonable* (if one formed one's belief on the basis of a normally reliable authority, say), but it isn't justified. Yet surely we think that someone *is* justified in taking a pain-killer for his phantom-limb pain (and is not merely acting reasonably in doing so), despite the fact that the pain misrepresents the presence of on-going damage in a non-existent limb. And we think that the justification here is direct—justified by the presence of the pain itself—and not merely because of the indirect "spammy" and disruptive effects that the experience of pain has on the rest of one's life, as Martínez (2015) claims (although that might be part of the reason: the patient wants to get his life back).

The concepts of justification that are applicable to actions are common-sense ones, however, not scientific ones. Yet the claim that phantom-limb pain is not only representational (having a content along the lines of, *bad quality there*), but represents incorrectly, is one that is warranted (if at all) by the best interpretation of the science. Attributing bodily damage correctness-conditions to (some) pain experiences is needed for scientific explanatory purposes, I have argued. It is not part of (nor intended to be part of) common-sense thinking about pain. It is no surprise, then, that common sense should treat actions that get rid of one's pain as justified if and only if they are rational from the perspective of the subject, for that is all common sense has to go on.

7.7 Conclusion

The value-representing theory of valence (pleasure and displeasure) developed in Chapters 5 and 6 has survived our discussion of the special case of sensory pain and painfulness fully intact; indeed, it has been strengthened. We have seen that it makes the best sense of the scientific data; and the resulting theory has the resources to respond successfully to all of the main arguments that have been thrown at it by critics.

The upshot is that motivational hedonism has finally been refuted. In the basic case, people act neither to secure intrinsically good (and avoid intrinsically bad) subjective feelings for themselves; nor is their decision-making all about competition among motor-urges or imperatives to obtain specific types of experience for themselves. Rather, people take decisions to secure a wide variety of valuable things, properties, and events (as well as to avoid disvaluable ones), where the common currency of the representations employed in decision-making is adaptive value and disvalue. From the perspective of the agent these representations manifest as impressions of some extent of (nonconceptual) *seeming goodness* and *seeming badness*. So people (and animals) take decisions to secure what seems good to them and to avoid what seems bad. Hence motivational pluralism has been vindicated. It remains to discuss how this translates into forms of moral motivation. That will form the topic of Chapter 8.

8

Moral Motivation

This final chapter will develop the value-representing theory of valence into an account of moral motivation, looking especially at the question of how much of moral motivation (if any) is "built in" (innate), as opposed to being culturally constructed via processes of conditioning and affective learning. I assume that previous chapters have established the truth of motivational pluralism, refuting hedonism and egoism. Our task, now, is to consider whether or not there are human-specific innate foundations for altruism and for motivation by moral norms.

What is it for a property of the mind to be innate? It means that it emerges in the course of normal development *without learning* (Ritchie 2021) or that it is *psychologically primitive* (Samuels 2004). Learning mechanisms themselves are innate, of course, as are the basic initial settings within those systems. (This need not mean that those settings are unalterable; an innate setting can be just an initial default, modifiable through subsequent learning.) Primary rewards and punishments, in particular, are innate, and provide the foundations for affective learning and conditioning thereafter. And in addition, of course, the mechanisms that underlie affective learning are themselves innate.

An important caveat: I intend to take no stand, in this chapter, on the question of what marks off moral judgments from other kinds of evaluative judgment, nor on what distinguishes moral norms from conventional ones. Although there is an extensive philosophical literature on the definition of morality, as well as an extensive empirical literature attempting to discover how people distinguish moral from conventional rules, the entire field is highly contested (Machery & Stich 2022). For present purposes I assume only that morality involves prosociality (a disposition to help, and not to harm, at least some others) as well as some set of intrinsically motivating norms.

8.1 Kinds of Moral Motivation

What are the sources of moral motivation? In Section 2.6 I suggested, for purposes of illustration, that people might have an innate or innately

Human Motives: Hedonism, Altruism, and the Science of Affect. Peter Carruthers, Oxford University Press.
© Peter Carruthers 2024. DOI: 10.1093/oso/9780198906131.003.0008

channeled desire for the good regard of community members. I suggested that if people are motivated to secure and/or enhance their reputations, then normal processes of affective conditioning and learning could explain how most people would end up being intrinsically motivated to be helpful to others, as well as intrinsically motivated to comply with the moral norms of the community. For since these things would be rewarded with social approval, and failures would be punished by the community's ill-regard, one would expect them to acquire value in their own right. Even if people start from a situation in which they have only self-interested desires, they would nevertheless end up assigning intrinsic value to the welfare of community members, and intrinsic value to acting in accordance with community norms. Hence egoism leads naturally to altruism and pluralism, *unless* it can be shown that the valence produced by these new values is itself self-regarding—either being an intrinsically good or bad feeling that decisions are taken to secure or avoid, or being constituted by a pair of experience-directed imperatives (*get more of this [experience]!* and *get less of this [experience]!*).

There is no doubt that people are, in general, motivated by reputational concerns, and that there are good evolutionary reasons why this should be so (Henrich 2017). People are more likely to act prosocially when their actions will be publicly known, and they seemingly treat efforts to obtain a good reputation as a kind of investment in the future, made to secure future benefits from others (Milinski 2016). Moreover, there is evidence that even uncalculating helpfulness is used to signal one's trustworthiness to observers, since people are more likely to engage in uncalculating cooperation when their decision-making process is itself observable to others (Jordan et al. 2016).

As we will see shortly, however, there is good evidence of prosocial impulses in infants and toddlers, whereas reputational concerns seem not to emerge until the age of about four or five (Engelmann & Rapp 2018; Rapp et al. 2019). But since this is about the age at which children first become capable of adjusting their behavior in anticipation of future events (Atance 2008), it is possible that infants, too, are intrinsically concerned with their reputations, but are incapable of pursuing them in a planful manner. At any rate, it does seem that infants at least find overt displays of approval from community members to be rewarding and signs of disapproval to be punishing. So it is possible that infants learn to assign intrinsic value to prosocial behavior through a process of social reward and punishment from what are, initially, things they see as good for themselves. We will return to this idea in due course.

There are a number of distinct forms of moral motivation, each of which sets humans apart from all other primates. One is greatly increased

166 Human Motives

prosociality—a willingness to help and share resources with non-kin (including strangers) and to cooperate with others, together with a willingness to engage in costly forms of punishment of those who act antisocially. Another is a sense of fairness, together with motivations to reward fairness and punish unfairness. And a third is a motivation to comply with specific moral and other norms, often motivated by anticipatory guilt for non-compliance. If there are innate bases for these motivations, they may have emerged in evolution in roughly the order mentioned, as we will see.

We begin with a discussion of prosociality in Section 8.2, followed by the sense of fairness in Section 8.3, before transitioning via a discussion of group-level cognition (Section 8.4) to the psychology of norms in Section 8.5. Section 8.6 will then briefly consider how all the different factors might "scale up" into full-blown adult forms of morality. Finally, Sections 8.7 and 8.8 will pull together the various strands of argument of the book and conclude.

8.2 Prosociality and Altruism

There is reason to think that increased prosociality developed along with cooperative breeding and alloparenting, perhaps beginning with the first emergence of relatively big-brained *Homo erectus* over a million and a half years ago (Hrdy 2009; Vaesen 2012; Rosenberg 2021). Cooperative breeding is extremely rare among primates generally, and outside of hominins is mostly confined to bi-parental care. Human infants, in contrast, are cared for by mothers, fathers, grandparents, and older siblings, as well as by unrelated females in the group. This pattern of care is necessitated by human infants' comparative immaturity at birth and their extended period of dependency. These in turn are partly necessitated by humans' larger head sizes, since altricial birth-timing is needed for the head to fit through the birth canal. (There are limits on how large the latter can become while still enabling normal locomotion.)

It is worth noting, too, that increases in head size/brain size in the genus *homo* may have been dependent on the capacity to create and control fire. For it was the invention of cooking that enabled our ancestors to swap out the large guts characteristic of other great apes for increased brain-size instead, since cooked food is much easier to digest (Wrangham 2009).[1] This

---

[1] Brains are energetically extremely expensive to run, which is why large brains are so rare in nature. Although the human brain accounts for only 2 percent of overall body weight, it consumes around 20 percent of the body's resting-state energy (Herculano-Houzel 2011). Note, however, that although there is

implies capacities for cultural learning. Humans don't have innate capacities to create and control fire, and nor are cooking abilities innate. Rather, these were early cultural innovations passed down from generation to generation that rapidly set in train a form of gene-culture co-evolution. So it seems that quite early on in human evolution, hominins were capable of learning complex skills from others and transmitting those abilities to other members of their social group.

Among adults, prosocial motivations are linked to fear-sensitivity. Extraordinary altruists (such as those who donate a kidney to a stranger) are better at recognizing fearful expressions, and have larger empathic responses to others' fear. Conversely, psychopaths are specifically deficient in recognizing fear in other people, and fail to respond emotionally to their fear (Marsh 2019). Moreover, fearful facial expressions, although traditionally thought to be negative stimuli, facilitate approach motivations rather than withdrawal ones (Marsh et al. 2005). And even subliminal priming with fearful faces increases people's motivation to be helpful in a follow-up task (Marsh et al. 2007). Consistent with the suggestion made above, that greatly increased human prosociality is linked to cooperative breeding and alloparenting, the fear-face in many respects resembles the face of a human infant, with raised brows, wider eyes, and a more-rounded overall appearance, for infant faces elicit interest, concern, and empathic behavior across cultures, which is seemingly an adaptation to support alloparenting.

In addition, a necessary condition for widespread alloparenting to evolve was reduced aggression among group members.[2] These evolutionary pressures likely led to a sort of self-domestication, with people seeking group-membership with, and preferentially mating with, whose who were less aggressive (and indeed, both men and women around the world today list kindness as one of the main factors they look for in a mate; Buss 1989). Moreover, comparisons with other species (domestic dogs, foxes bred for domesticity, and bonobos as contrasted with chimpanzees) show that one result of domestication (in addition to reduced aggression) is that facial morphology as a whole becomes more infant-like (Hare 2017). The same is true of human faces in comparison with other apes, especially among human

---

evidence of controlled use of fire by hominins from a million years ago or more (Berna et al. 2012; Hlubik et al. 2017; Wrangham 2017), the earliest direct evidence we have of cooking comes from 180,000 years ago (Zohar et al. 2022).

[2] As an illustration of just how different humans are from other great apes, imagine locking 200 chimpanzees—all strangers to one another—in a metal tube for a few hours: the result would be bloody mayhem. Yet humans routinely find themselves in this situation whenever they take a train or an airplane, mostly without incident.

females. So human faces in general will elicit some degree of prosocial motivation, as will the fear-face in particular.

There is also evidence that both fearfulness and fear-recognition abilities play important roles in human infants' prosocial development. Human infants are uniquely fearful and cautious of novelty among primates (Herrmann et al. 2011), and their fear responses are generally successful in eliciting adult concern and care-giving. There are individual differences in fearfulness among infants, too, which are significantly innate (Grossmann et al. 2011), and greater fearfulness predicts greater maternal protective behavior (Kiel & Buss 2011). Moreover, infants as a whole can discriminate fearful faces from faces displaying other emotions by as early as seven months, and individual differences in this ability correlate with the security of the child's attachment to the mother at fourteen months (Peltola et al. 2015). More striking still, attentional responses to fearful faces at seven months predicts cooperative helping behavior at 14 months (Grossmann et al. 2018), just as accurate identification of fearful expressions among both children and adults predicts prosocial behavior (Marsh et al. 2007; Rajhans et al. 2016).

It seems, then, that there might be a number of inter-linked adaptations underlying humans' prosocial motivations. One is an innate attraction to and protective motivation toward neotenous facial morphology (especially infants, children, and women, as well as anyone expressing fear). Another is automatic motor output from fear appraisal circuits to produce facial expressions mimicking or accentuating the main components of that morphology. A third is increased levels of fearfulness among human infants, combined with early-developing capacities to recognize fear in others. But the connections between this set of interlinked adaptations and innate altruism are not entirely clear. It would make the case stronger if there were direct evidence of early-developing prosociality. This is where we go next.

Grueneisen & Warneken (2022) review evidence that empathy drives the helpfulness of toddlers and young children, finding that their helping behavior only becomes more strategic (for example, influenced by reputational concerns) after the age of about five. Similarly, House et al. (2013) find that young children (ages three to five) across a diverse range of cultures (including hunter-gatherers) will engage in personally costly sharing of food items with familiar peers. Rates of sharing then drop dramatically with age across all cultures, before starting (around age eight) to approach and track the sharing rates characteristic of adults in the same culture (which vary considerably). What accounts for the drop in prosociality in the period between ages five and eight? It may be that younger children are naturally and spontaneously helpful, and make their offerings without thought or planning, but then become more capable of reflecting on the potential loss to themselves as they get older. This would be consistent with the finding with adults that spontaneous responses are more prosocial, with rates of helping in anonymous games dropping significantly when people have time to reflect (Rand 2016; Yamagishi et al. 2017). It would also fit with the finding that rates of helping are higher when people are placed under cognitive load, making reflection more difficult (Cornelissen et al. 2011; Schulz et al. 2014).

The suggestion of an innate, default, prosociality gains some further support from human toddlers' chronic helpfulness. If 14-month-old infants become aware that an adult is in need of instrumental help (for example, to reach an object dropped on the floor, or to open a cupboard door when the adult has his hands occupied), they will give up what they are doing and toddle over to help. And they do so even if what they are doing is intrinsically interesting and/or if helping is physically effortful, such as requiring the child to climb out of a ball-pool (Warneken & Tomasello 2009). Moreover, they do so in the absence of any extrinsic reward. Indeed, in experiments done with slightly older infants, it emerges that provision of external rewards actually undermines helping behavior rather than reinforcing it (Warneken & Tomasello 2008). In addition, measures of toddlers' arousal show that what motivates them is that someone who needs help should receive it, rather than that they themselves should be the ones to provide that help; for they appear equally satisfied whether the help is provided by themselves or by someone else (Hepach et al. 2012).

Furthermore, 18-month-olds will engage in altruistic sharing of a resource (such as a toy), in addition to instrumental helping (Svetlova et al. 2010; Dunfield et al. 2011). Indeed, infants as young as 15 months have been found to engage in altruistic sharing, with this behavior apparently being linked to a sense of fairness in a separate expectancy-violation task in which they were surprised by unequal distributions (Schmidt & Sommerville 2011). And 12-month-old infants (most of whom cannot yet walk, and so cannot be tested in standard instrumental-helping tasks) will use pointing appropriately, helpfully communicating facts to ignorant (but not to knowledgeable) adults engaged in a search task (Liszkowski et al. 2008).

Do these findings demonstrate that prosociality (operationalized in terms of a willingness to help and share resources and information with others) is innate? Not necessarily. It is difficult to exclude the suggestion that infants' helpfulness may have been conditioned by even earlier patterns of reward and/or punishment. And it does appear, at any rate, that helping behavior in 18-month-old infants is at least influenced and modified by cultural practices and expectations (Giner Torréns & Kärtner 2017). Hence the case for

170 Human Motives

innateness would be stronger if prosociality could be established even earlier in development.

While it is hard to demonstrate prosocial motivations in infants who are not yet mobile or capable of pointing, what one can do is test their evaluations of other prosocial and/or antisocial agents. An especially important early set of findings came from Hamlin et al. (2007), who showed that even six-month-old infants prefer an agent who has helped another to achieve its goal over one who has hindered its pursuit of the goal. (These experiments were done with seemingly animated toys, and infants' preferences were measured by their reaching for one character or the other in a subsequent forced-choice offer of a toy.) Indeed, six-month-olds also prefer a helpful agent to a neutral one, and a neutral agent to a hinderer.

Hamlin & Wynn (2011) were then able to show, using different materials and employing a number of control conditions, that even three-month-old and five-month-old infants overwhelmingly prefer an agent who has helped another over an agent who has hindered another. Likewise, Kanakogi et al. (2017) show that six-month-old infants prefer an agent who interferes to prevent one agent from harming another to an agent who fails to interfere. Such findings, when combined with data concerning the prosocial motivations of slightly older infants, seem to demonstrate the presence of an early-developing affective system that issues in positive and negative evaluations of prosocial and antisocial agents respectively, while also creating prosocial—helpful—motivations in the infants themselves.[3]

Taken all together, the evidence reviewed in this section amounts to a convincing case for the innateness of prosociality and altruism. Concern for the well-being of unrelated others seems to be an innate default, rather than a result of affective conditioning. Such concern may be restricted to those who one appraises as belonging to one's own social group, however, for it evolved to support alloparenting and other forms of cooperation within small-scale ethnolinguistic groups. And for sure we know that degrees of empathy for others are heavily influenced by cues of group-membership and by similarity to oneself (Cikara & Van Bavel 2014; Hackel et al. 2017). This point will be developed further in Section 8.4.

Notice that when one feels sympathy for someone in trouble, the thought of helping them will have positive valence attached—one will see the act of helping as (nonconceptually) good. And on the account of valence defended

---

[3] Remarkably, by the age of ten months, these prosocial evaluations are integrated with the output of infants' mentalizing systems, too, leading them to prioritize evaluations of other agents' intentions over the actual outcomes of their actions (Hamlin 2013; Kanakogi et al. 2017; Woo et al. 2017; Woo & Spelke 2023).

in Chapters 5 and 6, this means that helping the other person will have been often-enough adaptive to have stabilized the underlying evaluation. But how can saving a non-relative's life (say) increase one's own inclusive fitness? How could a prosocial affective system of this sort have evolved? There are two explanatory factors. The first is that small-scale hunter-gatherer groups are both fragile and highly interdependent, to the point that the fitness of any one individual partly depends on that of each other member of the group. The second is that prosociality is expected: acting prosocially will increase one's reputation, and failing to do so will attract at least informal punishment. Only the second of these factors is still operative in the developed world, however. Does this mean that when one now sees the act of helping a stranger as good one is to some degree *mis*representing it? In one sense, yes, possibly (depending on the strength of the prosociality norms in one's society), for positive valence may no longer be tracking what it was designed to track (adaptive value). But seeing the act of helping as good can still be an accurate expression of one's own stored values; and from one's own subjective perspective, one is just acting to secure what appears good to one, not what is adaptive.

On this point, recall the distinction drawn in Section 5.7 between the referential correctness-conditions of a nonconceptual signal, needed for explanatory purposes in cognitive science (here, adaptiveness), and the mode of presentation of those conditions to the subject (here, perceived goodness, an expression of the values one has acquired over one's lifetime, built through conditioning and social learning from species-general primary rewards and punishments). We need to see valence as representing adaptive value and disvalue in order to understand how and why the affective systems work as they do, and undergo learning and change in the ways that they do. But when seeking to explain the choices that individual people make in particular circumstances we need to appeal to the way in which signals of adaptive value and disvalue present themselves to the agent, which is as nonconceptual representations of goodness and badness.

8.3 Equality and Fairness

This section will examine the suggestion that humans have an innate sense of fairness. But first, a word about terminology. In some contexts fairness requires *equal* treatment, or *equal* reward; in others it requires what I shall call "equity," which is distribution in accordance with individual contributions or effort.

172 Human Motives

One initial line of support for an innate sense of fairness came from experiments purporting to show that other primates, too, are inequity-averse. Brosnan & de Waal (2003) found that capuchin monkeys refuse to participate in a task in which another monkey receives larger rewards from a human experimenter for performing the same work. The consensus in the field now, however, is that this behavior results not from a sense of fairness, but rather from feelings of frustration at receiving a lesser reward when a larger one is available. Thus Dubreuil et al. (2006) show that capuchins who are only allowed to access a less-preferred food when a more-preferred item is also placed on the same tray are likewise apt to refuse to participate, whether or not another animal is present. And Amici et al. (2012) come to a similar but more nuanced conclusion in a study involving a range of primate species. They show that tendencies to reject an offer when a conspecific receives a better payoff vary depending on the relative dominance of the two animals (less-dominant animals are more likely to accept a lower payoff, presumably because this is something they are used to). And they also show that species whose members are more socially tolerant, such that low-dominance individuals are more likely to be allowed by dominant ones to access resources, are more likely to *reject* an inequitable payoff (in this case, seemingly because it violates their expectations).

Finally, consider the study conducted by Engelmann et al. (2017) with chimpanzees, who are our nearest relatives amongst existing primates. They tested two versions of the inequity-aversion hypothesis: whether the aversion is to inequity as such (whatever the source), or to inequity in offers provided by another agent. The former hypothesis was tested using food rewards made available by a machine, either alone or with another chimpanzee receiving a higher reward from the machine. Here refusal-rates were extremely low, whether or not a partner chimpanzee was present performing the same task and getting larger rewards. So chimpanzees plainly aren't averse to inequity as such. In contrast, when it was a human experimenter who made only the lesser of two rewards available, chimpanzees rejected the offer at high rates; but refusal-rates were no higher when another chimpanzee was present and received a larger reward than when they were alone. What really seems to drive cases of refusal to participate is frustration at someone making a low offer when a better offer could have been provided.

If an innate sense of fairness wasn't inherited from our primate ancestors, then it would have to have evolved at some point in the hominin lineage. And it is true that hunter-gatherer groups (in contrast with troops of chimpanzees) are generally non-hierarchical in structure, with leadership conferred voluntarily on the basis of respect and prestige (Boehm 2001). But it is by no means clear that equality-preferences provide the best explanation of this difference. Rather, an unwillingness to blindly follow those whose judgments may well be untrustworthy, or are known to be untrustworthy, combined with the fission-fusion nature of hunter-gather groups, may be sufficient. For if any one individual (or small group of individuals) attempts to take control without earning the respect of the rest of the group, and cannot be discouraged from doing so by the gossip and ridicule of the others (a frequently adopted tactic), then the latter can simply decamp and leave.

Moreover, distributional principles among hunter-gatherers are by no means driven by egalitarianism, but split along gender lines (Marlowe 2005). Women and children forage and gather, with mostly predictable and stable daily returns. The results of female foraging are generally retained within the family group, thus insuring that family members get fed on a regular basis. Hunting, in contrast, is mostly conducted by males, and has highly variable and unpredictable rates of success. Since no family can consume an entire big-game animal before the meat spoils, and since sharing has the effect of distributing the risks of failure across all hunters, one would expect cultural norms to develop that require meat from hunting to be shared. And this is, indeed, just the pattern that we find.

Perhaps the strongest argument for why we should expect a sense of fairness to have evolved in the hominin line is that it is needed to sustain effective cooperation (Tomasello et al. 2012; Baumard et al. 2013). A good case can be made that we should expect to find (and do find) humans equipped with a "cheater-detection mechanism," in particular, for identifying free-riders and others who fail to make sufficient contributions to cooperative tasks (Cosmides & Tooby 1992; Fiddick et al. 2000; Stone et al. 2002). And free-riding is certainly a kind of unfairness—a free-rider attempts to take the benefits of cooperation without contributing to the cost, which is unfair. Likewise, attempting to secure more of the benefits from a cooperative task (to which others have contributed just as much) is a form of unfairness; and it, too, will undermine cooperation in the long run. It is unclear how this rationale for an innate sense of fairness would extend to an expectation that windfall (unearned) resources should be distributed equally, however, which is the paradigm form of fairness employed in most experimental investigations of the topic. But perhaps people construe situations in which agents equally contribute *zero* effort (a windfall) as limiting cases of those in which agents contribute *equal* effort, falling under the equitable-distribution norm as a result.

Turning now to experimental work with contemporary humans, results obtained with adults in the so-called "ultimatum game" have been thought to support an innate sense of fairness (Fehr & Gächter 2000). Individuals

174 Human Motives

play in pairs, generally anonymously, and normally in one-shot trials rather than in repeated ones. One participant is given an endowment of money to play with. That person is required to make an offer of some sort (no matter how small) to the other, who can either accept or reject the offer. If the offer is accepted, then each person keeps their respective portions. But if the offer is rejected, then neither of them gets anything. According to traditional (egoistic) economic models of rationality, the proposer should offer the smallest sum possible, which should then be accepted by the receiver (because it is better to get something rather than nothing). But no one, anywhere, behaves like this.

Cross-cultural work done in developed nations finds that the average initial offer is about 45 percent of the total stake (Roth et al. 1991). So people are much more generous than standard economic models would predict. But this finding is easily explicable in light of humans' innate prosociality and willingness to share resources with others, discussed in Section 8.2. We don't need to appeal to an innate sense of fairness to explain it. Much more interesting are the rejection-rates. In the same study it was found that people tended on average to reject offers below 20 percent. This is consistent with the idea that people balance a desire to punish unfair offers against their own likely losses if they do.

Cross-cultural work done in a wide range of small-scale societies has produced much more variable results, however (Henrich et al. 2001). The mean initial offers across these societies range from 26 percent to 58 percent. Rejection-rates are just as variable, with people in some societies accepting almost all offers, whatever their size, whereas in others even offers over 50 percent are frequently rejected. The authors suggest that the variations are explained, in part, by levels of cooperation and co-dependency within the cultures in question, as well as by their degree of market integration. But cultural norms also play a part. For example, those who reject high offers belong to cultures with a tradition of strategic gift-giving, in which there is often a reluctance to take on the unknown obligation that would be incurred from accepting a large gift.

Cultural norms also provide the main explanation for variations among children in the extent to which resources produced through a cooperative task get distributed equally, on the one hand, or equitably (in proportion to effort), on the other (Schäfer et al. 2015). Children in Germany—where people often interact with others in one-off tasks with no opportunities for later reciprocation—distribute outcomes in proportion to effort (equitably but unequally), whereas children from two small-scale societies—in which there would be frequent opportunities for fortunes to be reversed in future interactions—opt for equality, ignoring variations in contributions to the task in hand.

Of course, none of this demonstrates that a sense of fairness *isn't* innate. For everyone should allow that innate properties of the mind can subsequently be modulated by culture. But neither is the innateness-hypothesis supported. And in fact, even had the results been consistent across cultures, the findings could be explained in terms of innate prosociality alone (of the sort discussed for in Section 8.2). For prosocial people will be generous with resources, at least to other group members. And those on the receiving end will likewise have expectations of generosity. Hence someone receiving a low offer in the ultimatum game might evaluate their partner as a less-than-minimally-good person, and be inclined to punish on that basis, rather than because the offer was an unfair one. Consistent with this suggestion, Sznycer et al. (2017) find that support for redistribution from the rich to the poor across cultures is predicted by measures of people's compassion (for the poor), envy (of the rich), and self-interest (one's own likely gain or loss through redistribution), but not by two distinct measures of attitudes towards fairness (procedural and distributional).

If there is an experimental case to be made for an innate sense of fairness to back up the predictions from evolutionary psychology, then, it will have to be on the basis of studies conducted with human infants. A number of different labs have shown that infants (aged between four months and 19 months across studies) expect an agent to distribute windfall resources equally between two recipients (Schmidt & Sommerville 2011; Sloane et al. 2012; Meristo et al. 2016; Buyukozer Dawkins et al. 2019). That is, they look longer, showing surprise or additional interest, when the resources are distributed unequally rather than equally. Taken by themselves, however, it is not clear that the infants in these studies are responding specifically to the unfairness of the distribution, rather than to the mere fact of a difference in treatment. For infants might be operating with something resembling a "principle of (in)sufficient reason," expecting that actions with different outcomes should have different goals; in which case they look longer when the distribution is unequal, not because it is unfair, but because they are trying to figure out the reason for treating the two receivers differently.

More interesting—and more revealing—are studies of infants' expectations of third-parties' evaluations of fair and unfair agents. Thus DesChamps et al. (2015) show that 13-month-old and 15-month-old infants associate a fair distributor of resources with praise and an unfair distributor with admonishment. (In the test phase of the experiments just the faces of the distributors were shown alongside positive or negative utterances, so infants

176 Human Motives

were not responding to the outcomes as such.) Similarly, Surian & Franchin (2017) show that, at least by 20 months, infants expect a larger reward to be given to an agent who has helped another over an agent who has hindered another, which can be construed as an expectation of equity, thus suggesting that by this age expectations of fair (in the sense of equal) distributions are modulated by the deservingness of the agents.

Wang & Henderson (2018)—likewise working within an expectations-based looking-time paradigm—show that 17-month-old infants are surprised when one of two agents secures more of the fruits of a task to which both had contributed equally (which is inequitable). And in a separate experiment where the two agents made unequal contributions, 17-month-olds are surprised when the agent who had contributed less secures more of the proceeds; and they are also surprised when the lesser-contributor secures more of the proceeds than when the proceeds end up distributed equally. It seems that by this age, infants expect the rewards of cooperation to be distributed in proportion to the agents' respective contributions (equitably).

The findings discussed thus far have concerned infants' *expectations* of fairness, as well as their expectations regarding others' evaluations of fairness and unfairness. More important, if a claim about innate *values* is to be supported, are studies that assess the infants' *own* evaluations of fair and unfair agents. In the first such study of this kind, Burns & Sommerville (2014) showed that 15-month-old infants prefer to interact with (select a toy from) an agent who had distributed windfall resources equally between two others over an agent who had made an unequal distribution. (The same experiment also showed that infants' preferences are modulated by the race of the distributor and the race of the receivers.) Using a similar social-choice paradigm but focusing just on infants' evaluations of fairness, Lucca et al. (2018) show that both 13-month-old and 17-month-old infants prefer to interact with (accept a toy from) an agent who had distributed windfall resources equally over one who had distributed them unequally. Finally in this same vein of research, Ziv et al. (2021) find that 16-month-old infants choose to reward an agent who had distributed resources equally rather than unequally, either (in one experiment) by touching a screen to deliver verbal praise, or (in another) by touching the screen to deliver a cookie.

The evidence reviewed in this section provides some reason to think that a sense of fairness might be innate. It makes good evolutionary sense that humans might be adapted to track and evaluate fair versus unfair outcomes relative to contributions in cooperative tasks. And there is a significant amount of evidence that infants are doing just this during the second year of life. But it is hard to tell what learning might have taken place within families at earlier ages. So the case for innateness here is significantly less strong than was the case supporting innate prosociality discussed in Section 8.2, where much of the data concerned infants in the first six months or so of life.

8.4 Social-Group Cognition

Prior to the invention of agriculture just 10,000 years ago, human evolutionary history for the previous one and a half million years was comprised of hunting and gathering. Marlowe (2005) provides an analysis of extant hunter-gatherer groups, while also drawing on historical and archaeological sources, to offer a picture of what hominin life-ways were probably like through significant portions of that time, at least. Humans and their immediate ancestors would always have lived in groups, of two different sorts. First, they would have been members of a tribe or ethnolinguistic group, whose average size would have been somewhere around 1,500 adult individuals. Tribal membership would have been fixed by birth and by language, with perhaps some opportunities for incorporation of members of other tribes, either through warfare or immigration. But then second, within the tribe, people would have been members of a much smaller coalition of families, generally comprising around 30 adults, who hunt, gather, travel, and camp together. Importantly, most of the adults in the group would be unrelated or only distantly related, meaning that family networks would extend across multiple small groups (Hill et al. 2011). Membership of these smaller groups would display a "fission-fusion" pattern, with people frequently switching between groups, either to visit with relatives or for reasons having to do with the existing group dynamics. Depending on the cultural practices of the tribe, there might or might not be periodic gatherings of the entire tribal membership (perhaps for ritual purposes).

One might expect that an evolutionary history of this length would have left its mark on the human mind—people should be adapted to think in terms of groups and group-membership. And as we will see, there is extensive evidence that this is so. Most experimental studies fail to clarify whether their findings pertain to tribal psychology or small-group coalitional psychology, however, leaving this open to interpretation. Some of this ambiguity may result from the fact that contemporary large-scale societies are comprised of multiple overlapping and cross-cutting social groups. There are religious groups, ethnic groups, racial groups, political parties, fans of differing sports-teams, college alums, fraternity and sorority members, trade

178 Human Motives

unions and professional societies, and so on. Most people have multiple "identities," and transition back and forth between them depending on context. So one's religious affiliation, for example, will have some of the properties of a tribal group but also some of the properties of a shorter-term coalitional group.

Moreover, coalitional groups in hunter-gatherer societies would always have been formed from members of the same tribe. So when such groups are constructed by experimenters today, they are also providing participants with a powerful cue of shared tribal membership. This may be part of the explanation for why the so-called "minimal group effect" is so powerful and multifaceted (Dunham 2018), as we will see shortly. It may also be why the formation of mixed-race minimal groups can moderate or remove implicit racial biases (Van Bavel & Cunningham 2009; Pietraszewski et al. 2014).

Nevertheless, some of the findings in the literature seem most clearly relevant to tribal thinking, whereas others seem most plausibly relevant to more ephemeral coalitions or collaborative groups. We begin with what seems like a clear example of the latter: the minimal-group effect. This was initially an accidental discovery from what had been intended to be just a control condition (Tajfel 1970). The finding is that randomly created small groups (generally involving just three or four members) immediately issue in ingroup preferences and expectations. Groups can be visually marked (e.g. by being assigned to wear yellow T-shirts as opposed to green), or they can be more abstract (e.g. supposedly formed on the basis of shared artistic preferences); and membership can be known or left anonymous. One consistent finding is that minimal-group members will preferentially allocate resources to members of their own as opposed to another group. Another is that people have positive expectations of other minimal-group members specifically, especially regarding likely reciprocity.

The effect has been demonstrated in five-year-old children and younger, with resulting changes in both explicit and implicit liking of ingroup members, as well as more positive expectations of reciprocity and support from ingroup members (Dunham et al. 2011; Dunham 2018). The effect-sizes are about half as strong as those for within-gender preferences (which are quite strong at this age). Moreover, it seems that these effects with children result (at least initially) from immediately formed positive attitudes towards minimal-group members, rather than negative ones towards outgroup members (Buttelmann & Böhm 2014).

It is striking that becoming a member of a novel group should change not only one's explicit—avowed—attitudes towards group members, but also one's implicit evaluations. (These are often measured by reaction-time differences in a categorization task using pairings of ingroup or outgroup members with either positive or negative attributes.) For implicit attitudes have often been thought to be built slowly and associatively. It seems, rather, that they can result from changes in affective evaluation imposed immediately in a top-down manner, similar to the placebo-like effects of belief on value discussed in Section 2.7. And remarkably, these evaluations and resulting affective feelings are quite flexible, changing as one moves from one minimal group to another (Xiao & Van Bavel 2019).[4]

The minimal-group effect makes good sense as an instance of what I am calling "coalitional psychology," given that humans evolved in the context of fission-fusion hunting and foraging groups. For instance, imagine that you are a young man or woman who has just joined a new group—either through marriage, or because of personal conflicts with members of your natal group, perhaps. You will now depend on the cooperation and active support of your new group members to survive and flourish, and for your offspring to survive and flourish. An immediate, sincere (non-strategic), liking for and trust in the members of your new group is likely to help you integrate into that group, and help secure for you the support that you need, for people tend both to like, and to be willing to collaborate with, those who manifestly like them and trust them.

Group stereotyping, in contrast, seems best understood as an instance of tribal psychology. As is well known, people rapidly form stereotypes of social groups, especially those based on race, ethnicity, and gender. As with affective attitudes, stereotypes can be explicitly held and endorsed, or they can be present and influence one's unreflective expectations and behavior while being explicitly rejected. Almost everyone knows the common stereotypes that are attributed to a group, including members of the group themselves—hence the phenomena of stereotype-threat and stereotype-boost.[5]

Many common stereotypes are known to children by the age of five or six, with the strength of their endorsement linked to their tendency to *essentialize* the categories involved (Gelman 2003; Pauker et al. 2010; Rhodes & Mandalaywala 2017)—that is, to believe that members of the category share a hidden underlying nature or essence, which causes them to share

---

[4] Indeed, the findings are consistent with a view of implicit and explicit attitudes that sees them, not as distinct kinds of stored mental state, but rather as differing behavioral manifestations of one-and-the same underlying evaluative attitude, subject to different kinds of situational pressure (Carruthers 2018b).

[5] Stereotype-threat occurs when someone under-performs in a given domain because of the salience of a negative stereotype about their group's abilities in that domain (Spencer et al. 2016). Because black people are stereotyped as unacademic, they tend to under-perform in high-stakes tests of academic ability, for example, especially when their race is made salient to them. Stereotype-boost is the converse phenomenon, where someone's performance in a given domain can be enhanced by salient positive stereotypes about their group's abilities in the domain, such as "Asians are good at math."

180 Human Motives

similar surface properties. Moreover, stereotypes are a kind of generic belief, having the form, *Xs are F*, unqualified by quantifiers like "all," "some," or "most;" and there is evidence that humans are apt to store and retrieve memories in generic form, even when the initial information presented to them is actually qualified and more nuanced (Sutherland et al. 2015; Gelman et al. 2016).

These findings make sense as instances of an evolved tribal psychology (and given that traditional societies have always been heavily gendered in organization), since the members of any one tribe (and gender) would have shared a great many of their properties. (Members of any small fission-fusion group, in contrast, would have been a set of individuals with their own idiosyncratic natures, over-and-above the tribal properties that they share.) Tribal members would have shared a language, shared religious beliefs, engaged in the same rituals, prepared food in the same ways, decorated their bodies and/or clothing in similar ways, and so on. So if one learned a fact about one member of a hunter-gatherer tribe, the chances are that it would generalize to other members of the same tribe; in which case tribal thinking would have been highly adaptive, enabling one to form accurate expectations of any individual member of a neigh-boring tribe one comes across.

Particular stereotypes about tribal groups need to be learned, of course. But what about the learning mechanism itself? Is there an innate system, perhaps with some initial innate structure, for identifying and learning about social groups? There is evidence that language is an innate cue to group membership. Infants as young as six months prefer someone who speaks their native language over a foreign language (Kinzler et al. 2007). (Although infants this young cannot yet speak themselves, they can recognize the language that their care-givers use.) Moreover, 12-month-olds will choose to accept toys or snacks offered by a native speaker over a foreign speaker (Kinzler et al. 2012), and 14-month-olds prefer to imitate a novel action exhibited by a native speaker rather than a foreign speaker (Buttelmann et al. 2013). In addition, nine-month-old infants expect speakers of the same language to affiliate rather than disengage, whereas they are surprised when speakers of different languages thereafter affiliate with one another (Liberman et al. 2017). In contrast, human children fail to show any preference on the basis of race until around the age of five years (Kinzler & Spelke 2011). This is as one might expect, given that tribal differences would almost always have been marked by language among hunter-gatherers, but never by race, since nearby tribes would almost always have shared similar skin coloring and facial features with one's own tribal group.

Infants' conception of social/tribal grouping appears to be more abstract than simply being marked by spoken language, however; and other salient differences can cue infants' group-stereotype expectations. Thus when groups are composed of differently colored and geometrically shaped mobile agents (with eyes), eight-month-old infants expect members of the same group to behave similarly, and are surprised when they act differently (Powell & Spelke 2013).

Using a similar sort of expectancy-violation paradigm, also with differently colored geometric agents, Pun et al. (2021) show that 11-month-olds expect agents to come to the aid of a group member in cases where members of two groups have conflicting goals (attempting to cross a bridge in opposite directions at the same time), and are surprised if the agent helps an outgroup member instead. To similar effect, but using real human agents whose group-membership is marked by novel labels ("I'm a Bem" versus "I'm a Tig"), Jin & Baillargeon (2017) show that 17-month-old infants expect members of the same group to help one another, whereas they have no such expectations for members of different groups.

Something similar holds for infants' expectations of harming. They expect agents not to harm or interfere with the goals of a member of the same group, whereas they have no such expectations about not harming an agent from an outgroup (Ting et al. 2020). Furthermore, 12-month-old infants expect an observing bystander to withhold support from (to punish) someone who does something to harm another member of the bystander's group, but not when the harming agent herself belongs to the bystander's group and the victim is an outgroup member (Ting et al. 2019).

It is hard to see group-level/tribal cognition as anything other than innate, at least in its core properties. For infants in the first year of life would have had very few opportunities to observe interactions between members of differing tribal groups. This is because during this time the infant would have been surrounded almost exclusively by family members and coalitional-group members. So how could an infant learn that members of the same tribal group share properties and forms of behavior, whereas members of differing tribal groups tend not to? Indeed, how could an infant of this age even learn that there are such things as tribal groups?

As noted, people are disposed to assume that members of a given social group will share properties (especially when marked along ethnic lines), an assumption that would have been largely true and adaptive in our tribal past. And as is widely known, people tend to feel more warmly towards—that is, to like—members of their own social group (Mullen et al. 1992), beginning by six months of age (Kinzler et al. 2007). The converse also holds: people are

182 Human Motives

much less likely to feel empathy for the suffering of those who belong to an outgroup, especially when outgroup status is made salient (Cikara et al. 2011). Human prosociality is heavily modulated by group membership and is, by default, limited to members of one's own social/tribal group.

One might expect that people would also make the reverse inference: using shared properties to assign people to the same social/tribal group. If they do, then this would explain one of the best-established findings in social psychology, which is that people tend to like those who are similar to themselves (Byrne 1971; Krebs 1975). The phenomenon itself is present early in infancy. Within the first year of life, human infants prefer an agent who expresses the same food preference as themselves to one who has a different preference (Mahajan & Wynn 2012). Indeed, using the same food-liking paradigm, Hamlin et al. (2013) found that nine-month-olds will even prefer an agent who helps someone with the same food-preference as the infant over a different agent who hinders the person, while preferring an agent who *hinders* a *dis*similar other to one who helps a dissimilar other.

While ingroup preferences are pervasive, the default attitude towards outgroup members seems to be one of disregard rather that outright dislike (Brewer 1999; Balliet et al. 2014). This is what one might predict on evolutionary grounds, since relationships with surrounding hunter-gatherer tribes can range from cautious cooperativeness to murderous hostility. Denigration of outgroup members is something that needs to be learned, just as outgroup stereotypes need to be learned (Amodio & Cikara 2021). But evidence of competition with, or threat from, outgroups can be sufficient to transform disregard into outright hostility (Chang et al. 2016), as can the use of language that dehumanizes the outgroup (Haslam & Loughnan 2014).

It seems, then, that while humans are innately prosocial (as we saw in Section 8.2), their prosociality is modulated by perceived group membership. Humans are only innately disposed to empathize with, help, trust, and cooperate with members of their own social/tribal group. And the kind of tribal-group cognition that underlies this limitation is itself innate. Humans are innately disposed to identify social/tribal groups and to generalize on the basis of group membership. So while humans are innately altruistic towards ingroup members, they are also innately vulnerable to becoming prejudiced and heartless towards outgroup members.

8.5 Norm Psychology

All human cultures everywhere are imbued with norms, and probably have been for tens if not hundreds of thousands of years. These norms are rules that are enforced formally in developed societies by police forces and court systems, and informally in all societies through gossip, ostracism, and withdrawal of trust and collaboration. Some of these norms are recognizably moral ones, with variations on rules against lying, promise-breaking, stealing, and harming group members, as well as those regulating the fair distribution of resources. But cultural norms can (and do) concern all manner of behaviors, including whom one may marry or have sex with, how food must be prepared, how ceremonies should be conducted, how people should dress, whether and how bodies may be decorated, and so on. Such norms are generally treated no differently by members of the culture than recognizably moral ones: failure to obey them attracts formal or informal punishment, and people are apt to experience guilt-like emotions when infringing them and outrage when other people do. This has led some to propose that humans have evolved a distinctive "norm psychology," charged with learning, enforcing, and motivating norm-compliant behavior in general (Sripada & Stich 2006; Chudek & Henrich 2011).

There are good theoretical models of how an innate norm psychology might have evolved through a process of gene-culture co-evolution (Henrich 2017). One can suppose that collaboration in small hunter-gatherer groups was initially supported through forms of reciprocal altruism. People would be cooperating with known individuals over extended periods of time for mutual benefit, and would be able to identify those who fail to reciprocate, thereafter declining to cooperate with them again. Persistent free-riders would soon run out of people willing to cooperate with them. But enforcement of prosociality in such groups would have become much more powerful once it became reputation-based, with third-party observers likewise becoming disposed to withdraw cooperation from non-reciprocators (Feinberg et al. 2014). People who attempted to free-ride on the efforts of others would then have been widely ostracized, either entirely (being expelled from the group) or partially (being denied some of the benefits of group membership).

Notice that significant components of what is often called "third-party punishment" (in which observers impose costs of one sort or another on non-reciprocators) require only memory and some sort of character-based predictive inference. Having observed an individual fail to act prosocially towards another, one just has to recall that fact when there is an opportunity to collaborate with that individual oneself, predict likely further free-riding, and then choose to collaborate with someone else instead. All that this requires are capacities for memory and social foresight together with practical intelligence. As soon as people became capable of transmitting this information to others, however, gossiping about bad behavior, then reputations

184   Human Motives

could be widely shared, not only within the collaborative group but also with neighboring groups, and potentially throughout the entire tribe. The costs of free-riding would then have become a great deal higher. And indeed, some have even argued that the main impetus behind the evolution of language itself may have derived from the gains in social cohesion and cooperation that result from gossip (Dunbar 2004).

Once third-party punishment became fully established, then that would have created a powerful evolutionary pressure on individuals to learn the patterns of behavior that are expected within the group (and that will result in informal punishment if not followed). There would also have been pressure to imbue those patterns with intrinsic value, thereby internalizing the norms and becoming motivated to comply with them for their own sake (without having to calculate the likelihood of discovery or the likely severity of punishment for breaches of them). Having internalized the norms one will feel bad (guilty) if one breaches them, and one will feel angry (indignant) if others breach them. One would thus expect human affective systems to have become altered in such a way that learning that a given behavior is expected would immediately assign positive value to the performance of that behavior, as well as negative value to non-performance. The result is norm psychology: a disposition to look for, learn, and attach intrinsic value to the norms of one's local group.

Likewise, once third-party punishment became established, norms themselves could begin to proliferate. Where initially they might have been confined to norms of reciprocity, harm avoidance, and collaborative action, as soon as a new norm became widely accepted (for whatever reason) it would be stabilized, mandating the behavior in question (Boyd & Richerson 1992). Thereafter competition (either direct or indirect) among tribal groups would mean that groups whose norms produced beneficial effects for the group would tend to do better, with those groups either destroying, incorporating, our outlasting their neighbors. Norms that increase internal group cohesion, innovation, learning, and cooperation would then proliferate in the long term. But alongside these can be norms that are individually maladaptive, involving pointless but expensive rituals, for example.

The result would be just the sort of cross-cultural variation-with-commonalities that we now observe. All cultures have norms of the kind required to maintain collaboration and social cohesion, forbidding lying, promise-breaking, harming group members, mandating fair resource distribution, and so on (perhaps with culture-specific exceptions and variations). But cultures can differ widely in norms that have little impact on group success, such as what one should wear, what rituals one should observe when getting married, and so on. But these, too, would have been stabilized in place through third-party-punishment once they had been introduced.

Experimental evidence with adults supports all the main components of norm psychology predicted by this evolutionary account. Willingness to engage in costly punishment of those who act too selfishly in economic games is a human universal, although cultures vary in what they consider to be too selfish (Henrich et al. 2006). And people will engage in both direct and (preferably, if given the option) indirect punishment of strangers, not only in online economic games (Goette et al. 2006), but in real-life contexts (Balafoutas et al. 2014). Moreover, people find rewarding both norm-compliant action and punishment of others' failures to comply (Baumgartner et al. 2011; Buckholtz & Marois 2012; Ruff & Fehr 2014). Collaboration with others, too, is generally experienced as rewarding (Fareri et al. 2015), as is engaging in collaboration with someone who has a reputation for reciprocity (Phan et al. 2010).

None of this entails that norm psychology is innate, of course (although it does make it plausible). It is possible that only the core prosocial motivations (to help group members who need it, and not to hurt them) are innate, and the rest results from general-purpose learning and conditioning. It does at least seem that four-year-old children will invest in their own good reputations, however (Rapp et al. 2019); that five-year-old children will impose new conventional norms on each other across societies, correcting mistakes (Kanngiesser et al. 2022); and that children in the fourth year of life will set aside their own preferences when they learn that an activity is governed by a rule, whether that rule is provided by an adult or by another child (Li et al. 2021). But evidence from infants would provide much stronger support. That is what we consider next.

What should we be looking for if we seek evidence of innate dispositions to identify and learn social norms, as well as innate dispositions to positively-value norm-compliance in oneself and others and/or to negatively-value failures of norm-compliance in oneself and others? Social norms either pro-scribe actions as forbidden/wrong, or they prescribe them as obligatory/required, or else they allow that they are permissible without being forbidden or required. This three-way classification, and its attendant concepts, appears to be a human universal (Mikhail 2007). But how can we tell whether a prelinguistic infant thinks that an action is forbidden, required, or is merely permissible? For all one can measure in young infants is what they expect or what they find surprising, on the one hand, and what they find good or bad, on the other. The former can be measured using expectancy-violation looking-time experiments; the latter by studying infants' choice behavior.

186 Human Motives

While it is hard to see how one could test for the presence of concepts like FORBIDDEN and OBLIGATORY, as such, among prelinguistic infants, one can test for simpler concepts that are more-or-less extensionally equivalent to them. Thus one can roughly characterize a forbidden action in terms of two properties: it is an action that it would be bad for someone to do; and if someone *does* perform that action it would be good if others were to sanction them in some way, which we can operationalize as *doing bad to them*. Likewise, one can roughly characterize an obligatory action in terms of two properties: it is one that it would be bad for someone *not* to do; and if someone does fail to perform the action then it would be good if others were to sanction them/do bad to them. We do have some evidence of such attitudes in infants, at least in connection with forbidden actions.

Unfortunately, most studies with infants have used looking times, providing evidence of what they expect to happen, not of what they prefer—or think good—to happen. And we have already seen in Section 8.4 that infants have rich expectations of people's behavior within groups, some of which are likely to be innate. We noted, in particular, that 12-month-old infants expect a bystander to withhold support from (to punish) someone who does something to harm another member of the bystander's group, but not when the harming agent herself belongs to the bystander's group and the victim is an outgroup member (Ting et al. 2019). But this doesn't show that infants themselves share similar motivations, or feel that it is *good* to withhold support from someone who acts antisocially towards a member of their group.

In one of the few studies to test infants' own preferences, Hamlin et al. (2011) first familiarized eight-month-old infants with two puppets: a helpful puppet, who helped another protagonist open a box; and a nasty puppet, who jumped on the box to prevent it from being opened (potentially a forbidden action). One group of infants then saw the helpful puppet playing with a ball, which it dropped on a couple of occasions. On one such occasion the ball was returned to it by another helpful character (the Giver); whereas on another occasion it was taken away by an unhelpful character (the Taker). When offered a choice between the Giver and the Taker to play with, infants chose the helpful Giver. They thus seemingly think, either that someone who helps a good agent is good, or that someone who harms a good agent is bad, or both.

Another group of infants watched the nasty puppet (who had jumped on the box to prevent it being opened in the first scenario) in the same pair of events: dropping a ball it was playing with, which was then either returned to it by the Giver or taken away by the Taker. When offered a choice between the two characters, infants in this condition chose the *un*helpful one (the Taker). They thus seemingly think someone is good who does something bad to a bad agent (thereby engaging in something rather similar to punishing), or else they think that someone is bad who does something good for a bad agent, or both.[6]

In a follow-up experiment with toddlers (aged 19 to 23 months), the children were presented with the same initial scenario: a helpful puppet who helped an agent open a box, and a nasty puppet who jumped on top of the box to prevent it being opened. One group of toddlers was then given an opportunity to provide a treat to either the helpful or the nasty puppet, with most of them choosing to reward the helpful one. Another group of toddlers saw each of the helpful and nasty puppets already with a treat, but were introduced to a third character who didn't yet have one, and were invited to take a treat away from one of the other two puppets to give to him. They overwhelming chose to take the treat from the nasty puppet. They thus chose to do something bad to someone who had done something bad, in effect themselves imposing a punishment on the nasty puppet.

These experiments seem to show that infants think that it is good to do something bad to someone who has done something bad, suggesting that they have a concept a bit like FORBIDDEN. But I am not aware of any evidence showing that infants have a concept similar to OBLIGATORY. For this, we would need to show that infants think it is appropriate to do something bad to someone who *fails* to do something good. We do have evidence that 17-month-old infants *expect* someone with a leadership position in a group to intervene to prevent something bad happening to another group member (Stavans & Baillargeon 2019), but this is not really evidence that they think leaders *ought* (are obliged) to intervene.

The case is somewhat weaker for thinking that there is an innately structured norm psychology, then, than there is for thinking that prosociality towards group members is innate (as was argued in Section 8.2). And the present case is also weaker than exists for thinking that humans have innate expectations of groups and group behavior (as was argued in Section 8.4). While the evolutionary arguments are compelling that we should expect to find innate structures for learning and internalizing group norms, as well as dispositions towards third-party-punishment, we have only limited evidence thus far collected with infants to support such claims.

---

[6] Although this latter result was found with eight-month-olds, five-month-olds chose the helpful character in both conditions, no matter whether the puppet playing with the ball was itself a helper or a hinderer. One possible explanation is that the working-memory demands of the experiment (which are considerable) were too great for the younger infants.

8.6 Conclusion: Scaling Up

It is likely, then, that humans are innately prosocial: they have innate motivations to help and not to harm group members (as we saw in Section 8.2). It is also likely that humans are innately disposed to categorize and reason about the social world in terms of groups and group membership, both tribe-like and collaborative (Section 8.4). It is likely (albeit a bit less so, given current evidence) that humans are innately equipped to learn, internalize, and enforce the norms of their group (Section 8.5). And there is some reason to think, as well, that humans are innately disposed to track fairness and unfairness in both behavior and outcomes, and to evaluate these accordingly; although more evidence on this would be welcome (Section 8.3).

These initial innate factors (or some subset thereof) will vary to some significant degree across individuals, of course, just as do all other heritable properties. And they will then respond to cultural input of various sorts and interact with regular forms of evaluative learning that we share with other animals to issue in full-blown moral and normative systems of the kind that characterize all human cultures. The processes involved will be highly variable, both across individuals and across societies. One mechanism of learning will be straightforward evaluative conditioning, shared with almost all other creatures. Things or actions that are predictive of things or actions already found rewarding will come to be positively valued in their own right (likewise for acquiring new negative values). And these values can thereafter be sustained (prevented from extinguishing) by one's beliefs, as we noted in Section 2.7. This is because the belief that something is good or bad can lead one to experience it as such, altering (or sustaining) one's stored appraisals of its value thereafter.

A second mechanism of evaluative social learning is that observing evaluative behavior on the part of others will be apt to produce similar values in oneself. (Recall from Section 2.6 that observational value-learning is known to occur in both mammals and birds, and almost certainly occurs in humans too.) And then third, simply being told by others in one's group that something is good or bad (and accepting what they say) will be apt to both produce and store some degree of equivalently valenced affective value in oneself. (Recall from Section 2.7 that there are top-down effects of belief and expectation on value, and that such placebo and nocebo effects can be quite powerful.)

Putting these factors together in a variety of different combinations can result in a plethora of both cultural and individual values, just as we see across the world and over historical time. But it is not a complete free-for-all.

Moral Motivation **189**

There are constraints imposed by shared components of the innate starting state and of the mechanisms of evaluative learning; there are constraints imposed by local ecological conditions; and there are constraints on what social groups can value or disvalue while still remaining viable (let alone successful). So what we should expect to see (and what we do in fact see) are norms and values that are human universals (or nearly so) embedded within a kaleidoscope of cultural and individual variation (Brown 2001).

8.7 Addendum: Weak Humeanism

It is a consequence of the account of moral motivation developed in this book that the latter is, at bottom, affectively grounded. Indeed, the same is true of all motivation. So moral motivation is based on "the passions," as Blackburn (1999) persuasively argues on other grounds. The result is at least a weak form of Humeanism about motivation, and about moral motivation in particular (Rosati 2016). All motivation (at least, at the decision-making stage, as opposed to any goals and intentions that might result) requires a pairing of a belief or belief-like state with an affective state of some sort (a desire, perhaps, or anticipatory guilt or pride).

Note, however, that on the account defended here desires themselves are comprised of a number of distinct components. One is automatic motor-activation, whether expressive or instrumental, innate or learned. This will issue in action (in circumstances that afford action) unless inhibited. In contrast, the components of desires that are involved in decision-making (including decisions to inhibit or not to inhibit the motoric component) comprise two indicative-like representations with correctness-conditions—a representation of the desired outcome or action, paired with an analog-magnitude representation of its value, or its apparent goodness or badness.

The resulting account thus conflicts with some widely endorsed philosophical claims. One is that desires are directly motivating, comprising a disposition to bring about the desired state of affairs when paired with a means–ends belief. Although there is a kind of direct motivation embedded in the automatic motor-activation component of desires, the standard view falsely describes the way in which desires figure in decision-making processes. The components of desire that contribute to the latter are comprised entirely of indicative (belief-like and/or perception-like) representations, not imperative-like ones. The influence of desire on intentional action is indirect, resulting from processes that compute over and integrate values with likelihoods to issue in decisions and subsequent intentions. Moreover, desires are not (or not entirely) propositional attitudes. They always at least comprise a nonconceptual component (valence, which is an analog-magnitude representation of value), and they can often be wholly nonconceptual in content (as when a nonconceptual rehearsal of a motor plan is appraised positively and results in anticipatory pleasure bound into its content).

In some respects, then, the account defended here seems decidedly un-Humean. For decision-making can be comprised entirely of states with correctness-conditions and mind-to-world direction of fit, including beliefs, desires, and other affective states (albeit not when existing goals and intentions are involved, since these do have satisfaction-conditions and world-to-mind direction of fit). Note, too (in contrast with many forms of Humeanism), that a mere belief that something is good, or that an action is morally required, can issue in some degree of motivation independent of any pre-existing desire, for as we saw in Section 2.7, beliefs about value are apt to cause forms of affective valuation of the same general valence. So the upshot can be a kind of contingent moral internalism (Rosati 2016). Moral beliefs and moral judgments (however acquired) will be apt to produce some degree of matching affective valuation in a top-down manner.

Suppose, for example, that community members tell one that an action is morally forbidden, and one believes them. This may be enough for one to feel thereafter some degree of aversion to the thought of so acting. This is consistent with some characterizations of Humeanism (Smith 1987), but probably not with others (Sinhababu 2009), depending on whether or not the Humean allows that desires can result from reasoning that doesn't include desires amongst its premises. For although there might be a form of affective valuation involved in accepting what one is told, this will result from an appraisal of the community members' trustworthiness and good-will, rather than anything directly to do with the moral content itself.

In addition, one might reason one's way to a new moral principle or belief—or be persuaded by others—from premises that one already accepts, via innate or learned inferential steps, to a conclusion that one appraises and feels committed to accepting. Having endorsed it, that principle will thereafter operate somewhat as does a goal or intention: that is, as a "cold" rather than "hot" mental state that is apt to cause the corresponding actions directly (see Section 3.5). But like any other intention, it will be apt to interact with affective systems to produce positive valence at indications of progress towards fulfillment, and negative valence (frustration) in response to perceived obstacles. So in this respect the upshot may be what Blackburn (1999) would call a "Hume-friendly" conception of the role of reason in ethics.

In fact, the account that has emerged out of our consideration and interpretation of the science can be seen as a sort of hybrid between Humean and rationalist theories of motivation. On the one hand, all decision-making constitutively involves an affective state of some sort, whether a desire, a repulsion, or an emotion. On the other hand, the components of affective states that enter directly into decision-making (setting aside arousal and automatic motor-activation) are all indicative in nature (belief-like or perception-like), with correctness conditions. And moreover, beliefs and expectations can have a top-down influence on one's affective states, creating sources of motivation where none had previously existed.

8.8 Summary: The Case against Hedonism

One conclusion reached in this chapter is that humans are innately disposed to act helpfully towards unrelated group members. But it doesn't follow from this alone that altruism itself is innate, of course. For it might have been that the adults, children, and infants in these experiments act as they do because they anticipate that good feelings will result, and decide to be helpful in order to secure those feelings. Or it could have been the case that appraising a group member as needing help results in an action-motivating imperative aimed at securing the *experience* of helping. In short, whether or not the arguments presented in this chapter demonstrate innate altruism depends on the best overall account of the real nature of anticipatory positive and negative valence (pleasure and displeasure). That has been the topic of previous chapters.

We saw in Chapters 2 and 3 that pleasure and displeasure (or positive and negative valence more generally) are the common currency of all decision-making (whether conscious or unconscious), just as motivational hedonists have always maintained. But people don't select actions because they *believe* that those actions will secure pleasure or avoid displeasure (or at least, not in general—of course people *can* sometimes aim to secure or avoid pleasant or unpleasant experiences as such). Rather, the anticipated actions and/or their consequences are appraised by one's evaluative systems and result in some degree of pleasure or displeasure, now, that attaches to them. This drives decision-making directly. So actions that result from decision-making are motivated by anticip*atory* pleasure or displeasure, rather than anticip*ated* (believed in) future pleasure or displeasure. The future-directed character of the pleasures and displeasures involved in decision-making is implicit in

192 Human Motives

their binding to future-directed representations of actions and outcomes, as well as in the mechanisms that compare the actual pleasures and displeasures later experienced with the anticipatory ones, thereby updating one's evaluations of actions and outcomes of those sorts.

It is this fundamental fact about the workings of decision-making systems that renders motivational hedonism immune from many of the standard philosophical and experimental critiques, as we saw in Chapter 4. Others of those arguments are unsuccessful, as we also saw, in virtue of failing to draw a clear distinction between the contents (generally world-directed) whose appraisal gives rise to affective states, on the one hand, and the valence-signals (pleasure or displeasure) generated as output that get used in decision-making, on the other.

From the fact that anticipatory pleasure and displeasure are what drive all decision-making it doesn't follow that all decisions are taken *in order to secure* pleasure and avoid displeasure, of course. That depends on the nature of pleasure and displeasure themselves. If anticipatory pleasure is a representation of the goodness of the anticipated action or its consequences, and anticipatory displeasure is a representation of badness, then decisions are taken in order to secure good things and avoid bad ones. That is consistent with and (given minimal additional assumptions) entails motivational pluralism and altruism. In contrast, if anticipatory valence is comprised of intrinsically good or bad subjective feelings that decision-making systems are designed to secure and avoid, then motivational hedonism follows. And likewise if valence is comprised of experience-directed imperatives.

The question of motivational hedonism thus ultimately turns on the true nature of valence (pleasure and displeasure). Chapters 5 through 7 argued that the best overall account, providing the best theory that encompasses all of the scientific evidence, is the value-representing one. Consummatory pleasure is an analog-magnitude signal representing the current action or event as to some degree good; and anticipatory pleasure is an analog-magnitude representation of the degree of goodness of the future action or outcome currently being considered. Likewise, consummatory displeasure is an analog-magnitude representation of the degree of badness of the current action or event; and anticipatory displeasure is an analog-magnitude representation of the degree of badness of the action or outcome being anticipated. Valence is neither a decision-determining positive or negative subjective feeling attaching to experiences, nor is it comprised of experience-directed imperatives. Or so I have argued.

As we also saw in Chapter 5, however, the representational content (the correctness condition) of valence is adaptive value and disvalue. For this is what valence signals carry information about, and it is the fact that they carry that information, rather than any other information, that explains why valence has the roles that it does, and why systems of evaluative learning, valence-production, and valence-based decision-making operate as they do. This is what opens up the possibility of a kind of extended egoism, discussed in Section 5.7. For it might be said, in consequence, that all decisions are taken to maximize one's own inclusive fitness. But here the distinction between the referential correctness conditions of a signal (needed for explanatory purposes in cognitive science) and the mode of presentation of those conditions to the subject proves crucial. (This also turned out to be important in Section 7.5 when discussing the nature of sensory pain.) While valence represents (has as its correctness conditions) adaptive value and disvalue, the mode of presentation of those conditions to the subject is just as a sort of non-articulable—nonconceptual—analog-magnitude presentation of goodness and badness.

In conclusion, I claim that motivational hedonism has finally been refuted, for recall that I have employed the steel-man strategy throughout, attempting to formulate and critique the strongest, most defensible, forms of motivational hedonism. In fact, most people are genuinely altruistic (at least sometimes, and especially towards ingroup members); and most people are genuinely motivated by considerations of justice and fairness for their own sakes, as required by moral norms (because these things are represented nonconceptually as good, with failures represented nonconceptually as bad). Indeed, the evidence reviewed in the present chapter suggests that people are *innately* altruistic, and may also be innately disposed to learn, internalize, and comply with moral norms. But at the same time, as we have seen, our innately channeled forms of tribal cognition and tribal-group motivation leave humans vulnerable to both becoming and doing evil.

References

Adolphs, R. & Anderson, D.J. (2018). *The Neuroscience of Emotion*. Princeton University Press.

Ahrens, A., Singer, B., Fitzpatrick, C., Morrow, J., & Robinson, T. (2016). Rats that sign-track are resistant to Pavlovian but not instrumental extinction. *Behavioral Brain Research*, 296, 418–30.

Albers, A., Kok, P., Toni, I., Dijkerman, C., & de Lange, F. (2013). Shared representations for working memory and mental imagery in early visual cortex. *Current Biology*, 23, 1427–31.

Amici, F., Call, J., & Aureli, F. (2012). Aversion to violation of expectations of food distribution: The role of social tolerance and relative dominance in seven primate species. *Behavior*, 149, 345–68.

Amodio, D. & Cikara, M. (2021). The social neuroscience of prejudice. *Annual Review of Psychology*, 72, 439–69.

Amodio, P., Farrar, B., Krupenye, C., Ostojić, L., & Clayton, N. (2021). Little evidence that Eurasian jays protect their caches by responding to cues about a conspecific's desire and visual perspective. *eLife*, 10, e69647.

Anscombe, G.E. (1957). *Intention*. Blackwell.

Ashar, Y., Chang, L.J., & Wager, T. (2017). Brain mechanisms of the placebo effect: An affective appraisal account. *Annual Review of Clinical Psychology*, 13, 73–98.

Atance, C. (2008). Future thinking in young children. *Current Directions in Psychological Science*, 17, 295–98.

Aydede, M. (2019). Is the experience of pain transparent? Introspecting phenomenal qualities. *Synthese*, 196, 677–708.

Aydede, M. & Fulkerson, M. (2014). Affect: Representationalists' headache. *Philosophical Studies*, 170, 175–98.

Aydede, M. & Fulkerson, M. (2019). Reasons and theories of sensory affect. In D. Bain, M. Brady, & J. Corns (eds.), *The Philosophy of Pain*, Routledge.

Bain, D. (2013). What makes pains unpleasant? *Philosophical Studies*, 166, S69–S89.

Bain, D. (2017). Evaluativist accounts of pain's unpleasantness. In J. Corns (ed.), *Routledge Handbook of Philosophy of Pain*, Routledge.

Bain, D. & Brady, M. (2014). Pain, pleasure, and unpleasure. *Review of Philosophy and Psychology*, 5, 1–14.

Balafoutas, L., Nikiforakis, N., & Rockenbach, B. (2014). Direct and indirect punishment among strangers in the field. *Proceedings of the National Academy of Sciences*, 111, 15924–27.

Balleine, B., Delgado, M., & Hikosaka, O. (2007). The role of dorsal striatum in reward and decision-making. *Journal of Neuroscience*, 27, 8161–65.

Balliet, D., Wu, J., & De Drey, C. (2014). Ingroup favoritism in cooperation: A meta-analysis. *Psychological Bulletin*, 140, 1556–81.

Bandelow, B., Reitt, M., Röver, C., Michaelis, S., Görlich, Y., & Wedekind, D. (2015). Efficacy of treatments for anxiety disorders: A meta-analysis. *International Clinical Psychopharmacology*, 30, 183–92.

Barlassina, L. (2020). Beyond good and bad: Reflexive imperativism, not evaluativism, explains valence. *Thought*, 9, 274–84.

Barlassina, L. & Hayward, M. (2019a). Loopy regulations: The motivational profile of affective phenomenology. *Philosophical Topics*, 47, 233–61.

196 References

Barlassina, L. & Hayward, M. (2019b). More of me! Less of me!: Reflexive imperativism about affective phenomenal character. *Mind*, 128, 1013–44.

Barrett, H.C., Bolyanatz, A., Crittenden, A., Fessler, D., Fitzpatrick, S., Gurven, M., Henrich, J., Kanovsky, M., Kushnick, G., Pisor, A., Scelza, B., Stich, S., von Rueden, C., Zhao, W., & Laurence, S. (2016). Small-scale societies exhibit fundamental variation in the role of intentions in moral judgment. *Proceedings of the National Academies of Science*, 113, 4688–93.

Barrett, H.C., Broesch, T., Scott, R., He, Z., Baillargeon, R., Wu, D., Bolz, M., Henrich, J., Setoh, P., Wang, J., & Laurence, S. (2013). Early false-belief understanding in traditional non-Western societies. *Proceedings of the Royal Society B*, 280, 20122654.

Barrett, L. & Bar, M. (2009). See it with feeling: Affective predictions during object perception. *Philosophical Transactions of the Royal Society B*, 364, 1325–34.

Barrett, L., Lindquist, K., Bliss-Moreau, E., Duncan, S., Gendron, M., Mize, J. & Brennan, L. (2007). Of mice and men: Natural kinds of emotions in the mammalian brain? *Perspectives on Psychological Science*, 2, 297–312.

Barth, H., Kanwisher, N., & Spelke, E. (2003). The construction of large number representations in adults. *Cognition*, 86, 201–21.

Basbaum, A., Bautista, D., Scherrer, G., & Julius, D. (2009). Cellular and molecular mechanisms of pain. *Cell*, 139, 267–84.

Bateson, M., Desire, S., Gartside, S., & Wright, G. (2011). Agitated honey-bees exhibit pessimistic cognitive biases. *Current Biology*, 21, 1070–73.

Batson, C.D. (1991). *The Altruism Question*. Lawrence Erlbaum Associates.

Batson, C.D. (2019). *The Scientific Search for Altruism*. Oxford University Press.

Batson, C.D., Batson, J., Slingsby, J., Harrell, K., Peekna, H., & Todd, R. (1991). Empathic joy and the empathy-altruism hypothesis. *Journal of Personality and Social Psychology*, 61, 413–26.

Batson, C.D., Dyck, J., Brandt, J., Batson, J., Powell, A., McMaster, M., & Griffitt, C. (1988). Five studies testing two new egoistic alternatives to the empathy-altruism hypothesis. *Journal of Personality and Social Psychology*, 55, 52–77.

Baumard, N., André, J., & Sperber, D. (2013). A mutualistic approach to morality: The evolution of fairness by partner choice. *Behavioral and Brain Sciences*, 36, 59–78.

Baumgartner, T., Knoch, D., Hotz, P., Eisenegger, C., & Fehr, E. (2011). Dorsolateral and ventromedial prefrontal cortex orchestrate normative choice. *Nature Neuroscience*, 14, 1468–74.

Bays, P. (2015). Spikes not slots: Noise in neural populations limits working memory. *Trends in Cognitive Sciences*, 19, 431–38.

Benoit, R., Szpunar, K., & Schacter, D. (2014). Ventromedial prefrontal cortex supports affective future simulation by integrating distributed knowledge. *Proceedings of the National Academy of Sciences*, 111, 16550–55.

Berlucchi, G. & Aglioti, S. (1997). The body in the brain: Neural bases of corporeal awareness. *Trends in Neurosciences*, 20, 560–64.

Berna, F., Goldberg, P., Kolska Horwitz, L., Brink, J., Holt, S., Bamford, M., & Chazan, M. (2012). Microstratigraphic evidence of in situ fire in the Acheulean strata of Wonderwerk cave, Northern Cape province, South Africa. *Proceedings of the National Academy of Sciences*, 109, E1215–E1220.

Berridge, K. (2009). Wanting and liking: Observations from the neuroscience and psychology laboratory. *Inquiry*, 52, 378–98.

Berridge, K. & Kringelbach, M. (2008). Affective neuroscience of pleasure: Reward in humans and animals. *Psychopharmacology*, 199, 457–80.

Berridge, K. & Kringelbach, M. (2015). Pleasure systems in the brain. *Neuron*, 86, 646–64.

Berthier, M., Starkstein, S., & Leiguarda, R. (1988). Asymbolia for pain: A sensory-limbic disconnection syndrome. *Annals of Neurology*, 24, 41–49.

Bird, C. & Emery, N. (2009). Rooks use stones to raise the water level to reach a floating worm. *Current Biology*, 19, 1410–14.

Blackburn, S. (1999). *Ruling Passions*. Oxford University Press.

Blackwell, L., Trzesniewski, K., & Dweck, C. (2007). Implicit theories of intelligence predict achievement across an adolescent transition: A longitudinal study and an intervention. *Child Development*, 78, 246–63.

Boehm, C. (2001). *Hierarchy in the Forest*. Harvard University Press.

Bonnano, G. (2021). *The End of Trauma: How the New Science of Resilience Is Changing How We Think about PTSD*. Basic Books.

Botvinick, M., Huffstetler, S., & McGuire, J. (2009). Effort discounting in human nucleus accumbens. *Cognitive, Affective, & Behavioral Neuroscience*, 9, 16–27.

Boyd, R. & Richerson, P. (1992). Punishment allows for the evolution of cooperation (or anything else) in sizable groups. *Ethology and Sociobiology*, 13, 171–95.

Boyd, R.N. (1991). Realism, anti-foundationalism and the enthusiasm for natural kinds. *Philosophical Studies*, 61, 127–48.

Boyd, R.N. (1999). Kinds, complexity, and multiple realization. *Philosophical Studies*, 95, 67–98.

Brandt, R. (1979). *A Theory of the Good and the Right*. Oxford University Press.

Bratman, M. (1987). *Intentions, Plans, and Practical Reason*. Harvard University Press.

Bratman, M. (1999). *Faces of Intention*. Cambridge University Press.

Brewer, M. (1999). The psychology of prejudice: Ingroup love and outgroup hate? *Journal of Social Issues*, 55, 429–44.

Broad, C. (1952). *Ethics and the History of Philosophy*. Routledge and Kegan Paul.

Bromberg-Martin, E. & Hikosaka, O. (2009). Midbrain dopamine neurons signal preferences for advance information about upcoming rewards. *Neuron*, 63, 119–26.

Brosnan, S. & de Waal, F. (2003). Monkeys reject unequal pay. *Nature*, 425, 297–99.

Brown, D. (2001). *Human Universals*. McGraw-Hill.

Brownstein, M. (2019). Implicit bias. In E. Zalta (ed.), *Stanford Encyclopedia of Philosophy*. https://plato.stanford.edu/archives/fall2019/entries/implicit-bias/.

Buckholtz, J. & Marois, R. (2012). The roots of modern justice: Cognitive and neural foundations of social norms and their enforcement. *Nature Neuroscience*, 15, 655–61.

Buhle, J., Stevens, B., Friedman, J., & Wager, T. (2012). Distraction and placebo: Two separate routes to pain control. *Psychological Science*, 23, 246–53.

Bunce, S., Bernat, E., Wong, P., & Shevrin, H. (1999). Further evidence for unconscious learning: Preliminary support for the conditioning of facial EMG to subliminal stimuli. *Journal of Psychiatric Research*, 33, 341–47.

Burke, K., Franz, T., Miller, D., & Schoenbaum, G. (2008). The role of the orbitofrontal cortex in the pursuit of happiness and more specific rewards. *Nature*, 454, 340–45.

Burns, M. & Sommerville, J. (2014). "I pick you": The impact of fairness and race on infants' selection of social partners. *Frontiers in Psychology*, 5, #93.

Buschman, T., Siegel, M., Roy, J., & Miller, E. (2011). Neural substrates of cognitive capacity limitations. *Proceedings of the National Academy of Sciences*, 108, 11252–55.

Buss, D. (1989). Sex differences in human mate preferences: Evolutionary hypotheses tested in 37 cultures. *Behavioral and Brain Sciences*, 12, 1–49.

Butler, J. (1726). *Fifteen Sermons Preached at the Rolls Chapel*. W. Botham.

Buttelmann, D. & Böhm, R. (2014). The ontogeny of the motivation that underlies in-group bias. *Psychological Science*, 25, 921–27.

Buttelmann, D., Zmyj, N., Daum, M., & Carpenter, M. (2013). Selective imitation of in-group over out-group members in 14-month-old infants. *Child Development*, 84, 422–28.

Buyukozer Dawkins, M., Sloane, S., & Baillargeon, R. (2019). Do infants in the first year of life expect equal resource allocations? *Frontiers in Psychology*, 10, #116.

198 References

Byrne, D. (1971). *The Attraction Paradigm*. Academic Press.

Cammaerts, M. (2004). Operant conditioning in the ant *Myrmica sabuleti*. *Behavioral Processes*, 67, 417–25.

Carruthers, P. (1999). Sympathy and subjectivity. *Australasian Journal of Philosophy*, 77, 465–82.

Carruthers, P. (2011). *The Opacity of Mind*. Oxford University Press.

Carruthers, P. (2015). *The Centered Mind*. Oxford University Press.

Carruthers, P. (2017). Are epistemic emotions metacognitive? *Philosophical Psychology*, 30, 58–78.

Carruthers, P. (2018a). The causes and contents of inner speech. In P. Langland-Hassan & A. Vicente (eds.), *Inner Speech*, Oxford University Press.

Carruthers, P. (2018b). Implicit versus explicit attitudes: Differing manifestations of the same representational structures? *Review of Philosophy and Psychology*, 9, 51–72.

Carruthers, P. (2018c). Valence and value. *Philosophy and Phenomenological Research*, 97, 658–80.

Carruthers, P. (2018d). Basic questions. *Mind & Language*, 33, 130–47.

Carruthers, P. (2019). *Human and Animal Minds*. Oxford University Press.

Carruthers, P. (2020). Questions in development. In L. Butler, S. Ronfard, & K. Corriveau (eds.), *The Questioning Child: Insights from Psychology and Education*. Cambridge University Press.

Carruthers, P. (2021). Explicit nonconceptual metacognition. *Philosophical Studies*, 178, 2337–56.

Carruthers, P. (2023). On valence: Imperative or representation of value? *British Journal for the Philosophy of Science*, 74. https://doi.org/10.1086/714985.

Carruthers, P. (2024). The contents and causes of curiosity. *British Journal for the Philosophy of Science*, 75. In press.

Carruthers, P. (2025). *Explaining Action*. In preparation.

Carruthers, P. & James, S. (2008). Evolution and the possibility of moral realism. *Philosophy and Phenomenological Research*, 77, 237–44.

Carruthers, P. & Veillet, B. (2017). Consciousness operationalized, a debate realigned. *Consciousness and Cognition*, 55, 79–90.

Carruthers, P. & Williams, D.M. (2019). Comparative metacognition. *Animal Behavior and Cognition*, 6, 278–88.

Carruthers, P. & Williams, D.M. (2022). Model-free metacognition. *Cognition*, 225, 105117.

Chang, L., Krosch, A., & Cikara, M. (2016). Effects of intergroup threat on mind, brain, and behavior. *Current Opinion in Psychology*, 11, 69–73.

Cheeseman, J., Millar, C., Greggers, U., Lehmann, K., Pawley, M., Gallistel, C., Warman, G., & Menzel, R. (2014). Way-finding in displaced clock-shifted bees proves bees use a cognitive map. *Proceedings of the National Academy of Sciences*, 111, 8949–54.

Chib, V., Rangel, A., Shimojo, S., & O'Doherty, J. (2009). Evidence for a common representation of decision values for dissimilar goods in the human ventromedial prefrontal cortex. *Journal of Neuroscience*, 29, 12315–20.

Chikazoe, J., Lee, D., Kriegeskorte, N., & Anderson, A. (2014). Population coding of affect across stimuli, modalities, and individuals. *Nature Neuroscience*, 17, 1114–22.

Chudek, M. & Henrich, J. (2011). Culture-gene coevolution, norm-psychology and the emergence of human prosociality. *Trends in Cognitive Sciences*, 15, 218–26.

Cicchini, G., Anobile, G., & Burr, D. (2016). Spontaneous perception of numerosity in humans. *Nature Communications*, 7: 12536.

Cikara, M., Bruneau, E., & Saxe, R. (2011). Us and them: Intergroup failures of empathy. *Current Directions in Psychological Science*, 20, 149–53.

Cikara, M. & Van Bavel, J. (2014). The neuroscience of intergroup relations: An integrative review. *Perspectives on Psychological Science*, 9, 245–74.

Cisek, P. & Kalaska, J. (2010). Neural mechanisms for interacting with a world full of action choices. *Annual Review of Neuroscience*, 33, 269–98.

Clark, A. (2013). Whatever next? Predictive brains, situated agents, and the future of cognitive science. *Behavioral and Brain Sciences*, 36, 181–204.

Clark, J., Hollon, N., & Phillips, P. (2012). Pavlovian valuation systems in learning and decision making. *Current Opinion in Neurobiology*, 22, 1054–61.

Clement, J. (1982). Students' preconceptions in introductory mechanics. *American Journal of Physics*, 50, 66–70.

Cochrane, T. (2018). *The Emotional Mind*. Cambridge University Press.

Cohen, G. & Sherman, D. (2014). The psychology of change: Self-affirmation and social psychological intervention. *Annual Review of Psychology*, 65, 333–71.

Cona, G., Scarpazza, C., Sartori, G., Moscovitch, M., & Bisiacchi, P. (2015). Neural bases of prospective memory. *Neuroscience and Biobehavioral Reviews*, 52, 21–37.

Coninx, S. (2021). Strong representationalism and bodily sensations: Reliable causal covariance and biological function. *Philosophical Psychology*, 34, 210–32.

Contrò, V., Pieretta Mancuso, E., & Proia, P. (2016). Delayed onset muscle soreness (DOMS) management: Present state of the art. *Trends in Sports Sciences*, 3, 121–27.

Corbetta, M., Patel, G., & Shulman, G. (2008). The reorienting system of the human brain: From environment to theory of mind. *Neuron*, 3, 306–24.

Cornelissen, G., Dewitte, S., & Warlop, L. (2011). Are social value orientations expressed automatically? Decision making in the dictator game. *Personality and Social Psychology Bulletin*, 37, 1080–90.

Corns, J. (2014). Unpleasantness, motivational oomph, and painfulness. *Mind & Language*, 29, 238–54.

Cos, I., Duque, J., & Cisek, P. (2014). Rapid prediction of biomechanical costs during action decisions. *Journal of Neurophysiology*, 112, 1256–66.

Cosmides, L. & Tooby, J. (1992). Cognitive adaptations for social exchange. In J. Barkow, L. Cosmides, & J. Tooby (eds.), *The Adapted Mind*, Oxford University Press.

Cowan, N. (2001). The magical number 4 in short-term memory: A reconsideration of mental storage capacity. *Behavioral and Brain Sciences*, 24, 87–185.

Cuijpers, P., Driessen, E., Hollon, S., van Oppen, P., Barth, J., & Andersson, G. (2012). The efficacy of non-directive supportive therapy for adult depression: A meta-analysis. *Clinical Psychology Review*, 32, 280–91.

Cutrone, E., Heeger, D., & Carrasco, M. (2014). Attention enhances contrast appearance via increased input baseline of neural responses. *Journal of Vision*, 14: 16.

Cutter, B. & Tye, M. (2011). Tracking representationalism and the painfulness of pain. *Philosophical Issues*, 21, 90–109.

Cutter, B. & Tye, M. (2014). Pains and reasons: Why is it rational to kill the messenger? *Philosophical Quarterly*, 64, 423–33.

Damasio, A. (1994). *Descartes' Error*. Putnam Press.

D'Arms, J. & Jacobson, D. (2000). The moralistic fallacy: On the "appropriateness" of emotions. *Philosophy and Phenomenological Research*, 61, 65–90.

Dayan, P. & Berridge, K. (2014). Model-based and model-free Pavlovian reward learning: Revaluation, revision, and revelation. *Cognitive and Affective Behavioral Neuroscience*, 14, 473–92.

de Araujo, I., Rolls, E., Velazco, M., Margot, C., & Cayeux, I. (2005). Cognitive modulation of olfactory processing. *Neuron*, 46, 671–79.

de Araujo, I., Schatzker, M., & Small, D. (2020). Rethinking food reward. *Annual Review of Psychology*, 71, 139–64.

De Sousa, R. (1987). *The Rationality of Emotion*. MIT Press.

de Vignemont, F. (2010). Body schema and body image—Pros and cons. *Neuropsychologia*, 48, 669–80.

Dehaene, S. (2014). *Consciousness and the Brain*. Viking Press.

Dennett, D. (1978). Why you can't make a computer that feels pain. *Synthese*, 38, 415–56.

200 References

Deonna, J. & Teroni, F. (2015). Emotions as attitudes. *Dialectica*, 69, 293–311.

DesChamps, T., Eason, A., & Sommerville, J. (2015). Infants associate praise and admonishment with fair and unfair individuals. *Infancy*, 20, 1–27.

Dichter, G., Smoski, M., Kampov-Polevoy, A., Gallop, R., & Garbutt, J. (2010). Unipolar depression does not moderate responses to the sweet taste test. *Depression and Anxiety*, 27, 859–63.

Dickinson, A. & Balleine, B. (1994). Motivational control of goal-directed action. *Animal Learning and Behavior*, 22, 1–18.

Dickinson, A. & Balleine, B. (2002). The role of learning in the operation of motivational systems. In C.R. Gallistel (ed.), *Stevens Handbook of Experimental Psychology*, John Wiley and Sons.

DiFeliceantonio, A. & Berridge, K. (2016). Dorsolateral neostriatum contribution to incentive salience: Opioid or dopamine stimulation makes one reward cue more motivationally attractive than another. *European Journal of Neuroscience*, 43, 1203–18.

Doll, B., Simon, D., & Daw, N. (2012). The ubiquity of model-based reinforcement learning. *Current Opinion in Neurobiology*, 22, 1075–81.

Döring, S. (2003). Explaining action by emotion. *The Philosophical Quarterly*, 53, 214–30.

Doris, J., Stich, S., & Walmsley, L. (2020). Empirical approaches to altruism. In E. Zalta (ed.), *Stanford Encyclopedia of Philosophy*. https://plato.stanford.edu/archives/spr2020/entries/altruism-empirical/.

Dretske, F. (1988). *Explaining Behavior*. MIT Press.

Dretske, F. (1995). *Naturalizing the Mind*. MIT Press.

Dubreuil, D., Silvia Gentile, M., & Visalberghi, E. (2006). Are capuchin monkeys (*Cebus apella*) inequity averse? *Proceedings of the Royal Society B*, 273, 1223–28.

Dunbar, R. (2004). Gossip in evolutionary perspective. *Review of General Psychology*, 8, 100–110.

Dunfield, K., Kuhlmeier, V., O'Connell, L., & Kelley, E. (2011). Examining the diversity of prosocial behavior: Helping, sharing, and comforting in infancy. *Infancy*, 16, 227–47.

Dunham, Y. (2018). Mere membership. *Trends in Cognitive Sciences*, 22, 780–93.

Dunham, Y., Baron, A., & Carey, S. (2011). Consequences of "minimal" group affiliations in children. *Child Development*, 82, 793–811.

Eippert, F., Finsterbusch, J., Binkel, U., & Büchel, C. (2009). Direct evidence for spinal cord involvement in placebo analgesia. *Science*, 326, 404.

Eisenberg, N. & Miller, P. (1987). Empathy and prosocial behavior. *Psychological Bulletin*, 101, 91–119.

Eisenberger, N., Lieberman, M., & Williams, K. (2003). Does rejection hurt? An fMRI study of social exclusion. *Science*, 302, 290–92.

Eisenberger, R. (1992). Learned industriousness. *Psychological Review*, 99, 248–67.

Ekman, P. (1992). Are there basic emotions? *Psychological Review*, 99, 550–53.

Eldar, E., Pessiglione, M., & van Dillen, L. (2021). Positive affect as a computational mechanism. *Current Opinion in Behavioral Sciences*, 39, 52–57.

Eldar, E., Rutledge, R., Dolan, R., & Niv, Y. (2016). Mood as representation of momentum. *Trends in Cognitive Sciences*, 20, 15–24.

Engelmann, J., Clift, J., Herrmann, E., & Tomasello, M. (2017). Social disappointment explains chimpanzees' behavior in the inequity aversion task. *Proceedings of the Royal Society B*, 284, 20171502.

Engelmann, J. & Rapp, D. (2018). The influence of reputational concerns on children's prosociality. *Current Opinion in Psychology*, 20, 92–95.

Fanselow, M., Lester, L., & Helmstetter, F. (1988). Changes in feeding and foraging patterns as an antipredator defensive strategy: A laboratory simulation using aversive stimulation in a closed economy. *Journal of the Experimental Analysis of Behavior*, 50, 361–74.

Fareri, D., Chang, L., & Delgado, M. (2015). Computational substrates of social value in interpersonal collaboration. *Journal of Neuroscience*, 35, 8170–80.

Fehr, E. & Gächter, S. (2000). Fairness and retaliation: The economics of reciprocity. *Journal of Economic Perspectives*, 14, 159–81.

Feinberg, J. (1984). Psychological egoism. In S. Cahn, P. Kitcher, & G. Sher (eds.), *Reason at Work*, Harcourt, Brace, and Jovanovich.

Feinberg, M., Willer, R., & Schultz, M. (2014). Gossip and ostracism promote cooperation in groups. *Psychological Science*, 25, 656–64.

Feinstein, J., Buzza, C., Hurlemann, R., Follmer,R., Dahdaleh,N., Coryell,W., Welsh, M., Tranel, D., & Wemmie, J. (2013). Fear and panic in humans with bilateral amygdala damage. *Nature Neuroscience*, 16, 270–72.

Feldman, F. (1997). Two questions about pleasure. In F. Feldman (ed.), *Utilitarianism, Hedonism, and Desert*, Cambridge University Press.

Feldman, F. (2004). *Pleasure and the Good Life*. Oxford University Press.

Fernqvist, F. & Ekelund, L. (2014). Credence and the effect on consumer liking of food—A review. *Food Quality and Preference*, 32, 340–53.

Ferrer, R., Maclay, A., Litvak, P., & Lerner, J. (2016). Revisiting the effects of anger on risk-taking: Empirical and meta-analytic evidence for differences between males and females. *Journal of Behavioral Decision Making*. https://doi.org/10.1002/bdm.1971.

Fiddick, L., Cosmides, L., & Tooby, J. (2000). No interpretation without representation: The role of domain-specific representations and inferences in the Wason selection task. *Cognition*, 77, 1–79.

Flagel, S., Clark, J., Robinson, T., Mayo, L., Czuj, A., Willuhn, I., Akers, C., Clinton, S., Phillips, P., & Akil, H. (2011). A selective role for dopamine in stimulus-reward learning. *Nature*, 469, 53–57.

Fodor, J. (1990). *A Theory of Content and Other Essays*. MIT Press.

Frank, R., Gilovich, T., & Regan, D. (1993). Does studying economics inhibit cooperation? *Journal of Economic Perspectives*, 7, 159–71.

Frankish, K. (2004). *Mind and Supermind*. Cambridge University Press.

Frankish, K. (2009). Systems and levels: Dual-system theories and the personal-subpersonal distinction. In J.S.T.B. Evans & K. Frankish (eds.), *In Two Minds*, Oxford University Press.

Frankish, K. (2016). Illusionism as a theory of consciousness. *Journal of Consciousness Studies*, 23 (11–12), 11–39.

Frijda, N. (2010). Impulsive action and motivation. *Biological Psychiatry*, 84, 570–79.

Frith, C., Blakemore, S.-J., & Wolpert, D. (2000). Abnormalities in the awareness and control of action. *Philosophical Transactions of the Royal Society of London B*, 355, 1771–88.

Fulkerson, M. (2020). Emotional perception. *Australasian Journal of Philosophy*, 98, 16–30.

Galea, J., Vazquez, A., Pasricha, N., Orban de Xivry, J.-J., & Celnik, P. (2011). Dissociating the roles of the cerebellum and motor cortex during adaptive learning: The motor cortex retains what the cerebellum learns. *Cerebral Cortex*, 21, 1761–70.

Gallistel, R., Mark, T., King, A., & Lantham, P. (2001). The rat approximates an ideal detector of rates of reward. *Journal of Experimental Psychology: Animal Behavior Processes*, 27, 354–72.

Gan, Z., Gangadharan, V., Liu, S., Körber, C., Tan, L.L., Li, H., Oswald, M., Kang, J., Martin-Cortecero, J., Männich, D., Groh, A., Kuner, T., Wieland, S., & Kuner, R. (2022). Layer-specific pain relief pathways originating from primary motor cortex. *Science*, 378, 1336–43.

Gandevia, S. (2001). Spinal and supraspinal factors in human muscle fatigue. *Physiological Reviews*, 81, 1725–89.

Gard, D., Kring, A., Gard, M., Horan, W., & Green, M. (2007). Anhedonia in schizophrenia: Distinctions between anticipatory and consummatory pleasure. *Schizophrenia Research*, 93, 253–60.

202 References

Gasper, K. & Clore, G. (2000). Do you have to pay attention to your feelings to be influenced by them? *Personality and Social Psychology Bulletin*, 26, 698–711.

Gelman, S. (2003). *The Essential Child*. Oxford University Press.

Gelman, S., Sánchez Tapia, I., & Leslie, S.-J. (2016). Memory for generic and quantified sentences in Spanish-speaking children and adults. *Journal of Child Language*, 43, 1231–44.

Gianaros, P. & Wager, T. (2015). Brain-body pathways linking psychological stress and physical health. *Current Directions in Psychological Science*, 24, 313–21.

Gibbons, M., Versace, E., Crump, A., Baran, B., & Chittka, L. (2022). Motivational trade-offs and modulation of nociception in bumblebees. *Proceedings of the National Academy of Sciences*, 119, e2205821119.

Gigerenzer, G., Todd, P., & the ABC Research Group (1999). *Simple Heuristics that Make Us Smart*. Oxford University Press.

Gilbert, D. & Wilson, T. (2007). Prospection: Experiencing the future. *Science*, 317, 1351–54.

Gilbert, D. & Wilson, T. (2009). Why the brain talks to itself: Sources of error in emotional prediction. *Philosophical Transactions of the Royal Society B*, 364, 1335–41.

Giner Torréns, M. & Kärtner, J. (2017). The influence of socialization on early helping from a cross-cultural perspective. *Journal of Cross-Cultural Psychology*, 48, 353–68.

Gläscher, J., Daw, N., Dayan, P., & O'Doherty, J. (2010). Prediction error signals underlying model-based and model-free reinforcement learning. *Neuron*, 66, 585–95.

Glimcher, P. & Rustichini, A. (2004). Neuroeconomics: The consilience of brain and decision. *Science*, 206, 447–52.

Gneezy, A., Gneezy, U., & Lauga, D. (2014). A reference-dependent model of the price-quality heuristic. *Journal of Marketing Research*, 51, 153–64.

Godfrey-Smith, P. (2016). *Other Minds*. Farrar, Straus, and Giroux.

Goette, L., Huffman, D., & Meier, S. (2006). The impact of group membership on cooperation and norm enforcement: Evidence using random assignment to real social groups. *American Economic Review*, 96, 212–16.

Goldstein, I. (2002). Are emotions feelings? A further look at hedonic theories of emotion. *Consciousness and Emotion*, 3, 21–33.

Gollwitzer, P. (1999). Implementation intentions: Strong effects of simple plans. *American Psychologist*, 54, 493–503.

Gollwitzer, P. & Sheeran, P. (2006). Implementation intentions and goal achievement: A meta-analysis of effects and processes. *Advances in Experimental Social Psychology*, 38, 69–119.

Gould, J. & Gould, C. (1994). *The Animal Mind*. Scientific American Library.

Grabenhorst, F. & Rolls, E. (2011). Value, pleasure and choice in the ventral prefrontal cortex. *Trends in Cognitive Sciences*, 15, 56–67.

Grabenhorst, F., Rolls, E., & Bilderbeck, A. (2008). How cognition modulates affective responses to taste and flavor: Top-down influences on the orbitofrontal and pregenual cingulate cortices. *Cerebral Cortex*, 18, 1549–59.

Green, E.J. (2022a). The puzzle of cross-modal shape experience. *Noûs*, 56, 867–96.

Green, E.J. (2022b). Representing shape in sight and touch. *Mind & Language*, 37, 694–714.

Greenspan, P. (1988). *Emotions and Reasons*. Routledge.

Greenwald, A. & De Houwer, J. (2017). Unconscious conditioning: Demonstration of existence and difference from conscious conditioning. *Journal of Experimental Psychology: General*, 146, 1705–21.

Gregg, A., Seibt, B., & Banaji, M. (2006). Easier done than undone: Asymmetry in the malleability of implicit preferences. *Journal of Personality and Social Psychology*, 90, 1–20.

Gross, J. (2015). Emotion regulation: Current status and future prospects. *Psychological Inquiry*, 26, 1–26.

Grossmann, T., Johnson, M.H., Vaish, A., Hughes, D., Quinque, D., Stoneking, M., & Friederici, A. (2011). Genetic and neural dissociation of individual responses to emotional expressions in human infants. *Developmental Cognitive Neuroscience, 1,* 57–66.

Grossmann, T., Missana, M., & Krol, K. (2018). The neurodevelopmental precursors of altruistic behavior in infancy. *PLoS Biology,* 16, e2005281.

Gruber, R., Schiestl, M., Boeckle, M., Frohnwieser, A., Miller, R., Gray, R., Clayton, N., & Taylor, A. (2019). New Caledonian crows use mental representations to solve metatool problems. *Current Biology,* 29, 686–92.

Grueneisen, S. & Warneken, F. (2022). The development of prosocial behavior—From sympathy to strategy. *Current Opinion in Psychology,* 43, 323–28.

Hackel, L., Zaki, J., & Van Bavel, J. (2017). Social identity shapes social evaluation: Evidence from prosocial behavior and vicarious reward. *Social Cognitive and Affective Neuroscience,* 12, 1219–28.

Hagger, M., Chatzisarantis, N., Alberts, H., Anggono, C., Batailler, C., Birt, A., Brand, R., Brandt, M., Brewer, G., Bruyneel, S., Calvillo, D., Campbell, W., Cannon, P., Carlucci, M., Carruth, N., Cheung, T., Crowell, A., De Ridder, D., Dewitte, S., Elson, M., Evans, J.R., Fay, B., Fennis, B., Finley, A., Francis, Z., Heise, E., Hoemann, H. Inzlicht, M., Koole, S., Kopel, L., Kroese, F., Lange, F., Lau, K., Lynch, B., Martijn, C., Merckelbach, J., Mills, N., Michirev, A., Miyake, A., Mosser, A., Muise, M., Muller, D., Muzi, M., Nalis, D., Nurwanti, R., Otgaar, H., Philipp, M., Primoceri, P., Rentzsch, K., Ringos, L., Schlinkert, C., Schmeichel, B., Schoch, S., Schrama, M., Schütz, A., Stamos, A., Tinghög, G., Ullrich, J., vanDellen, M., Wimbarti, S., Wolff, W., Ysainy, C., Zerhouni, O., & Zwienenberg, M. (2016). A multilab preregistered replication of the ego-depletion effect. *Perspectives on Psychological Science,* 11, 546–73.

Hahn, L., Balakhonov, D., Fongaro, E., Nieder, A., & Rose, J. (2021). Working memory capacity of crows and monkeys arises from similar neuronal computations. *eLife,* 10, e72783.

Hamilton, W.D. (1963). The evolution of altruistic behavior. *American Naturalist,* 97, 354–56.

Hamlin, J.K. (2013). Failed attempts to help and harm: Intention versus outcome in preverbal infants' social evaluations. *Cognition,* 128, 451–74.

Hamlin, J.K., Mahajan, N., Liberman, Z., & Wynn, K. (2013). Not like me = bad: Infants prefer those who harm dissimilar others. *Psychological Science,* 24, 589–94.

Hamlin, J.K. & Wynn, K. (2011). Young infants prefer prosocial to antisocial others. *Cognitive Development,* 26, 30–39.

Hamlin, J.K., Wynn, K., & Bloom, P. (2007). Social evaluation by preverbal infants. *Nature,* 450, 557–60.

Hamlin, J.K., Wynn, K., Bloom, P., & Mahajan, N. (2011). How infants and toddlers react to antisocial others. *Proceedings of the National Academy of Sciences,* 108, 19931–36.

Han, W., Tellez, L., Perkins, M., Perez, I., Qu, T., Ferreira, J., Ferreira, T., Quinn, D., Liu, Z.-W., Gao, X.-B., Kaelberer, M., Bohórquez, D., Shammah-Lagnado, S., Lartigue, Gu., & de Araujo, I. (2018). A neural circuit for gut-induced reward. *Cell,* 175, 665–78.

Hanus, D., Mendes, N., Tennie, C., & Call, J. (2011). Comparing the performances of apes (*Gorilla gorilla, pan troglodytes, Pongo pymaeus*) and human children (*Homo sapiens*) in the floating peanut task. *PLoS One,* 6, e19555.

Hardcastle, V. (1999). *The Myth of Pain.* MIT Press.

Hare, B. (2017). Survival of the friendliest: *Homo sapiens* evolved via selection for prosociality. *Annual Review of Psychology,* 68, 155–86.

Haslam, N. & Loughnan, S. (2014). Dehumanization and infrahumanization. *Annual Review of Psychology,* 65, 399–423.

Havermans, R. & Jansen, A. (2007). Increasing children's liking of vegetables through flavor-flavor learning. *Appetite,* 48, 259–62.

204 References

Heathwood, C. (2007). The reduction of sensory pleasure to desire. *Philosophical Studies*, 133, 23–44.

Henrich, J. (2017). *The Secret of Our Success*. Princeton University Press.

Henrich, J., Boyd, R., Bowles, S., Camerer, C., Fehr, E., Gintis, H., & McElreath, R. (2001). In search of *Homo Economicus*: Behavioral experiments in 15 small-scale societies. *American Economic Review*, 91, 73–78.

Henrich, J., McElreath, R., Barr, A., Ensminger, J., Barrett, C., Bolyanatz, A., Camilo Cardenas, J., Gurven, M., Gwako, E., Henrich, N., Lesorogol, C., Marlowe, F., Tracer, D., & Ziker, J. (2006). Costly punishment across human societies. *Science*, 312, 1767–70.

Hepach, R., Vaish, A., & Tomasello, M. (2012). Young children are intrinsically motivated to see others helped. *Psychological Science*, 23, 967–72.

Herculano-Houzel, S. (2011). Scaling of brain metabolism with a fixed energy budget per neuron: Implications for neuronal activity, plasticity and evolution. *PLoS ONE*, 6, e17514.

Herrmann, E., Hare, B., Cissewski, J., & Tomasello, M. (2011). A comparison of temperament in nonhuman apes and human infants. *Developmental Science*, 14, 1393–405.

Heyes, C. (2015). Animal mindreading: What's the problem? *Psychonomic Bulletin and Review*, 22, 313–27.

Hill, K., Walker, R., Božičević, M., Eder, J., Headland, T., Hewlett, B., Hurtado, A.M., Marlowe, F., Wiessner, P., & Wood, B. (2011). Co-residence patterns in hunter-gatherer societies show unique human social structure. *Science*, 331, 1286–89.

Hlubik, S., Berna, F., Feibel, C., Braun, D., & Harris, J.W.K. (2017). Researching the nature of fire at 1.5 Mya on the site of FxJj20 AB, Koobi Fora, Kenya, using high-resolution spatial analysis and FTIR spectrometry. *Current Anthropology*, 58, S16.

Holroyd, J. (2012). Responsibility for implicit bias. *Journal of Social Philosophy*, 43, 274–306.

Holton, R. & Berridge, K. (2013). Addiction between compulsion and choice. In N. Levy (ed.), *Addiction and Self-Control*, Oxford University Press.

Hosking, J., Crocker, P., & Winstanley, C. (2016). Prefrontal cortical inactivations decrease willingness to expend cognitive effort on a rodent cost/benefit decision-making task. *Cerebral Cortex*, 26, 1529–38.

House, B., Silk, J., Henrich, J., Barrett, H.C., Scelza, B., Boyette, A., Hewlett, B., McElreath, R., & Laurence, S. (2013). Ontogeny of prosocial behavior across diverse societies. *Proceedings of the National Academy of Sciences*, 110, 14586–91.

Hrdy, S. (2009). *Mothers and Others*. Harvard University Press.

Hsieh, N-h. & Andersson, H. (2021). Incommensurable values. In E. Zalta (ed.), *Stanford Encyclopedia of Philosophy*. https://plato.stanford.edu/archives/fall2021/entries/value-incommensurable.

Huang, J., Zhang, Z., Feng, W., Zhao, Y., Aldanado, A., de Brito Sanchez, M., Paoli, M., Rolland, A., Li, Z., Nie, H., Lin, Y. Zhang, S., Guifa, M., & Su, S. (2022). Food wanting is mediated by transient activation of dopaminergic signaling in the honey bee brain. *Science*, 376, 508–12.

Hunt, L. & Hayden, B. (2017). A distributed, hierarchical and recurrent framework for reward-based choice. *Nature Reviews Neuroscience*, 16, 172–82.

Huys, Q., Cools, R., Gölzer, M., Friedel, E., Heinz, A., Dolan, R., & Dayan, P. (2011). Disentangling the roles of approach, activation and valence in instrumental and Pavlovian responding. *PLoS Computational Biology*, 7, e1002028.

Inzlicht, M., Shenhav, A., & Olivola, C. (2018). The effort paradox: Effort is both costly and valued. *Trends in Cognitive Sciences*, 22, 337–49.

Izard, C. (2007). Basic emotions, natural kinds, emotion schemas, and a new paradigm. *Perspectives on Psychological Science*, 2, 260–80.

Izard, V., Sann, C., Spelke, E., & Streri, A. (2009). Newborn infants perceive abstract numbers. *Proceedings of the National Academy of Sciences*, 106, 10382–85.

James, W. (1890). *Principles of Psychology*. Henry Holt.

Jankowski, M., Rau, K., Ekmann, K., Anderson, C., & Koerber, H. (2013). Comprehensive phenotyping of group III and IV muscle afferents in mouse. *Journal of Neurophysiology*, 109, 2374–81.

Jeannerod, M. (2006). *Motor Cognition*. Oxford University Press.

Jensen, K., Kaptchuk, T., Chen, X., Kirsch, I.C., Ingvar, M., Gollub, R., & Kong, J. (2015). A neural mechanism for nonconscious activation of conditioned placebo and nocebo responses. *Cerebral Cortex*, 25, 3903–10.

Jensen, K., Kaptchuk, T., Kirsch, I., Raicek, J., Lindstrom, K., Berna, C., Gollub, R., Ingvar, M., & Kong, J. (2012). Nonconscious activation of placebo and nocebo pain responses. *Proceedings of the National Academy of Sciences*, 109, 15959–64.

Jeong, H., Taylor, A., Floeder, J., Lohmann, M., Mihalas, S., Wu, B., Zhou, M., Burke, D., & Namboodri, V. (2022). Mesolimbic dopamine release conveys causal associations. *Science*, 378, eabq6740.

Jin, K-s. & Baillargeon, R. (2017). Infants possess an abstract expectation of ingroup support. *Proceedings of the National Academy of Sciences*, 114, 8199–204.

Job, V., Walton, G., Bernecker, K., & Dweck, C. (2015). Implicit theories about willpower predict self-regulation and grades in everyday life. *Journal of Personality and Social Psychology*, 108, 637–47.

Jonas, W., Crawford, C., Colloca, L., Kaptchuk, T., Moseley, B., Miller, F., Kriston, L., Linde, K., & Meissner, K. (2016). To what extent are surgery and invasive procedures effective beyond a placebo response? A systematic review with meta-analysis of randomized, sham controlled trials. *British Medical Journal Open*, 5, e009655.

Jones, J.L., Esber, G., McDannald, M., Gruber, A., Hernandez, A., Mirenzi, A., & Schoenbaum, G. (2012). Orbitofrontal cortex supports behavior and learning using inferred but not cached values. *Science*, 338, 953–56.

Jordan, J., Hoffman, M., Nowak, M., & Rand, D. (2016). Uncalculating cooperation is used to signal trustworthiness. *Proceedings of the National Academy of Sciences*, 113, 8658–63.

Jordan, K., MacLean, E., & Brannon, E. (2008). Monkeys match and tally quantities across senses. *Cognition*, 108, 617–25.

Juechems, K. & Summerfield, C. (2019). Where does value come from? *Trends in Cognitive Sciences*, 23, 836–50.

Kahneman, D. (2011). *Thinking, Fast and Slow*. Farrar, Straus, and Giroux.

Kanakogi, Y., Inoue, Y., Matsuda, G., Butler, G., Hiraki, K., & Myowa-Yamakoshi, M. (2017). Preverbal infants affirm third-party interventions that protect victims from aggressors. *Nature Human Behavior*, 1, 0037.

Kanngiesser, P., Schäfer, M., Herrmann, E., Zeidler, H., Haun, D., & Tomasello, M. (2022). Children across societies enforce conventional norms by in culturally variable ways. *Proceedings of the National Academy of Sciences*, 119, e211251118.

Keleman, D., Rottman, J., & Seston, R. (2013). Professional physical scientists display tenacious teleological tendencies: Purpose-based reasoning as a cognitive default. *Journal of Experimental Psychology: General*, 142, 1074–83.

Keltner, D., Kogan, A., Piff, P., & Saturn, S. (2014). The sociocultural appraisals, values, and emotions (SAVE) framework of prosociality: Core processes from gene to meme. *Annual Review of Psychology*, 65, 425–60.

Kennedy, A. (2022). An emergent encoding of aggressive motivation in neurons in the hypothalamus. *Science*, 484, 484–85.

Kennedy, D., McNeil, C., Gandevia, S., & Taylor, J. (2014). Fatigue-related firing of distal muscle nociceptors reduces voluntary activation of proximal muscles in the same limb. *Journal of Applied Physiology*, 116, 385–94.

206 References

Khan, A., Faucett, J., Lichtenberg, P., Kirsch, I., & Brown, W.A. (2012). A systematic review of the comparative efficacy of treatments and controls for depression. *PLoS ONE*, 7, e41778.

Kiel, E. & Buss, K. (2011). Prospective relations among fearful temperament, protective parenting, and social withdrawal: The role of maternal accuracy in a moderated mediation framework. *Journal of Abnormal Child Psychology*, 39, 953–66.

Kind, A. (2013). The case against representationalism about moods. In U. Kriegel (ed.), *Current Controversies in Philosophy of Mind*, Routledge.

King, M. & Carruthers, P. (2012). Moral responsibility and consciousness. *Journal of Moral Philosophy*, 9, 200–228.

King, M. & Carruthers, P. (2022). Responsibility and consciousness. In D. Nelkin & D. Pereboom (eds.), *Handbook of Moral Responsibility*, Oxford University Press.

Kinzler, K., Dupoux, E., & Spelke, E. (2007). The native language of social cognition. *Proceedings of the National Academy of Sciences*, 104, 12577–80.

Kinzler, K., Dupoux, E., & Spelke, E. (2012). "Native" objects and collaborators: Infants' object choices and acts of giving reflect favor for native over foreign speakers. *Journal of Cognition and Development*, 13, 67–81.

Kinzler, K. & Spelke, E. (2011). Do infants show social preferences for people differing in race? *Cognition*, 119, 1–9.

Klein, C. (2015). *What the Body Commands*. MIT Press.

Knutson, B. & Greer, S. (2008). Anticipatory affect: Neural correlates and consequences for choice. *Philosophical Transactions of the Royal Society B*, 363, 3771–86.

Kobayashi, K. & Hsu, M. (2019). Common neural code for reward and information value. *Proceedings of the National Academy of Sciences*, 116, 13061–66.

Kobayashi, S., Kojima, S., Yamanaka, M., Sadamoto, H., Nakamura, H., Fujito, Y., Kawai, R., Sakakibara, M., & Ito, E. (1998). Operant conditioning and escape behavior in the pond snail, *Lymnaea stagnalis*. *Zoological Science*, 15, 683–90.

Kohl, J. (2018). Circuits for care: A small population of hypothalamic neurons orchestrates parenting behaviors. *Science*, 362 (6411), 168–69.

Korsgaard, C. (1996). *The Sources of Normativity*. Cambridge University Press.

Kosslyn, S., Thompson, W., & Ganis, G. (2006). *The Case for Mental Imagery*. Oxford University Press.

Krebs, D. (1975). Empathy and altruism. *Journal of Personality and Social Psychology*, 32, 1134–46.

Krieglmeyer, R., Deutsch, R., De Houwer, J., & De Raedt, R. (2010). Being moved: Valence activated approach-avoidance behavior independently of evaluation and approach-avoidance intentions. *Psychological Science*, 21, 607–13.

Kupers, R., Konings, H., Adriaensen, H., & Gybels, J. (1991). Morphine differentially affects the sensory and affective pain ratings in neurogenic and idiopathic forms of pain. *Pain*, 47, 5–12.

Kurzban, R. (2010). Does the brain consume additional glucose during self-control tasks? *Evolutionary Psychology*, 8, 244–59.

Kurzban, R., Duckworth, A., Kable, J., & Myers, J. (2013). An opportunity cost model of subjective effort and task performance. *Behavioral and Brain Sciences*, 36, 661–726.

Labukt, I. (2012). Hedonic tone and the heterogeneity of pleasure. *Utilitas*, 24, 172–99.

Lambie, J. & Marcel, A. (2002). Consciousness and the varieties of emotion experience. *Psychological Review*, 109, 219–59.

Landrieu, P., Said, G., & Allaire, C. (1990). Dominantly transmitted congenital indifference to pain. *Annals of Neurology*, 27, 574–78.

Larsen, J., McGraw, A., Mellers, B., & Cacioppo, J. (2004). The agony of victory and the thrill of defeat: Mixed emotional reactions to disappointing wins and relieving losses. *Psychological Science*, 15, 325–30.

Lau, H., Michel, M., LeDoux, J., & Fleming, S.M. (2022). The mnemonic basis of subjective experience. *Nature Reviews Psychology*, 1, 479–88.

LeDoux, J. (2012). Rethinking the emotional brain. *Neuron*, 73, 653–76.

Legg, E. & Clayton, N. (2014). Eurasian jays (*Garrulus glandarius*) conceal caches from onlookers. *Animal Cognition*, 17, 1223–26.

Legg, E., Ostojić, L., & Clayton, N. (2016). Caching at a distance: A cache protection strategy in Eurasian jays. *Animal Cognition*, 19, 753–58.

Leknes, S., Berna, C., Lee, M., Snyder, G., Biele, G., & Tracey, I. (2013). The importance of context: When relative relief renders pain pleasant. *Pain*, 154, 402–10.

Leknes, S. & Tracey, I. (2008). A common neurobiology for pain and pleasure. *Nature Reviews Neuroscience*, 9, 314–20.

Lerner, J., Li, Y., Valdesolo, P., & Kassam, K. (2015). Emotion and decision making. *Annual Review of Psychology*, 66, 33.1–33.25.

Levy, D. & Glimcher, P. (2012). The root of all value: A neural common currency for choice. *Current Opinion in Neurobiology*, 22, 1027–38.

Levy, N. (2014). *Consciousness and Moral Responsibility*. Oxford University Press.

Lewis, M. (2015). *The Biology of Desire*. Perseus Books.

Lhermitte, F. (1983). "Utilization behavior" and its relation to lesions of the frontal lobe. *Brain*, 106, 237–55.

Lhermitte, F. (1986). Human autonomy and the frontal lobes, II. Patient behavior in complex and social situations: the "environmental dependency syndrome." *Annals of Neurology*, 19, 335–43.

Li, L., Britvan, B., & Tomasello, M. (2021). Young children conform more to norms than to preferences. *PLoS ONE*, 16, e0251228.

Li, M., Tan, H.-E., Lu, Z., Tsang, K., Chung, A., & Zuker, C. (2022) Gut-brain circuits for fat preference. *Nature*, 610, 722–30.

Liberman, Z., Woodward, A., & Kinzler, K. (2017). Preverbal infants infer third-party social relationships based on language. *Cognitive Science*, 41, 622–34.

Liebenberg, L. (1990). *The Art of Tracking: The Origin of Science*. David Philip Publishers.

Lindström, B., Jangard, S., Selbing, I., & Olsson, A. (2018). The role of a "common is moral" heuristic in the stability and change of moral norms. *Journal of Experimental Psychology: General*, 147, 228–42.

Liszkowski, U., Carpenter, M., & Tomasello, M. (2008). Twelve-month-olds communicate helpfully and appropriately for knowledgeable and ignorant partners. *Cognition*, 108, 732–39.

Liu, Y.-Z., Wang, Y.-X., & Jiang, C.-L. (2017). Inflammation: The common pathway in stress-related diseases. *Frontiers in Human Neuroscience*, 11, #316.

Loewenstein, G., Rick, S., & Cohen, J.D. (2008). *Annual Review of Psychology*, 59, 647–72.

Lucca, K., Pospisil, J., & Sommerville, J. (2018). Fairness informs social decision making in infancy. *PLoS ONE*, 13, e0192848.

McCabe, C., Rolls, E., Bilderbeck, A., & McGlone, F. (2008). Cognitive influences on the affective representation of touch and the sight of touch in the human brain. *Social Cognitive and Affective Neuroscience*, 3, 97–108.

McCloskey, M. (1983). Naïve theories of motion. In D. Gentner & A. Stevens (eds.), *Mental Models*, Erlbaum.

McDaniel, M., LaMontagne, P., Beck, S., Scullin, M., & Braver, T. (2013). Dissociable neural routes to successful prospective memory. *Psychological Science*, 24, 1791–800.

McGuire, M., Fawzy, F., Spar, J., Weigel, R., & Troisi, A. (1994). Altruism and mental disorders. *Ethology and Sociobiology*, 15, 299–321.

Machery, E. & Stich, S. (2022). The moral/conventional distinction. In E. Zalta (ed.), *Stanford Encyclopedia of Philosophy*. https://plato.stanford.edu/archives/sum2022/entries/moral-conventional/.

208 References

McNamara, J. & Houston, A. (1986). The common currency for behavioral decisions. *The American Naturalist*, 127, 358–78.

McNamee, D. & Wolpert, D. (2019). Internal models in biological control. *Annual Review of Control, Robotics, and Autonomous Systems*, 2, 339–64.

Mahajan, N. & Wynn, K. (2012). Origins of "us" versus "them": Prelinguistic infants prefer similar others. *Cognition*, 124, 227–33.

Mancini, F., Nash, T., Iannetti, G.-D., & Haggard, P. (2014). Pain relief by touch: A quantitative approach. *Pain*, 155, 635–42.

Maravita, A., Spence, C., & Driver, J. (2003). Multisensory integration and the body schema: Close to hand and within reach. *Current Biology*, 13, R531–R539.

Marlowe, F. (2005). Hunter-gatherers and human evolution. *Evolutionary Anthropology*, 14, 54–67.

Marsh, A. (2019). The caring continuum: Evolved hormonal and proximal mechanisms explain prosocial and antisocial extremes. *Annual Review of Psychology*, 70, 1–25.

Marsh, A. & Ambady, N. (2007). The influence of the fear facial expression on prosocial responding. *Cognition and Emotion*, 21, 225–47.

Marsh, A., Ambady, N., & Kleck, R. (2005). The effects of fear and anger facial expressions on approach- and avoidance-related behaviors. *Emotion*, 5, 119–24.

Marsh, A., Kozak, M., & Ambady, N. (2007). Accurate identification of fear facial expressions predicts prosocial behavior. *Emotion*, 7, 239–51.

Martin Braunstein, L., Gross, J., & Ochsner, K. (2017). Explicit and implicit emotion regulation: A multi-level framework. *Social Cognitive and Affective Neuroscience*, 12, 1545–57.

Martínez, M. (2011). Imperative content and the painfulness of pain. *Phenomenology and the Cognitive Sciences*, 10, 67–90.

Martínez, M. (2015). Pains as reasons. *Philosophical Studies*, 172, 2261–74.

Masicampo, E. & Baumeister, R. (2008). Toward a physiology of dual-process reasoning and judgment. *Psychological Science*, 19, 255–60.

May, J. (2018). *Regard for Reason in the Moral Mind*. Oxford University Press.

Maynard Smith, J. (1964). Group selection and kin selection. *Nature*, 201, 1145–47.

Melzack, R. (1996). Gate control theory: On the evolution of pain concepts. *Pain Forum*, 5, 128–38.

Mendes, N., Hanus, D., & Call, J. (2007). Raising the level: Orangutans use water as a tool. *Biology Letters*, 3, 453–55.

Mendola, J. (2006). Intuitive hedonism. *Philosophical Studies*, 128, 441–77.

Menon, V. & Uddin, L. (2010). Saliency, switching, attention and control: A network model of insula function. *Brain Structure and Function*, 214, 655–67.

Mercer, M. (2001). In defense of weak psychological egoism. *Erkenntnis*, 55, 217–37.

Mercier, H. & Sperber, D. (2017). *The Enigma of Reason*. Harvard University Press.

Merel, J., Botvinick, M., & Wayne, G. (2019). Hierarchical motor control in mammals and machines. *Nature Communications*, 10: 5489.

Meristo, M., Strid, K., & Surian, L. (2016). Preverbal intants' ability to encode the outcome of distributive actions. *Infancy*, 21, 353–72.

Metcalfe, J. & Mischel, W. (1999). A hot/cool-system analysis of delay of gratification: Dynamics of willpower. *Psychological Review*, 106, 3–19.

Mikhail, J. (2007). Universal moral grammar: Theory, evidence and the future. *Trends in Cognitive Sciences*, 11, 143–52.

Milinski, M. (2016). Reputation, a universal currency for human social interactions. *Philosophical Transactions of the Royal Society B*, 371, 20150100.

Miller, E., Shankar, M., Knutson, B., & McClure, S. (2014). Dissociating motivation from reward in human striatal activity. *Journal of Cognitive Neuroscience*, 26, 1075–84.

Miller, K., Shenhav, A., & Ludvig, E. (2019). Habits without values. *Psychological Review*, 126, 292–311.

⸳an, R. (1984). *Language, Thought, and Other Biological Categories*. MIT Press.

Millikan, R. (1989). Biosemantics. *The Journal of Philosophy*, 86, 281–97.

Millikan, R. (1995). Pushmi-pullyu representations. *Philosophical Perspectives*, 9 [AI, Connectionism and Philosophical Psychology], 185–200.

Milo, R. (1995). Contractarian constructivism. *The Journal of Philosophy*, 92, 181–204.

Miloyan, B. & Suddendorf, T. (2015). Feelings of the future. *Trends in Cognitive Sciences*, 19, 196–200.

Mizumura, K. & Taguchi, T. (2016). Delayed onset muscle soreness: Involvement of neurotrophic factors. *Journal of Physiological Sciences*, 66, 43–52.

Mobbs, D. (2018). The ethological deconstruction of fear(s). *Current Opinion in Behavioral Sciences*, 24, 32–37.

Mobbs, D., Headley, D., Ding, W., & Dayan, P. (2020). Space, time, and fear: Survival computations along defensive circuits. *Trends in Cognitive Sciences*, 24, 228–41.

Moller, D. (2011). Anticipated emotions and emotional valence, *Philosophers Imprint*, 9, 1–16.

Momennejad, I. & Haynes, J.-D. (2013). Encoding of prospective tasks in the human prefrontal cortex under varying task loads. *Journal of Neuroscience*, 33, 17342–49.

Montague, P.R. & Berns, G. (2002). Neural economics and the biological substrates of valuation. *Neuron*, 36, 265–84.

Moore, G.E. (1903). *Principia Ethica*. Cambridge University Press.

Moors, A., Ellsworth, P., Scherer, K., & Frijda, N. (2013). Appraisal theories of emotion: State of the art and future development. *Emotion Review*, 5, 119–24.

Morales, I. & Berridge, K. (2020). "Liking" and "wanting" in eating and food reward: Brain mechanisms and clinical implications. *Physiology & Behavior*, 227, 113152.

Morillo, C. (1995). *Contingent Creatures*. Rowman & Littlefield.

Morrison, S., Bamkole, M., & Nicola, S. (2015). Sign tracking, but not goal tracking, is resistant to outcome devaluation. *Frontiers in Neuroscience*, 9, #468.

Mullen, B., Brown, R., & Smith, C. (1992). Ingroup bias as a function of salience, relevance and status: An integration. *European Journal of Social Psychology*, 22, 103–22.

Müri, R. (2016). Cortical control of facial emotion. *Journal of Comparative Neurology*, 524, 1578–1585.

Murphy, D. & Stich, S. (2000). Darwin in the madhouse: Evolutionary psychology and the classification of mental disorders. In P. Carruthers, S. Lawrence, & S. Stich (eds.), *Evolution and the Human Mind*, Cambridge University Press.

Muthukrishna, M. & Henrich, J. (2016). Innovation in the collective brain. *Philosophical Transactions of the Royal Society B*, 371, 20150192.

Mysore, S. & Knudsen, E. (2013). A shared inhibitory circuit for both exogenous and endogenous control of stimulus selection. *Nature Neuroscience*, 16, 473–78.

Nagasako, E., Oaklander, A., & Dworkin, R. (2003). Congenital insensitivity to pain: An update. *Pain*, 101, 213–19.

Nagel, T. (1970). *The Possibility of Altruism*. Oxford University Press.

Nathan, C. & Ding, A. (2010). Nonresolving inflammation. *Cell*, 140, 871–82.

Neander, K. (2017). *A Mark of the Mental*. MIT Press.

Negri, G., Rumiati, R., Zadini, A., Ukmar, M., Mahon, B., & Caramazza, A. (2007). What is the role of motor simulation in action and object recognition? Evidence from apraxia. *Cognitive Neuropsychology*, 24, 795–816.

Nguyen, D., Naffziger, E., & Berridge, K. (2021). Positive affect: Nature and brain bases of liking and wanting. *Current Opinion in Behavioral Sciences*, 39, 72–78.

Noakes, T. (2011). Time to move beyond a brainless exercise physiology: The evidence for complex regulation of human exercise performance. *Applied Physiology, Nutrition, and Metabolism*, 36, 23–35.

Norbury, R., Smith, S.A., Burnley, M., Judge, M., & Mauger, A. (2022). The effect of elevated muscle pain on neuromuscular fatigue during exercise. *European Journal of Applied Physiology*, 122, 113–26.

Nozick, R. (1974). *Anarchy, State, and Utopia*. Basic Books.

Nussbaum, M. (2001). *Upheavals of Thought*. Cambridge University Press.

O'Connor, P. & Cook, D. (1999). Exercise and pain: The neurobiology, measurement, and laboratory study of pain in relation to exercise in humans. *Exercise and Sport Sciences Reviews*, 27, 119–66.

O'Doherty, J., Cockburn, J., & Pauli, W. (2017). Learning, reward, and decision making. *Annual Review of Psychology*, 68, 73–100.

Oddie, G. (2005). *Value, Reality, and Desire*. Oxford University Press.

Odic, D., Libertus, M., Feigenson, L., & Halberda, J. (2013). Developmental change in the acuity of approximate number and area representations. *Developmental Psychology*, 49, 1103–12.

Ogilvie, R. & Carruthers, P. (2016). Opening up vision: The case against encapsulation. *Review of Philosophy and Psychology*, 7, 721–42.

Olney, J., Warlow, S., Naffzinger, E., & Berridge, K. (2018). Current perspectives on incentive salience and applications to clinical disorders. *Current Opinion in Behavioral Sciences*, 22, 59–69.

Olsson, A., McMahon, K., Papenberg, G., Zaki, J., Bolger, N., & Ochsner, K. (2016). Vicarious fear learning depends on empathic appraisals and trait empathy. *Psychological Science*, 27, 25–33.

Orsini, C., Moorman, D., Young, J., Setlow, B., & Floresco, S. (2015). Neural mechanisms regulating different forms of risk-related decision-making: Insights from animal models. *Neuroscience and Biobehavioral Reviews*, 58, 147–67.

Orvell, A., Vicker, B., Drake, B., Verduyn, P., Ayduk, O., Moser, J., Jonides, J., & Kross, E. (2021). Does distanced self-talk facilitate emotion regulation across a range of emotionally intense experiences? *Clinical Psychological Science*, 9, 68–78.

Panksepp, J. & Watt, D. (2011). What is basic about basic emotions? Lasting lessons from affective neuroscience. *Emotion Review*, 3, 387–96.

Papineau, D. (1987). *Reality and Representation*. Blackwell.

Parfit, D. (2011). *On What Matters*. Oxford University Press.

Pauker, K., Ambady, N., & Apfelbaum, E. (2010). Race salience and essentialist thinking in racial stereotype development. *Child Development*, 81, 1799–813.

Paul, L.A. (2014). *Transformative Experience*. Oxford University Press.

Pautz, A. (2014). The real trouble with phenomenal externalism: New empirical evidence for a brain-based theory of consciousness. In R. Brown (ed.) *Consciousness Inside and Out, Studies in Brain and Mind*, volume 6, Springer.

Peltola, M., Forssman, L., Puura, K., van Ijzendoorn, M., & Leppänen, J. (2015). Attention to faces expressing negative emotion at 7 months predicts attachment security at 14 months. *Child Development*, 86, 1321–32.

Peng, Y., Gillis-Smith, S., Jin, H., Tränkner, D., Ryba, N., & Zuker, C. (2015). Sweet and bitter taste in the brain of awake behaving animals. *Nature*, 527, 512–15.

Penn, D., Holyoak, K., & Povinelli, D. (2008). Darwin's mistake: Explaining the discontinuity between human and nonhuman minds. *Behavioral and Brain Sciences*, 30, 109–78.

Persichetti, A., Aguirre, G., & Thompson-Schill, S. (2015). Value is in the eye of the beholder: Early visual cortex codes monetary value of objects during a diverted attention task. *Journal of Cognitive Neuroscience*, 27, 893–901.

Peters, J. & Büchel, C. (2011). The neural mechanisms of inter-temporal decision-making: Understanding variability. *Trends in Cognitive Sciences*, 15, 227–39.

Petrie, K. & Rief, W. (2019). Psychobiological mechanisms of placebo and nocebo effects: Pathways to improve treatments and reduce side effects. *Annual Review of Psychology*, 70, 599–625.

References   211

Pfabigan, D., Alexopoulos, J., Bauer, H., & Sailer, U. (2011). Manipulation of feedback expectancy and valence induces negative and positive reward prediction error signals manifest in event-related potentials. *Psychophysiology*, 48, 656–64.

Phan, K.L., Sripada, C., Angstadt, M., & McCabe, K. (2010). Reputation for reciprocity engages the brain reward center. *Proceedings of the National Academy of Sciences*, 107, 13099–104.

Pichon, S., de Gelder, B., & Grézes, J. (2012). Threat prompts defensive brain responses independently of attentional control. *Cerebral Cortex*, 22, 274–85.

Pietraszewski, D., Cosmides, L., & Tooby, J. (2014). The content of our cooperation, not the color of our skin: An alliance detection system regulates categorization by coalition and race, but not by sex. *PLoS ONE*, 9, e88534.

Pietroski, P. & Rey, G. (1995). When other things aren't equal: saving *ceteris paribus* laws from vacuity. *The British Journal for the Philosophy of Science*, 46, 81–110.

Pinotsis, D., Buschman, T., & Miller, E. (2019). Working memory load modulates neuronal coupling. *Cerebral Cortex*, 29, 1670–81.

Plassmann, H., O'Doherty, J., Shiv, B., & Rangel, A. (2008). Marketing actions can modulate neural representations of experienced pleasantness. *Proceedings of the National Academy of Sciences*, 105, 1050–54.

Ploner, M., Freund, H.-J., & Schnitzler, A. (1999). Pain affect without pain sensation in a patient with a postcentral lesion. *Pain*, 81, 211–14.

Poppenk, J., Moscovitch, M., McIntosh, A., Ozcelik, E., & Craik, F. (2010). Encoding the future: Successful processing of intentions engages predictive brain networks. *NeuroImage*, 49, 905–13.

Powell, L. & Spelke, E. (2013). Preverbal infants expect members of social groups to act alike. *Proceedings of the National Academy of Sciences*, 110, E3965–E3972.

Prather, R. (2014). Numerical discrimination is mediated by neural coding variation. *Cognition*, 133, 601–10.

Prinz, J. (2004). *Gut Reactions*. Oxford University Press.

Prinz, J. (2012). *The Conscious Brain*. Oxford University Press.

Pun, A., Birch, S., & Barron, A. (2021). The power of allies: Infants' expectations of social obligations during intergroup conflict. *Cognition*, 211, 104630.

Pyke, G., Pulliam, H., & Charnov, E. (1977). Optimal foraging: A selective review of theory and tests. *Quarterly Review of Biology*, 52, 137–54.

Qi, S., Hassabis, D., Sun, J., Guo, F., Daw, N., & Mobbs, D. (2018). How cognitive and reactive fear circuits optimize escape decisions in humans. *Proceedings of the National Academy of Sciences*, 115, 3186–91.

Quirk, G. & Mueller, D. (2008). Neural mechanisms of extinction learning and retrieval. *Neuropsychopharmacology*, 33, 56–72.

Railton, P. (2017). At the core of our capacity to act for a reason: The affective system and model-based learning and control. *Emotion Review*, 9, 335–42.

Rajhans, P., Altvater-Mackensen, N., Vaish, A., & Grossmann, T. (2016). Children's altruistic behavior in context: The role of emotional responsiveness and culture. *Scientific Reports*, 6, 24089.

Rand, D. (2016). Cooperation, fast and slow: Meta-analytic evidence for a theory of social heuristics and self-interested deliberation. *Psychological Science*, 27, 1192–206.

Rapp, D., Engelmann, J., Herrmann, E., & Tomasello, M. (2019). Young children's reputational strategies in a peer group context. *Developmental Psychology*, 55, 329–36.

Raz, J. (1986). *The Morality of Freedom*. Oxford University Press.

Rhodes, M. & Mandalaywala, T. (2017). The development and developmental consequences of social essentialism. *WIREs Cognitive Science*, 8, e1437.

212 References

Richerson, P. & Boyd, R. (2004). *Not by Genes Alone*. University of Chicago Press.

Ritchie, J.B. (2021). What's wrong with the minimal conception of innateness in cognitive science? *Synthese*, 199, 159–76.

Roberts, R. (2003). *Emotions*. Cambridge University Press.

Robinson, T. & Flagel, S. (2009). Dissociating the predictive and incentive motivational properties of reward-related cues through the study of individual differences. *Biological Psychiatry*, 65, 869–73.

Rolls, E. (1999). *The Brain and Emotion*. Oxford University Press.

Rolls, E. (2014). *Emotion and Decision Making Explained*. Oxford University Press.

Rolls, E. (2015). Limbic systems for emotion and for memory, but no single limbic system. *Cortex*, 62, 119–57.

Rosati, C. (2016). Moral motivation. In E. Zalta (ed.), *Stanford Encyclopedia of Philosophy*. https://plato.stanford.edu/archives/win2016/entries/moral motivation/.

Rosenberg, K. (2021). The evolution of human infancy: Why it helps to be helpless. *Annual Review of Anthropology*, 50, 423–40.

Rosenthal, D. (2010). How to think about mental qualities. *Philosophical Issues*, 20, 368–93.

Roth, A., Prasnikar, V., Okuno-Fujiwara, M., & Zamir, S. (1991). Bargaining and market behavior in Jerusalem, Ljubljana, Pittsburgh, and Tokyo: An experimental study. *American Economic Review*, 81, 1068–95.

Rubins, J. & Friedman, E. (1948). Asymbolia for pain. *Archives of Neurology and Psychiatry*, 60, 554–73.

Ruff, C. & Fehr, E. (2014). The neurobiology of rewards and values in social decision-making. *Nature Reviews Neuroscience*, 15, 549–62.

Runeson, E., Boynton, G., & Murray, S. (2013). Effects of task and attentional selection on responses in human visual cortex. *Journal of Neurophysiology*, 109, 2606–17.

Rupert, R. (2018). Representation and mental representation. *Philosophical Explorations*, 21, 204–25.

Russell, J. (2003). Core affect and the psychological construction of emotion. *Psychological Review*, 110, 145–72.

Sadacca, B., Jones, J.L., & Schoenbaum, G. (2016). Midbrain dopamine neurons compute inferred and cached value prediction errors in a common framework. *eLife*, 5, e13665.

Samuels, R. (2004). Innateness in cognitive science. *Trends in Cognitive Sciences*, 8, 136–41.

Saul, J. (2013). Unconscious influences and women in philosophy. In F. Jenkins & K. Hutchison (eds.), *Women in Philosophy*, Oxford University Press.

Scanlon, T. (1982). Contractualism and utilitarianism. In A. Sen & B. Williams (eds.), *Utilitarianism and Beyond*, Cambridge University Press.

Scanlon, T. (1998). *What We Owe to Each Other*. Harvard University Press.

Schäfer, M., Haun, D., & Tomasello, M. (2015). Fair is not fair everywhere. *Psychological Science*, 26, 1252–60.

Schafer, S., Colloca, L., & Wager, T. (2015). Conditioned placebo analgesia persists when subjects know they are receiving a placebo. *Journal of Pain*, 16, 412–20.

Schafer, S., Geuter, S., & Wager, T. (2018). Mechanisms of placebo analgesia: A dual-process model informed by insights from cross-species comparisons. *Progress in Neurobiology*, 160, 101–22.

Schilder, P. & Stengel, E. (1932). Asymbolia for pain. *Archives of Neurology*, 25, 598–600.

Schmidt, L., Skvortsova, V., Kullen, C., Weber, B., & Plassmann, H. (2017). How context alters value: the brain's valuation and affective regulation system link price cues to experienced taste pleasantness. *Nature Scientific Reports*, 7, 8098.

Schmidt, M. & Sommerville, J. (2011). Fairness expectations and altruistic sharing in 15-month-old human infants. *PLoS ONE*, 6, e23223.

Schrittwieser, J., Antonoglou, I., Hubert, T., Simonyan, K., Sifre, L., Schmitt, S., Guez, A., Lockhart, E., Hassabis, D., Graepel, T., Lillicrap, T., & Silver, D. (2020). Mastering Atari, Go, chess and shogi by planning with a learned model. *Nature*, 588, 604–12.

Schroeder, T. (2004). *The Three Faces of Desire*. Oxford University Press.

Schulz, J., Fischbacher, U., Thöni, C., & Utikal, V. (2014). Affect and fairness: Dictator games under cognitive load. *Journal of Economic Psychology*, 41, 77–87.

Scott, S. (2012). The computational and neural basis of voluntary motor control and planning. *Trends in Cognitive Sciences*, 16, 541–49.

Searle, J. (1983). *Intentionality*. Cambridge University Press.

Seligman, M., Railton, P., Baumeister, R., & Sripada, C. (2013). Navigating into the future or driven by the past. *Perspectives on Psychological Science*, 8, 119–41.

Sescousse, G., Li, Y., & Dreher, J.-C. (2015). A common currency for the computation of motivational values in the human stratum. *Social Cognitive and Affective Neuroscience*, 10, 467–73.

Sestieri, C., Shulman, G., & Corbetta, M. (2010). Attention to memory and the environment: Functional specialization and dynamic competition in human posterior parietal cortex. *The Journal of Neuroscience*, 30, 8445–56.

Shargel, D. (2015). Emotions without objects. *Biology & Philosophy*, 30, 831–44.

Sharim, J. & Pouratian, N. (2016). Anterior cingulotomy for the treatment of chronic intractable pain: A systematic review. *Pain Physician*, 19, 537–50.

Sharot, T., De Martino, B., & Dolan, R. (2009). How choice reveals and shapes expected hedonic outcome. *Journal of Neuroscience*, 29, 3760–65.

Sharot, T., Fleming, S.M., Yu, X., Koster, R., & Dolan, R. (2012). Is choice-induced preference change long-lasting? *Psychological Science*, 10, 1123–29.

Shea, N. (2018). *Representation in Cognitive Science*. Oxford University Press.

Shechner, T., Hong, M., Britton, J., Pine, D., & Fox, N. (2014). Fear conditioning and extinction across development: Evidence from human studies and animal models. *Biological Psychology*, 100, 1–12.

Shenhav, A. & Buckner, R. (2014). Neural correlates of dueling affective reactions to win-win choices. *Proceedings of the National Academy of Sciences*, 11, 10978–83.

Shenhav, A., Musslick, S., Lieder, F., Kool, W., Griffiths, T., Cohen, J.D., & Botvinick, M. (2017). Toward a rational and mechanistic account of mental effort. *Annual Review of Neuroscience*, 40, 99–124.

Shenhav, A., Straccia, M., Cohen, J.D., & Botvinick, M. (2014). Anterior cingulate engagement in a foraging context reflects choice difficulty, not foraging value. *Nature Neuroscience*, 17, 1249–54.

Shenhav, A., Straccia, M., Musslick, S., Cohen, J.D., & Botvinick, M. (2018). Dissociable neural mechanisms track evidence accumulation for selection of attention versus action. *Nature Communications*, 9, 2485.

Sherdell, L., Waugh, C., & Gotlib, I. (2012). Anticipatory pleasure predicts motivation for reward in major depression. *Journal of Abnormal Psychology*, 121, 51–60.

Shizgal, P. & Conover, K. (1996). On the neural computation of utility. *Current Directions in Psychological Science*, 5, 37–43.

Shmuelof, L. & Krakauer, J. (2012). Are we ready for a natural history of motor learning? *Neuron*, 72, 469–76.

Siegel, H., Sands, M., Van den Noortgate, W., Condon, P., Chang, Y., Dy, J., Quigley, K., & Barrett, L. (2018). Emotion fingerprints or emotion populations? A meta-analytic investigation of autonomic features of emotion categories. *Psychological Bulletin*, 144, 343–93.

Sinhababu, N. (2009). The Humean theory of motivation reformulated and defended. *Philosophical Review*, 118, 465–500.

214 References

Sloane, S., Baillargeon, R., & Premack, D. (2012). Do infants have a sense of fairness? *Psychological Science*, 23, 196–204.

Small, D. & DiFeliceantonio, A. (2019). Processed foods and food reward: Processed foods compromise the fidelity of gut-brain signaling of food reinforcement. *Science*, 363, 346–47.

Smith, A. (1759). *The Theory of Moral Sentiments*. Penguin Classics (2010).

Smith, M. (1987). The Humean theory of motivation. *Mind*, 96, 36–61.

Smith, K.S., Berridge, K., & Aldridge, J.W. (2011). Disentangling pleasure from incentive salience and learning signals in brain reward circuitry. *Proceedings of the National Academy of Sciences*, 108, E255–E264.

Smith, J.D., Couchman, J., & Beran, M. (2014). Animal metacognition: A tale of two comparative psychologies. *Journal of Comparative Psychology*, 128, 115–31.

Smuts, A. (2011). The feels good theory of pleasure. *Philosophical Studies*, 155, 241–65.

Sober, E. & Wilson, D.S. (1998). *Unto Others*. Harvard University Press.

Solomon, R. (1976). *The Passions*. Anchor Press.

Spencer, S., Logel, C., & Davies, P. (2016). Stereotype threat. *Annual Review of Psychology*, 67, 415–37.

Sripada, C. (2022). Impaired control in addiction involves cognitive distortions and unreliable self-control, not compulsive desires and overwhelmed self-control. *Behavioural Brain Research*, 418, 113639.

Sripada, C. & Stich, S. (2006). A framework for the psychology of norms. In P. Carruthers, S. Laurence, and S. Stich (eds.), *The Innate Mind volume 2: Culture and cognition*, Oxford University Press.

Stampe, D. (1987). The authority of desire. *Philosophical Review*, 96, 335–81.

Stavans, M. & Baillargeon, R. (2019). Infants expect leaders to right wrongs. *Proceedings of the National Academy of Sciences*, 116, 16292–301.

Stich, S., Doris, J., & Roedder, E. (2010). Altruism. In J. Doris and The Moral Psychology Research Group (eds.), *The Moral Psychology Handbook*, Oxford University Press.

Stocks, E., Lishner, D., & Decker, S. (2009). Altruism or psychological escape: Why does empathy promote prosocial behavior? *European Journal of Social Psychology*, 39, 649–65.

Stone, V., Cosmides, L., Tooby, J., & Knight, R. (2002). Selective impairment of reasoning about social exchange in a patient with bilateral limbic system damage. *Proceedings of the National Academy of Sciences*, 99, 11531–36.

Storbeck, J. & Clore, G. (2008). Affective arousal as information: How affective arousal influences judgments, learning, and memory. *Social and Personality Psychology Compass*, 2, 1824–43.

Strait, C., Blanchard, T., & Hayden, B. (2014).Reward value comparison via mutual inhibition in ventromedial prefrontal cortex. *Neuron*, 82, 1357–66.

Surian, L. & Franchin, L. (2017). Infants reason about deserving agents: A test with distributive actions. *Cognitive Development*, 44, 49–56.

Sutherland, S., Cimpian, A., Leslie, S.-J., & Gelman, S. (2015). Memory errors reveal a bias to spontaneously generalize to categories. *Cognitive Science*, 39, 1021–46.

Sutton, R. & Barto, A. (1998). *Reinforcement Learning*. MIT Press.

Svetlova, M., Nichols, A., & Brownell, C. (2010). Toddlers' prosocial behavior: From instrumental to empathic to altruistic helping. *Child Development*, 81, 1814–27.

Sznycer, D., Lopez Seal, M., Sell, A., Lim, J., Porat, R., Shalvi, S., Halperin, E., Cosmides, L., & Tooby, J. (2017). Support for redistribution is shaped by compassion, envy, and self-interest, but not a taste for fairness. *Proceedings of the National Academy of Sciences*, 114, 8420–25.

Sznycer, D., Tooby, J., Cosmides, L., Porat, R., Shalvi, S., & Halperin, E. (2016). Shame closely tracks the threat of devaluation by others, even across cultures. *Proceedings of the National Academy of Sciences*, 113, 2625–30.

Sznycer, D., Xygalatas, D., Agey, E., Alami, S., An, X.-F., Ananyeva, K., Atkinson, Q. Broitman, B., Conte, T., Flores, C., Fuushima, S., Hitokoto, H., Kharitonov, A., Onyishi, C., Onyishi, I., Romero, P., Schrock, J., Snodgrass, J., Sugiyama, L., Takemura, K., Townsend, C., Zhuang, J.-Y., Aktipis, C.A., Cronk, L., Cosmides, L., & Tooby, J. (2018). Cross-cultural invariances in the architecture of shame. *Proceedings of the National Academy of Sciences*, 115, 9702–07.

Tajfel, H. (1970). Experiments in intergroup discrimination. *Scientific American*, 223, 96–102.

Tamietto, M. & de Gelder, B. (2010). Neural bases of the non-conscious perception of emotional signals. *Nature Reviews Neuroscience*, 11, 697–709.

Tappolet, C. (2012). Emotions, perceptions, and emotional illusions. In C. Calabi (ed.), *Perceptual Illusions*, Palgrave Macmillan.

Tappolet, C. (2016). *Emotions, Values, and Agency*. Oxford University Press.

Taylor, A., Elliffe, D., Hunt, G., & Gray, R. (2010). Complex cognition and behavioral innovation in New Caledonian crows. *Proceedings of the Royal Society B: Biological Sciences*, 277, 2637–43.

Thompson, B. (2009). Senses for senses. *Australasian Journal of Philosophy*, 87, 99–117.

Tiemann, L., Hohn, V., Ta Dinh, S., May, E., Nickel, M., Gross, J., & Ploner, M. (2018). Distinct patterns of brain activity mediate perceptual and motor and autonomic responses to noxious stimuli. *Nature Communications*, 9, 4487.

Ting, F., Dawkins, M., Stavans, M., & Baillargeon, R. (2020). Principles and concepts of early moral cognition. In J. Decety (ed.), *The Social Brain*, MIT Press.

Ting, F., He, Z., & Baillargeon, R. (2019). Toddlers and infants expect individuals to refrain from helping an ingroup victim's aggressor. *Proceedings of the National Academy of Sciences*, 116, 6025–34.

Todorov, E. & Jordan, M. (2002). Optimal feedback control as a theory of motor coordination. *Nature Neuroscience*, 5, 1226–35.

Tomasello, M., Melis, A., Tennie, C., Wyman, E., & Herrmann, E. (2012). Two key steps in the evolution of human cooperation: The interdependence hypothesis. *Current Anthropology*, 53, 673–92.

Tracey, W.D. (2017). Nociception. *Current Biology*, 27, R129–R133.

Treede, R.-D., Kenshalo, D., Gracely, R., & Jones, A.K. (1999). The cortical representation of pain. *Pain*, 79, 105–11.

Trivers, R. (1973). The evolution of reciprocal altruism. *Quarterly Review of Biology*, 46, 35–57.

Tye, M. (1995). *Ten Problems of Consciousness*. MIT Press.

Tye, M. (2000). *Consciousness, Color, and Content*. MIT Press.

Tye, M. (2002). Representationalism and the transparency of experience. *Noûs*, 36, 137–51.

Tye, M. (2017). *Tense Bees and Shell-Shocked Crabs*. Oxford University Press.

Vadillo, M., Gold, N., & Osman, M. (2016). The bitter truth about sugar and willpower: The limited evidential value of the glucose model of ego depletion. *Psychological Science*, 27, 1207–14.

Vaesen, K. (2012). Cooperative feeding and breeding, and the evolution of executive control. *Biology & Philosophy*, 27, 115–24.

Van Bavel, J. & Cunningham, W. (2009). Self-categorization with a novel mixed-race group moderates automatic social and racial biases. *Personality and Social Psychology Bulletin*, 35, 321–35.

van Dantzig, S., Pecher, D., & Zwaan, R. (2008). Approach and avoidance as action effects. *Quarterly Journal of Experimental Psychology*, 61, 1298–306.

Van den Stock, J., Tamietto, M., Sorger, B., Pichon, S., Grézes, J., & de Gelder, B. (2011). Cortico-subcortical visual, somatosensory, and motor activations for perceiving dynamic whole-body emotional expressions with and without striate cortex (V1). *Proceedings of the National Academy of Sciences*, 108, 16188–93.

References

Vasconcelos, M., Monteiro, T., & Kacelnik, A. (2015). Irrational choice and the value of information. *Nature Scientific Reports*, 5:13874.

Vetter, P., Smith, F., & Muckli, L. (2014). Decoding sound and imagery content in early visual cortex. *Current Biology*, 24, 1256–62.

Voisin, J., Bidet-Caulet, A., Bertrand, O., & Fonlupt, P. (2006). Listening in silence activates auditory areas: An fMRI study. *NeuroImage*, 17, 1623–33.

von Bayern, A., Danel, S., Auersperg, A., Mioduszewska, B., & Kacelnik, A. (2018). Compound tool construction by New Caledonian crows. *Nature Scientific Reports*, 8, 15676.

Wallis, J. (2007). Orbito-frontal cortex and its contribution to decision-making. *Annual Review of Neuroscience*, 30, 31–56.

Wang, Y. & Henderson, A. (2018). Just rewards: 17-month-old infants expect agents to take resources according to the principles of distributive justice. *Journal of Experimental Child Psychology*, 172, 25–40.

Warneken, F. & Tomasello, M. (2008). Extrinsic rewards undermine altruistic tendencies in 20-month-olds. *Developmental Psychology*, 44, 1785–88.

Warneken, F. & Tomasello, M. (2009). Varieties of altruism in children and chimpanzees. *Trends in Cognitive Sciences*, 13, 397–402.

Weijers, D. (2014). Nozick's experience machine is dead, long live the experience machine! *Philosophical Psychology*, 27, 513–35.

Whiting, D. (2011). The feeling theory of emotion and the object-directed emotions. *European Journal of Philosophy*, 19, 281–303.

Wilson, T., Dunn, D., Bybee, J., Hyman, D., & Rotondo, J. (1984). Effects of analyzing reasons on attitude-behavior consistency. *Journal of Personality and Social Psychology*, 47, 5–16.

Wilson, T., Dunn, D., Kraft, D., & Lisle, D. (1989). Introspection, attitude change, and attitude-behavior consistency: The disruptive effects of explaining why we feel the way we do. *Advances in Experimental Social Psychology*, 22, 287–343.

Wilson, T., Lisle, D., Schooler, J., Hodges, S., Klaaren, K., & LaFleur, S. (1993). Introspecting about reasons can reduce post-choice satisfaction. *Personality and Social Psychology Bulletin*, 19, 331–39.

Wilson, T. & Schooler, J. (1991). Thinking too much: Introspection can reduce the quality of preferences and decisions. *Journal of Personality and Social Psychology*, 60, 181–92.

Winkielman, P., Berridge, K., & Wilbarger, J. (2005). Unconscious affective reactions to masked happy versus angry faces influence consumption behavior and judgements of value. *Personality and Social Psychology Bulletin*, 31, 121–35.

Winstanley, C. & Floresco, S. (2016). Deciphering decision making: Variation in animal models of effort- and uncertainty-based choice reveals distinct neural circuitries underlying core cognitive processes. *Journal of Neuroscience*, 36, 12069–79.

Woo, B. & Spelke, E. (2023). Eight-month-old infants' social evaluations of agents who act on false beliefs. *Proceedings of the Annual Meeting of the Cognitive Science Society*, 44. https://escholarship.org/uc/item/8k02x1mx.

Woo, B., Steckler, C., Le, D., & Hamlin, J.K. (2017). Social evaluation of intentional, truly accidental, and negligently accidental helpers and harmers by 10-month-old infants. *Cognition*, 168, 154–63.

Wood, W. & Rünger, D. (2016). Psychology of habit. *Annual Review of Psychology*, 67, 289–314.

Wrangham, R. (2009). *Catching Fire*. Basic Books.

Wrangham, R. (2017). Control of fire in the paleolithic: Evaluating the cooking hypothesis. *Current Anthropology*, 58, S16.

Xiao, Y.J. & Van Bavel J. (2019). Sudden shifts in social identity swiftly shape implicit evaluation. *Journal of Experimental Social Psychology*, 83, 55–69.

Yamagishi, T., Matsumoto, Y., Kiyonari, T., Takagishi, H., Li, Y., Kanai, R., & Sakagami, M. (2017). Response time in economic games reflects different types of decision conflict for prosocial and proself individuals. *Proceedings of the National Academy of Sciences*, 114, 6394–99.

Yarkoni, T., Poldrack, R., Nichols, T., Van Essen, D., & Wager, T. (2011). Large-scale automated synthesis of human functional neuroimaging data. *Nature Methods*, 8, 665–70.

Yeomans, M., Leitch, M., Gould, N., & Mobini, S. (2008). Differential hedonic, sensory and behavioral changes associated with flavor-nutrient and flavor-flavor learning. *Physiology & Behavior*, 93, 798–806.

Ziv, T., Whiteman, J., & Sommerville, J. (2021). Toddlers' interventions towards fair and unfair individuals. *Cognition*, 214, 104781.

Zohar, I., Alperson-Afil, N., Goren-Inbar, N., Prévost, M., Tütken, T., Sisma-Ventura, G., Hershkovitz, I., & Najorka, J. (2022). Evidence for the cooking of fish 780,000 years ago at Gesher Benot Ya'aqov, Israel. *Nature Ecology & Evolution*. https://doi.org/10.1038/s41559-022-01910-z.

Zucco, G., Paolini, M., & Schaal, B. (2009). Unconscious odor conditioning 25 years later: Revisiting and extending "Kirk-Smith, Van Toller, and Dodd." *Learning and Motivation*, 40, 364–75.

Index

For the benefit of digital users, indexed terms that span two pages (e.g., 52–53) may, on occasion, appear on only one of those pages.

actor/critic model 27–8
affective states 11
  as natural kinds 11–12
  automatic motor outputs of 15–19, 125–6
  inputs versus outputs of 15, 39, 75, 83–6, 105–6
  learning and 26–34
  top-down influences on 34–9
  see also appraisal, arousal, displeasure, emotion, moods, pain, pleasure, valence
affective system 17n.4
altruism
  evolutionary 64
  innateness of 64–5, 166–71
  motivational 64
  psychological *see* motivational
  see also moral motivation, prosociality
appraisal 10–14, 87–8
arousal 19–20
  as essence of emotion 20
  in decision-making 20
Aydede, M. 116, 153, 157–8

Barlassina, L. 91, 117, 120n.2, 130–1, 134–8
Batson, C.D. 76–81
behavior
  affect-caused 15–19
  expressive 15–17
  instrumental 16–17
  intention-caused 18
Berridge, K. 29

Cochrane, T. 120n.3
commitment 58–9
consciousness, representational theory of 93–4, 157–9
cultural learning 37–8, 184

decision-making 19, 59–60
  in animals 43–4
  prospection in 40–3, 62–3
  theories of valence and 127
  unconscious 51–2
  verbal 56–9
desire 28, 189–90
  as future-directed pleasure 52–3, 72–4
  imperativism and 122
  non-conceptual content of 72–4, 91–2
  not a propositional attitude 189–90
  see also incentive-salience
displeasure 1–2, 11, 192
  see also pleasure, pain, punishment
dopamine, role of 22n.6

egoism
  extended 109–10, 192–3
  motivational 1–2, 33–4
  psychological *see* motivational
  see also hedonism
egoist 2
emotion
  correctness-conditions for 101–6
  in animals 101–3, 105
  natural kinds of 11–12
  normative errors in 106
  outward-focus of 88
  perceptual theories of 102–5
empathy
  experimental manipulation of 76–7
  increases helping behavior 76–7
  modulated by group membership 181–2
  see also altruism, prosociality
evaluativism *see* value-representing theory of valence
event-file 49
experience-machine 74–6
extinction 30, 38–9

220 Index

felt-quality theory of valence *see*
 intrinsic-feeling theory of valence
forward model, sensory 16
Fulkerson, M. 116, 153

Gilbert, D. 41, 46–7, 89–90
gut-brain pathway 25, 136–7

habit 17–18, 31
Hayward, M. 91, 117, 120n.2, 130–1, 134–8
Heathwood, C. 128–9
hedonic utilitarianism 3
hedonism 2–4, 16–17, 19, 25–6, 47
 desire-satisfaction argument against 72–4
 empirical evidence against 76–81
 evolutionary argument against 65–8
 experience-machine argument
  against 74–6
 motivational 1–2, 16–17, 40–1, 63
 self-sacrifice as objection to 68–72
 summary of case against 191–3
 without belief in future pleasure 47–9,
  67–8, 70–1, 78–80, 84
 see also intrinsic-feeling theory of valence,
  imperative theory of valence,
  prospection
hedonist 2–3, 76
Humean theory of motivation 7, 91,
 159–60, 189–91

imperative theory of valence
 avoids previous objections to
  hedonism 81–3
 brain networks and 132–4
 decision-making and 118
 evaluative learning and 118–19
 experience-directed forms of 81, 116–20
 hedonism and 120–1
 incentive-salience and 120n.2, 130–1
 pleasure and 127–32
 pluralism and 120
 reflexive form of 117
 theories of content and 121–7, 131
 theories of desire and 122–3
 world-directed form of 116–17
incentive-salience 16, 21–2, 28–9, 31
 see also desire
inclusive fitness 86
innateness 164
intention 17–18, 55–6
 formation of 18

implementational 55–6
 in moral evaluation 4–6
intrinsic-feeling theory of valence 40, 81, 85,
 100, 109
 anticipatory versus anticipated
  feelings 43, 46–7
 evolution and 85–6
 future-directed feelings 47–9
 neuroeconomics and 42
 phenomenology and 52–4
 prospection and 40–1
 summary of case against 114
 unconscious valence and 25, 50–2
 verbally-based decision-making and 56–9
 see also valence, value-representing theory
  of valence
intuition, unreliability of 8, 91–2, 160–1

Kringelbach, M. 29

minimal-group effect 178–9
model-free metacognition 118
Moller, D. 90
moral internalism 38–9, 190
moral motivation
 conditioned learning of 32–3
 cultural learning and 188–9
 forms of 165–6
 see also norm cognition, prosociality,
  sense of fairness
Morillo, C. 43

neuroeconomics 42, 89
nocebo effect 35
norm cognition
 concepts in infancy 186–7
 evolution of 182–5, 187

Odie, G. 87

pain
 asymbolia 143
 congenital indifference to 142–3
 congenital insensitivity to 141–2
 distinct sensory and affective
  components 142–3
 erroneous 157–8
 imperative content of 147–8, 152–3
 intrinsic-feeling theory of 145–7, 153–4
 nerve fibers for 141
 nociceptors for 140–1

placebo effects on 144–5
reason-giving nature of 159–63
representational contents of 146–52, 154–5
transparency of 157–9
two pathways for 142
placebo effect 35–6, 144–5
pleasure 1–2
anticipatory 21–2, 29, 47–9
brain-networks for 133
consummatory 26–8, 128
desire-theory of 52, 73–4
erroneous 106–9
momentary 128–9
phenomenology of 52–4
sub-personal forms of 109
task-completion and 129
unconscious 25, 51
see also intrinsic-feeling theory of valence, imperative theory of valence, valence, value-representing theory of valence
pluralism about motives 1
summary of argument for 192–3
Prinz, J. 104
prosociality
evolution of 64–5, 166–8, 170–1
in infancy 168–70
innateness of 170
see also altruism, empathy
prospection 40–3
in animals 43–5
in decision-making 40, 46–7
unconscious 51–2
punishment 8–9, 21, 24–6
primary 14, 21
secondary 30, 32–3
third-party 183–4
see also displeasure, pain, valence

representation, informational
theories of 95–7
reward 8–9
learning 21–2, 26–7
primary 21, 29–30, 97
secondary 29–33, 98
see also pleasure, valence

Schroeder, T. 86n.1
self-fulfilling theory 6–7
selfishness 2

sense of fairness
cooperation and 173
evolution of 166–8, 170–1
in infancy 168–70
innateness of 170, 176–7
in primates 172
ultimatum game and 173–5
sign-tracking 31–2
Sober, E. 65–6
social learning of value 32
social-group cognition
evolution of 177–8
small-group psychology and 178–9
stereotyping and 179–81
tribal psychology and 179
see also minimal-group effect, stereotypes
Stampe, D. 87
steel-man strategy 9, 39–40, 115, 193
stereotypes
as tribal psychology 179–80
in infancy 180–1
innateness and 181
Stroop test 80

transformative decision 62

ultimatum game 173–5

valence 20–6
analog-magnitude nature of 24, 53–4, 86–7
and pleasure / displeasure 24–5
and reward / punishment 25–6
anticipatory 26–8, 45–6
as analog-magnitude tag 51
as cause versus goal 47–9
as common currency 22–3, 61, 98–9
as intrinsic feeling 49–50
believed / predicted 41, 43, 46–7
consummatory 26–8
future-directed 43, 47–9
in incentive-salience 21–2
phenomenology of 52–4, 111
reference versus mode of presentation of 110–12
transparency of 94
two scales of 23–4
unconscious 25, 50–1
see also imperative theory of, intrinsic-feeling theory of, value-representing theory of

222 Index

value-representing theory of valence 86-9, 97-9, 113-14
  adaptive value and 97-9
  altruism and 92, 112-13
  consciousness and 94
  counter-examples to 134-8
  desire and 91-2, 123
  guilt and 90, 92
  incentive-salience and 132, 136-7
  information and 97-8, 124, 126-7
  misrepresentation and 100-1, 104-6
  moods and 134-5
  neurological damage and 135-6
  pluralism and 89
  self-sacrifice and 91-2
  theories of representation and 97
values 14-15
  adaptive 14, 97-8
  cached 30-1
  expected 24
  incommensurable 60-1
  learning of 26, 29-30, 32, 38, 42n.1
  natural 99
  other-regarding 34
  see also appraisal

Wilson, D. 65-6
Wilson, T. 41, 46-7, 89-90